The Arno Press Cinema Program

THE SILENT PARTNER
The History of the
American Film
Manufacturing Company
1910-1921

Timothy James Lyons

ARNO PRESS
A NEW YORK TIMES COMPANY
New York • 1974

This volume was selected for the
Dissertations on Film Series
of the ARNO PRESS CINEMA PROGRAM
by Garth S. Jowett, Carleton University

First publication in book form, Arno Press, 1974

Copyright © 1972 by Timothy James Lyons

THE ARNO PRESS CINEMA PROGRAM
For complete listing of cinema titles see last pages

Manufactured in the United States of America

Library of Congress Cataloging in Publication Data

Lyons, Timothy James.
   The silent partner.

   (Dissertations on film series of the Arno Press
cinema program)
   Originally presented as the author's thesis.
   1. American Film Manufacturing Company. I. Title.
II. Series: Dissertations on film series.
PN1999.A5L9   1974   338.7'61'79143   73-21590
ISBN 0-405-04872-6

THE SILENT PARTNER:

THE HISTORY OF THE AMERICAN FILM MANUFACTURING COMPANY,

1910-1921

by

Timothy James Lyons

A thesis submitted in partial fulfillment of the
requirements for the degree of Doctor of Philosophy
in the Department of Speech and Dramatic Art
in the Graduate College of
The University of Iowa

May, 1972

Thesis supervisor: Professor Richard Dyer MacCann

DEDICATION

In memory of two fine teachers:
Paul E. Wiggin and James E. Lyons.

ACKNOWLEDGMENTS

This thesis owes a note of thanks for the guidance and counsel given by members of my committee: Richard Dyer MacCann, Samuel L. Becker, Alexander C. Kern, David Knauf, Anthony Adams, and J. Dudley Andrew. I would particularly like to thank Professor William R. Reardon of the University of California at Santa Barbara for his help in the beginnings of this study. The following members of the film industry were willing to share some of their thoughts and information about the topics covered in this study: Peter Bogdanovich, Isaac Bonilla, Kevin Brownlow, Joel Conway, Allan Dwan, Kent D. Eastin, Robert Florey, Henry King, Kalton C. Lahue, George Marshall, Vaughn Obern, Mrs. Brandon O'Hilderbrandt, Mrs. Robert Phelan, Edward Sloman, Charles Tarbox, and Clark Wilkinson. The staffs from the following libraries aided in making resources available: the Academy of Motion Picture Arts and Sciences, the University of California at Santa Barbara, the University of Iowa, and the Library of Congress Motion Picture Section. I would also like to thank Karen Baum for her typing of this manuscript. Finally, to my wife, Judith, a note of gratitude; without her help and encouragement, this thesis could not have been written.

TABLE OF CONTENTS

CHAPTER		Page
	LIST OF TABLES	vi
	LIST OF FIGURES	vii
I	INTRODUCTION	1
II	THE MOTION PICTURE INDUSTRY, 1896-1921	15
	Early Monopoly Control, 1896-1910	17
	Expansion and Competition, 1910-1917	28
	The Second Monopoly, 1917-1921	36
	Summary	39
III	THE AMERICAN FILM MANUFACTURING COMPANY AS A BUSINESS	43
	Introduction	43
	The Beginnings: Western Film Exchange and the Independent Movement (1906-1910)	48
	The Exchanges Form Production Companies (1910-1912)	58
	Harry Aitken's Mutual and the American (1912-1915)	70
	John R. Freuler's Mutual and the American (1915-1918)	82
	American Distributes Where It Can (1918-1921) . . .	89
IV	AMERICAN'S PERSONNEL	95
	Introduction	95
	The Executive Branch, 1910-1921	97
	Directors	103
	Scenarists	111
	Actors and Actresses	120
	Production Personnel	128
	Summary	129
V	AMERICAN'S FILMS	132
	Introduction	132
	Western Comedy	138
	Western Drama	146
	Contemporary Social Comedy	154
	Contemporary Social Drama	157
	Period Drama	163
	Summary	168

TABLE OF CONTENTS (Cont'd.)

CHAPTER			Page
VI	CONCLUSIONS		172
	BIBLIOGRAPHY		186
	APPENDICES		197
	A	EXCERPTS FROM PHOTOPLAY ART, II (AUGUST 1916)	198
	B	FILMOGRAPHY	216
	C	PERSONNEL	250

LIST OF TABLES

TABLE		Page
1	AMERICAN FILM PRODUCTION: 1910-1921	87
2	RECAPITULATION OF INVENTORY: DECEMBER 31, 1919	93
3	AMERICAN SCENARIOS--AUGUST 18-DECEMBER 18, 1913	113
4	FILM TYPES RELEASED BY AMERICAN, 1910-1921	136
5	ELEMENTS OF AMERICAN'S FILMMAKING	170

LIST OF FIGURES

FIGURE		Page
1	ORGANIZATIONAL CHART: MUTUAL FILM CORPORATION	101
2	AMERICAN FILMS, 1910-1921: NUMBER OF FILMS, REELS, AND COPYRIGHT	137

CHAPTER I

INTRODUCTION

During the 1960's, the period of the giant motion picture studios was coming to an end. The five or six major companies which had dominated the film industry for over forty years were being infiltrated by outside conglomerates while small independent firms were taking over the majority of production responsibilities. From an era of "bigness" and monopoly, the industry was slowly returning to a condition of modest facilities and plurality of participation.

Those who are confused by this recent development would benefit from a close look at the early structure of the industry. From 1896 to 1908, film production in this country had yet to develop into a complex industry: a handful of companies provided short films for the developing mass culture with little effort toward systematization or industrial organization. In 1908, however, the situation began to change with the formation of the Motion Picture Patents Company. This was the first attempt to stablize film production (and later, distribution and exhibition) in this country. With this effort also came a parallel movement by independent companies to challenge the dominance of the Patents' monopoly. By 1920, the independents had succeeded in sapping the strength of the Patents' Trust; they had joined together into the major companies which were to dominate the field until only recently. Today's industrial scene in Hollywood can be viewed as not totally unlike the business picture of 1908: today, however, the roles are reversed--the "new independents" are challenging the "old independents."

To understand the workings of the film industry in this country is to discover a basic fact of motion picture history: small companies have always attempted to amalgamate into big companies; and big companies have always faced the challenges of small companies. One particular producing firm, the American Film Manufacturing Company, which prospered from 1910 to 1921, can serve as a good example of 1) the independent challenge to the Patents' Company; 2) the move toward amalgamation among the independents; and 3) the failure of those companies unable to compete with the progressive activities of the surviving independents.

Historical treatment of the American Film Manufacturing Company reveals not only the scarcity of coverage this company has received but also some of the major trends in silent film history writing. Of the traditionally accepted sources, only Terry Ramsaye's *A Million and One Nights*[1] and Jean Mitry's *Histoire du Cinéma*[2] mention American in any detail. Few other sources do more than simply note that the

---

[1] New York: Simon and Schuster, 1926; rpt. London: Cass, 1964.

[2] Vols. I (1895-1915) and II (1915-1925) (Paris: Editions Universitaires, 1967).

company existed,[3] while other historians cover American peripherally in their treatment of topics such as the moving picture serial,[4] silent film personalities,[5] or other producing companies.[6] One major reason for the lack of information is the scarcity of primary sources dealing with the company's operation. Another reason can be found in the major types of film historical writing.

The period of the silent film in this country has been treated by historians from a number of vantage points. For the investigator interested in the technological aspects of film production, his study will stress the development of the mechanical capabilities of film-making during the silent period.[7] A study which tries to uncover the nature of the personalities involved will reveal an emphasis on human

---

[3]The standard histories include Benjamin Hampton, History of the American Film Industry (New York: Covici-Friede, 1931; rpt. New York: Dover, 1970); Gertrude Jobes, Motion Picture Empire (Hamden, Connecticut: Archon, 1966); Kenneth Macgowan, Behind the Screen (New York: Delacorte, 1965); and Georges Sadoul, Histoire Générale du Cinéma, Vols. I, II, and III (Paris: Denoël, 1952).

[4]Kalton C. Lahue, Continued Next Week: A History of the Moving Picture Serial (Norman: University of Oklahoma, 1964).

[5]Kevin Brownlow, The Parade's Gone By (New York: Knopf, 1968).

[6]Fred J. Balshofer and Arthur C. Miller, One Reel a Week (Berkeley: University of California, 1967).

[7]See, for example, C. W. Ceram, Archaeology of the Cinema (New York: Harcourt, Brace, and World, 1965) and Raymond Fielding (ed.), A Technological History of Motion Pictures and Television (Berkeley: University of California, 1967).

activity rather than the machines.[8] Another type of film history will aim at enlightening the business operation of the various companies.[9] The cultural historian will treat film as an index to the larger societal operations.[10] And a large number of silent film historians will stress the films themselves as the chief topic of investigation.

While many of these approaches overlap, they are differentiated not only by subject matter but also by the particular questions to be answered, the methodologies employed in terms of types of evidence gathered, and the kinds of conclusions possible from their approaches to historical events. The level of causation discerned in each approach

---

[8] Examples are Brownlow; Ezra Goodman, The Fifty-Year Decline and Fall of Hollywood (New York: Simon and Schuster, 1961); and the numerous "film buff" books on silent film directors and stars.

[9] See Balshofer and Miller; Bosley Crowther, The Lion's Share: The Story of an Entertainment Empire (New York: Dutton, 1957); Robert Grau, The Theatre of Science: A Volume of Progress and Achievement in the Motion Picture Industry (New York: Broadway, 1914; rpt. New York: Blom, 1969); Hampton; Jobes; Macgowan; Albert E. Smith and Phil Koury, Two Reels and a Crank (New York: Doubleday, 1952).

[10] Works which attempt to blend the industrial aspects of film into a larger consideration of culture are Thomas H. Guback, The International Film Industry (Bloomington: Indiana University, 1969); George A. Huaco, The Sociology of Film Art (New York: Basic Books, 1965); Ian Jarvie, Movies and Society (New York: Basic Books, 1969). A more direct relationship between business and society is found in the sophisticated Marxist approach of John Howard Lawson, Film in the Battle of Ideas (New York: Masses and Mainstream, 1953) and his Film: The Creative Process (New York: Hill and Wang, 1967). See also Howard T. Lewis, The Motion Picture Industry (New York: Van Nostrand, 1933); John Harley, World-Wide Influences on the Cinema (Los Angeles: University of Southern California, 1960); and Georges Sadoul, Histoire du Cinéma mondial (Paris: Flammarion, 1949).

seems also to differentiate one approach from the other. By far the most abundant type of history dealing with the silent era has been the approach which concentrates on the personalities or "stars." The least work has been done in the area of "business histories" which stress the operation of a company as one involving many facets of film-making activity.

What is lacking in most film historical writing is an approach which integrates a discussion of not only the technical aspects of film production but also film as business, the personalities involved, and the films produced. Most writing of film history establishes a chronological chart by which to trace a particular aspect of the period, usually disregarding tangential influences. This study of the American Film Company hopes to provide an integrated account necessary for a complete understanding of an historical event.

A number of questions are raised by the existence of the American and other small independent companies: How did they start, and why? How were they run as businesses? Why did some fail while others survived? Each of these general questions also raises other questions about the operation of these independent companies: What was the general economic picture of the industry, and what part did these companies play in the industry's general business development? How did the utilization of personnel by these companies influence their business structures? What effect did the types and quality of films produced have on the companies' operation? Given these questions, some conclusions will be possible about the American Film Company specifically, and the independent companies in general.

For this study, there will be four areas of investigation: 1) the economic picture, 1896-1921; 2) the business operation of the American Film Manufacturing Company; 3) the personnel of American, with some attention to their careers before and after their work with American; and 4) the films produced by this company. Each of the four topics will be treated in an individual chapter; the concluding chapter will bring together the findings in each area with some general conclusions about American's place in film history.

For this study to have implications beyond simply one company, the first section will sketch a broad economically-based picture of the film industry from 1896 to 1921, the topic for Chapter II. A forecast to this discussion would reveal a period of rapid industrialization, in which some newcomers to film production gained tremendous wealth, while others disappeared just as quickly. In this period, the men who fought for control of the field began to recognize the necessity of major participation in all three branches of the industry: production, distribution, exhibition. A company producing high-quality films had little chance for success without equally well-handled distribution and control of theatres.

The American Film Manufacturing Company was born out of a film exchange business; like many other companies, its founders saw the need to control the supply of film if their film exchange interests were to be successful. With the pressure of the Motion Picture Patents' Trust, many exchangemen were forming their own producing companies to insure a steady supply of product for their distribution activities. Further development of the industry then demanded a control over exhibition; those companies which managed this extension were able to survive the fierce business competition, while those who did not--like American--fell by the wayside.

The years 1896 to 1921 also saw the motion picture move from a ten-minute curiosity to an hour-long entertainment. The feature film rapidly became the dominant product. This extension in scope also brought about financial considerations such as the need for stars and increased production time, which meant larger budgets and a greater dependence upon wide distribution and exhibition to insure adequate return and profit.

Chapter II will give a general coverage of the film industry so that any particular findings about American can be placed into a wider context. After establishing the state of the industry from 1896 to 1921, the study can then turn toward an analysis of the American Film Manufacturing Company as a business, the topic for Chapter III. From a small producing company, American developed into a large multi-faceted producing firm affiliated with one of the largest distributing chains in the country, Mutual Film Corporation. And from this vantage point, the company fell to the level of producing a few features sporadically, finally re-releasing its old products through any available source before succumbing to mounting competition.

Business records for American are all but lost. A segment of those that do exist help in determining the daily operations of this company.[11] Other information, such as reports in the contemporary press, interviews, and investigations by other historians, also helps to discern the changing structure of the company during its twelve year existence.[12] The number of films produced, the number of these copyrighted, the extent of advertising in the trade journals, the size and capacity of producing facilities--all of this information aids in an understanding of American's operation as a business.

Another facet of American's operation, the make-up of its personnel, will be covered in Chapter IV. The majority of American's employees remained with the company throughout its existence. However, some

---

[11] Those business records which do exist are found in the collection of Joel Conway of Santa Barbara, California, who purchased the American Film Company studio in the late 1940's. When Conway sold the land and buildings, he retained some of the production schedules, bankbooks, and inventories. A segment of these were made available for this study by Conway, although only a small amount of the records were actually put at my disposal. From these, I can make some general conclusions about how American was run; the records, however, failed to provide much of the detail necessary for a complete account of American's financial and production activities. When these records do aid in elaborating a particular point, they will be cited specifically; for the most part, though, they served more as background material.

[12] Care must be taken in the ways such information is used. Like the differing approaches to film history, each of these sources has its own credibility. Instead of reviewing here the methodology employed for each chapter, the study will comment upon the advantages and some of the drawbacks to these sources whenever they are brought into direct use in a chapter. In this manner, the approaches for the chapters will be somewhat differentiated from one another.

moved from American to greater heights, while others found their ways to obscurity. In this chapter, individuals hired by American will be investigated with the following questions in mind:

1) What background did these people have before joining American?
2) How did their career and production responsibilities develop during their stay with American?
3) For individuals who left American, how did their careers develop?

A sampling[13] will be made from the over five thousand people who worked for American in the following capacities:

1) Executives
2) Directors
3) Scenarists
4) Actors and Actresses
5) Production Personnel

Some conclusions about American can be based on the hiring practices of the company, the level of talent employed, the length of stay

---

[13]The selection was made on the basis of the three types of personnel employed by American: 1) those who remained with American throughout the company's career; 2) personnel who stayed with the company only temporarily and whose career ended after their stay with American; and 3) those who after leaving American achieved success with other firms. Less than fifty of the personnel will be treated; these were selected because they typified a large number of similar employees. In addition to the personnel selected for discussion, a comprehensive listing of the company's staff will be found in Appendix C.

an employee had with the company, and the general utilization of personnel by American.

With information about the general picture of the film industry, the business structure of American, and the personnel employed by the company, attention can then be given in Chapter V to the films produced by American. In its twelve years of operation, American released 1,228 films made up of 2,196 reels or 2,196,000 feet of market product. Slightly more than half of these films were registered for copyright with the Library of Congress. Today, only eleven of American's films are available for this study. To supplement the existing films, there is also material available to discover some evidence of the connection between the products and the operation of this company.

Trade journals reported the story synopsis for each film released by American, and criticism at the time evaluated these films, providing an indication of how the films related in quality to the output of other companies. From these two sources, some idea can be gained of the place American's films held in the industry, in terms of quality and quantity. The extant films--three features (1916, 1918, and 1919) and eight shorts (1911-1918)--will serve as examples of American's released products.

As American developed, it tended to form individual units devoted to producing specific types of films, eventually for specific stars. These subsidiary producing units roughly define the types of films produced by the Company. Originally American had three producing companies (American #1, #2, and #3), one located in the Southwest producing Westerns, and the other two in Chicago concentrating on Westerns and social comedies. Within two years, the Chicago companies had been disbanded, and a second company specializing in social comedy was added to the Western unit in Santa Barbara, California. By 1914, this second company had become known as the "Beauty" brand, continuing the speciality of "society plays." In the peak production years of 1915 and 1916, there were six major units at work in the Santa Barbara studio, each having its own subsidiary groups producing films of a specific kind: 1) <u>Mutual Masterpictures</u> (also known as Mutual Star Features, American Star Features, Mutual Masterpieces, and Masterpictures deLuxe), specializing in five-reel features; 2) <u>North American</u>, a company established to produce <u>The Diamond from the Sky</u>, a successful thirty-episode (two reels each) serial, and later <u>The Secret of the Submarine</u>, a war-preparedness serial; 3) <u>Flying A</u> and 4) <u>Mustang</u>, both concentrating on Westerns; 5) <u>Clipper</u>, a short-lived unit producing social dramas; and 6) <u>Beauty</u>, which supplied the light comedy series. By late 1916, most of the production activity was in features (Mutual Masterpictures) with different units organized around the individual stars; in this year, too, the production output was supplemented by re-releasing short films from 1911-1914. During this transitional period, American changed its name from the American Film Manufacturing Company, known in the trade journals as "Flying A," to the American Film Company, Inc.

The films produced by American can be categorized by the following types:[14]

   I. <u>Western Comedy</u>: usually short, one- or two-reel films built around a humorous situation occurring on the ranch or in some realm of the cowboy's daily existence.

  II. <u>Western Drama</u>: longer stories of the adventure and intrigue of frontier settlement.

 III. <u>Contemporary Social Comedy</u>: comic episodes, often slapstick, revolving about some social error or a situation readily identified with contemporary daily life.

  IV. <u>Contemporary Social Drama</u>: earnest portrayals of stories based on incidents promoting the serious, realistic themes of contemporary society.

   V. <u>Period Drama</u>: excursions into the past and to remote locales for a romantic or allegorical view of historical or fictitious events.[15]

The first section of Chapter V will deal with the individual companies, showing the types of films each produced, the number and lengths of films, with some attention to those types American found to be most successful. From this general coverage, the approach will cover an analysis of the eleven available examples:

---

[14] A few documentaries were attempted in the first two years of operation. These, however, appear to have been merely "fillers," used to complete a thousand-foot reel with a split-reel comedy or Western. They will not be covered in this study.

[15] A further delineation of the elements involved in each type will be found in Chapter V.

    I. __Western Comedy__:
        __Three Million Dollars__ (1911)
        __Calamity Anne's Trust__ (1913; re-released 1916)
        __Courage of Sorts__ (1913)
        __The Deacon's Card__ (1914)

   II. __Western Drama__:
        __Six Feet Four__ (feature; 1919)

  III. __Contemporary Social Comedy__:
        __The Borrowed Flat__ (1911)
        __Ella Wanted to Elope__ (1913)

   IV. __Contemporary Social Drama__:
        __What Her Diary Told__ (1913)
        __The Eyes of Julia Deep__ (feature; 1919)

    V. __Period Drama__:
        __Everyheart__ (1915)
        __The Pearl of Paradise__ (feature; 1916)

From this general look at the films and the specific analysis of the samples, some conclusions will be offered about the types of films each company produced and how these might figure into the success or failure of the American Film Company.

After the discussion of the various factors influencing American's operation, some conclusions about the company will be offered which attempt to answer the basic questions of this study. How American was operated, and why, will be placed into the general context of industrial development in this period. The last chapter will compare American's operation to the general practices employed by other companies.

This investigation of American proceeds from the general to the specific, from the economic picture of the industry to the business operation of one company. The final chapter is a return to the general coverage of the period, relating American to the industry as a whole. Aside from this direction of the study, Chapters III, IV, and V cover the same chronological period and events but from different vantage points. In Chapter III, American is viewed as an industrial concern whose business policies determine the inner workings of the company. Chapter IV looks at the individuals who shape and are influenced by these policies. And Chapter V concentrates on the products of the business policies and the personnel--the films themselves.

The history of the American Film Company should correct a partial void in historical film study. From this look at an independent company, we should be able to gain an understanding of an important factor in the development of the industry we know today. From the study of a little-known company, hopefully we can begin to see the part played not just by American but by a number of other companies which struggled behind the scenes, "silent partners" in the development of a major entertainment industry.

CHAPTER II

THE MOTION PICTURE INDUSTRY, 1896-1921

In 1937, the Englishmen Klingender and Legg suggested a useful division for viewing the progression of the film industry in America:

> The development of American film finance...can be summarized as a spiral movement from early monopoly control at a time when the industry...was but a minor sphere of economic life and when its undreamed of possibilities of expansion threatened to be stifled by that monopoly hold, through a phase of meteoric expansion coupled with violent competition back again to monopoly control. It is a movement which is never for one moment basically deflected by the unceasing obligatto of government anti-trust actions that enliven its progress.[1]

The early development of this entertainment industry in America is not only a capsule history of "gamblers" vs. "conservatives,"[2] struggling for control of a wholly new business phenomenon, but also a time in which the industrial framework for the motion picture business was formulated and strengthened, influencing not only the products of this system but also the society which served as consumer.

A "business history" approach to the American silent film era entails the understanding of the period as one in which the major interest was in machines necessary for motion picture production and

---

[1] F. D. Klingender and Stuart Legg, Money Behind the Screen (London: Lawrence and Wishart, 1937), p. 78. My italics serve to point out the division this chapter will use.

[2] See Richard Griffith's introduction to the reprint edition of Hampton.

projection. The inventors' interest in the nature of the films produced and the methods of organizing distribution and exhibition interests was a later development, one which was not evident until the formation of the Patents Company in 1908. This conglomerate was the means by which the manufacturers attempted to control the industry.

What the manufacturers found, however, was a breed of men who saw distribution as the major position of strength in the industry. These "independents," called so because they stood apart from the licensed Patents members, had strength in film distribution exchanges throughout the country providing an intermediary between the producers and the exhibitors. With the source of supply dried up, due to estrangement from the Patents Company, the independents formed their own producing units. The Patents were now challenged on two fronts: the independents not only distributed films but were also in the production business. The area which was still dominated by the Patents, however, was that of exhibition: through the required fees for use of licensed projectors, theatre owners were at the mercy of the Patents Company policies.

When the validity of the Patents claim of control over machinery began to be doubted by the courts, the independents saw the chance to move into the exhibition business, and their accumulation of theatres began. This development, however, took place over a long period of time. Changes in the business climate, increased demand for the supply of both more films and better films, a growing desire for longer films, the government's scrutiny of the film industry--for over two decades the film industry was influenced by these developments, the details of which are covered in the discussion below.

Early Monopoly Control, 1896-1910

The history of the American film industry begins not with the artists but with the inventors and the businessmen. From 1896[10] to 1908,[11] the motion picture business in America "was dominated by companies interested primarily in the manufacture and sale of motion picture equipment."[12] The major figure in this battle was the inventor

---

[10] The generally recognized date for the first commercial exhibition of motion pictures in America is April 23, 1896, when Thomas Armat demonstrated his and Thomas A. Edison's Vitascope for the Koster and Bial Music Hall audience in New York City. See Ramsaye, pp. 231-32; Hampton, pp. 11-12; Lewis Jacobs, The Rise of the American Film (New York: Columbia University Teachers College, 1968), pp. 3-4; Arthur Knight, The Liveliest Art (New York: Macmillan, 1957), p. 18; and Macgowan, p. 122. Most of these sources seem to base their use of this date on The New York Daily Mirror, April 25, 1896, p. 20.

[11] "The Motion Picture Patents Company was incorporated on September 8, 1908." Ralph Cassady, Jr., "Monopoly in Motion Picture Production and Distribution: 1908-1915," Southern California Law Review, XXXII (Summer 1959), 329. As my discussion will suggest, the formation of the Patents Company was a major development in a hitherto unorganized industry. Cassady's coverage of the Patents Company and its effects on the industry is based primarily on court cases and contemporary evidence, and is by far the most accurate and dependable research done on the economic and legal aspects of this era. The source for much of Cassady's material is the Transcript of Record of United States vs. Motion Picture Patents Company, in the District Court of the United States for the Eastern District of Pennsylvania (1915) to be referred throughout this study as Record. His article will be a major reference and influence in this chapter.

[12] Mae D. Huettig, Economic Control of the Motion Picture Industry (Philadelphia: University of Pennsylvania, 1944), p. 3. Italics mine.

Thomas A. Edison, who held control over important film, camera, and projector patents.[13] Opposing Edison and his licensees[14] were the American Mutoscope and Biograph[15] with its own licensees.[16] For the first thirteen years of the film industry, each camp kept the other involved in court suits over the right to manufacture and sell film equipment.[17]

During this time, the number of actual film production companies grew steadily. Before the turn of the century, the industry was

---

[13] Edison's film patents (nos. 12038 and 12192) and camera patent (no. 12037) were not his only assets. His associates were Thomas Armat, who held projector patents (nos. 578,185--the star-wheeled intermittent motion device; 580,749; 586,953--the "Phantoscope"--with Charles Francis Jenkins; 588,916, from William G. Steward and Ellis F. Frost; and 673,992--the "Vitascope"), and Albert E. Smith, of Vitagraph, who had projector patents (nos. 673,329--framing device; 744,251; 770,937; 771,280; 785,205, from William Ellwood; and 785,237). Edison's role as an inventor of motion pictures has received a serious debunking in Gordon Hendricks, The Edison Motion Picture Myth (Berkeley: University of California, 1961).

[14] Essanay Film Manufacturing Company, Kalem Film Manufacturing Company, Lubin Manufacturing Company, Gaston Méliès, Pathé Frères, Selig Polyscope Company, and Vitagraph Company of America.

[15] "Biograph," as the AMBC was called, held camera patent no. 629,063 (an intermittent motion device from Herman Casler) and projector patents nos. 707,934 (from Woodville Latham, on the film loading method popularly known as "the Latham Loop") and 722,382 (from John A. Pross, on the shutter mechanism).

[16] "The Biograph's licensees, unlike the Edison licensees, were importers rather than domestic producers" (Cassady, p. 328). These included Williams, Brown and Earle; Kleine Optical Company; Charles E. Dressler; and Thomas Armat. Until the Patents Company was formed, Armat held contractual Agreements with both Edison and Biograph.

[17] For a list and description of some of these litigations, see Cassady, p. 328; also Michael Conant, Antitrust in the Motion Picture Industry (Berkeley: University of California, 1960), pp. 16-21; and Lewis, pp. 1-27.

represented by four major studies: Edison (1893), American Mutoscope and Biograph (1896), Lubin (1897), and Vitagraph (1897). By 1907, other studios had been formed to compete in the growing market. George Kleine, whose Optical Company had been importing the films of Gaumont and Urban Eclipse, joined with Samuel Long and Francis Marion in 1905 to form a production company, entitled "Kalem," utilizing the first letters of the three men's last names. In the next year, Colonel William N. Selig formed his Polyscope Company, and George K. Spoor with actor Gilbert W. Anderson organized the Essanay (S. and A.) Film Manufacturing Company. When 1908 arrived, eight major companies and a few small producing units were vying with importing firms to fill the demands of the market.

As studio activity increased, so too did the length of the films produced. Beginning as a peep-show curiosity viewed through the Edison Kinetoscope and Biograph's Mutoscope, the films grew from a few feet in length to the standard 1000 foot reel which ran about fourteen minutes. With the increased length also came the possibility for story-telling. By 1903, with Edwin S. Porter's The Great Train Robbery, most film producers recognized that the dominant appeal of the commercial motion picture was in its narrative capacity.

The move of films from the nickelodeons and vaudeville theatres as "fillers" to theatres in which they were the sole source of entertainment also called for increased efficiency of distribution. Before 1904, exhibitors bought films directly from producers or their appointed agents.[18] However, people like the Miles Brothers of San Francisco quickly recognized the opportunities of exchange businesses which would purchase a number of prints from producing firms and then rent them to exhibitors. By 1907, between 125 and 150 film exchanges had sprung up around the country,[19] handling distribution on states right agreement.[20] Among the new members of the film exchange business were men destined to become major figures in the industry's development: Carl Laemmle, whose exchange interests and IMP company would seriously challenge the Motion Picture Patents Company;[21] William Fox, whose Greater New York Film Rental Company was the one licensed exchange to challenge the Patents' attempt at controlling all licensed

---

[18] Before the exchange system was initiated, the distribution of films was in the hands of the producers themselves. A few producing companies, however, had agencies which would handle this end of the business for them; for example, Edison appointed Frank R. Gammon and Norman C. Raff as his exclusive representatives. Such agents took on the responsibilities of getting their client's products into the theatres, while also protecting the patents held by their clients.

[19] Huettig, p. 13.

[20] Jobes, p. 43. She explains the term "states right" to mean that each exchange "purchased pictures with the understanding he might rent them only in states agreed upon in the deal."

[21] For an "authorized"--and somewhat generous--biography of Laemmle, see John Drinkwater, The Life and Adventures of Carl Laemmle (New York: Putnam, 1931). Contrary to some sources, IMP was not founded in 1907 but instead in May, 1909; see Moving Picture World, IV (May 29, 1909), 740, for Laemmle's announcement of Independent Motion Pictures.

exchanges;[22] Harry and Sam Warner, two of the Warner Brothers; John R. Freuler and Harry Aitken, who together later formed the Mutual Film Corporation; plus a number of others who would form production companies to challenge the Patents group.

By 1908, the film industry in America--though far from achieving the industrial complexity it would eventually encompass--contained all of the elements necessary to grow and to prosper. Ten major companies were producing the majority of films,[23] although Edison involved many of them--particularly Biograph--in court suits over violation of patents; film exchanges were functioning throughout the nation; and, perhaps over 8,000 theatres[24] were available to exhibit the product to a

---

[22] An extremely biased biography in favor of Fox and against the film industry is Upton Sinclair, <u>Upton Sinclair Presents William Fox</u> (Los Angeles: By the author, 1933).

[23] American Mutoscope and Biograph Company; Edison Film Manufacturing Company; Essanay Film Manufacturing Company; Kalem Company, Inc.; Kleine Optical Company (importers of Gaumont and Urban Eclipse films); Lubin Manufacturing Company; Gaston Méliès (representing Georges Méliès' Star Films); Pathé Frères; Selig Polyscope Company; and Vitagraph Company of America.

[24] Jobes, p. 55. The source does not cite where this information was found, and it is difficult to believe the number is completely accurate. No government census for theatres covers this early period; in fact, actual census information is not available until 1921, and then only for production firms. In 1909, a Patents Company official testified later, there were approximately 6,000 theatres in the country; these, however, were theatres devoted solely to the exhibition of motion pictures. During 1908, many legitimate theatres would feature films along with the live dramatic or vaudeville presentations. It is highly possible that Jobes' figure includes both legitimate theatres and motion picture houses. The point here is that, without accurate statistical data for this period, all numbers are approximate. Another factor--one which this study will constantly confront--is that the industry was rapidly changing. In 1912, <u>The Moving Picture World</u> underlined this fact in noting, "Until the year 1912 a list of motion picture theatres in any one city might be correct on the day it was

society hungry for cheap mass entertainment. In this field of potential splendor, some members of the industry could see the possibility for real industrial stability by collecting the three areas of the business--production, distribution, exhibition--under one umbrella. For this stability to occur, peace had to break out between the two warring camps of Edison and Biograph.

In September of 1908, this peace was effected by the formation of the Motion Picture Patents Company. This "holding company"[25] controlled all the important camera and projector patents[26] necessary for film production. A major function of the company was the collection of royalties from anyone making use of equipment falling under the Company's patents. The collection activities were of three types: machine royalties (cameras), exhibitor royalties (projectors), and film royalties. By early 1909, the Patents Company had "entered into agreement with...(a) the supplier of raw film [Eastman Kodak Company], (b) the

---

[24] Continued. made but a week later could not be relied upon, so constant was the changing of the ownership of theatres." Moving Picture Annual and Yearbook for 1912 (New York: Moving Picture World, 1913), p. 39. See also note 29 below.

[25] "Holding Company" has the following legal definition: "A super-corporation which owns or at least controls such a dominant interest in one or more other corporations that it is enabled to dictate their policies through voting power; a corporation organized to hold the stock of other corporations; any company, incorporated or unincorporated, which is in a position to control or materially influence the management of one or more other companies by virtue, in part at least, of its ownership or securities in the other companies." Black's Law Dictionary, 4th ed. (St. Paul: West, 1968), p. 865.

[26] See notes 7 and 9 above.

most important producers of motion pictures,[27] (c) the several manufacturers of projecting machines,[28] (d) the great bulk of rental exchanges, and (e) the leading exhibitors."[29] In the summer of 1909, the members of the Patents Company could view themselves as partners in a prosperous, trouble-free future--almost.

The potential control by the Patents Company seemed to many a most favorable development in the industry.[30] The roles of the Patents Company appeared to be soundly determined:

---

[27] By July, the following had signed agreements with the Patents Company, all of whom--with the exception of Méliès--were charter members: Biograph, Edison, Essanay, Kalem, Kleine, Lubin, Méliès, Pathé, Selig, and Vitagraph.

[28] Edison, Lubin, Selig, and George K. Spoor (of Essanay)--all of these also producing films--, Armat, Edengraph, Enterprise Optical, Nicholas Power, Eberhard Schneider, American Moving Picture Machine, Gaumont, Biograph, and Precision Machine.

[29] Cassady, p. 332. It would be difficult to provide an accurate list of both exchanges and exhibitors: "The Motion Picture Patents Company in an Exhibitors' Bulletin dated January 22, 1909, listed 111 licensed exchanges throughout the United States" (Cassady, p. 340; the list is available in 1 <u>Record</u> 87-94). Also, "according to the testimony of Harry M. Marvin, Vice-President of the Motion Picture Patents Company, there were approximately 6,000 exhibitors in the United States in 1909, and he estimated that three or four thousand of these became licensees [1 <u>Record</u> 27]. However, those remaining outside the fold were for the most part, no doubt, small and relatively unimportant" (Cassady, pp. 342-43).

[30] "In a report of a special committee of the Film Service Association (made up of erstwhile Edison exchange licensees) dated January 9, 1909, the new exchange agreement was judged in the main satisfactory and it stated '...that the Patents Company's license should prove desirable to all members who wished to build up the business along legitimate lines'," (Cassady, p. 339; 1 <u>Record</u> 499-500).

(a) holding title of patents governing motion picture films, cameras, and projectors;

(b) licensing individuals and companies to conduct motion picture operations under its jurisdiction;

(c) regulating the conduct of business of those licensed;

(d) preventing infringement by those not licensed by the Patents Company; and

(e) collecting royalties from various functionaries in exchange for the privilege of operating as licensed companies in the field.[31]

But other aspects of this period undermined the Patents' security. The Patents Company was formed in a period of trust-breaking. The American public had showed in a previous election, and would continue to show in the future, an adverse feeling about monopolies--Presidents Roosevelt, Taft, and Wilson followed the public's mandate in attacking the trusts. Two years after the forming of the Patents Company, the Supreme Court would hold Standard Oil in violation of the Sherman Anti-Trust Law and order the corporation to dissolve. This was also the period of unlimited opportunity in business, a period in which penniless immigrants became _dramatis personae_ in real-life Horatio Alger success stories. Strong figures entered the motion picture field, men who were not easily controlled and who were unwilling to be partners in the Patents Company scheme.

---

[31] Cassady, p. 345.

Two of these rebels--Carl Laemmle and William Fox--have received adequate coverage in other sources.[32] Laemmle achieved his fame by challenging the Trust policies in his advertisements for his unlicensed film exchange business in which he openly called for resistance from exhibitors.[33] Fox refused to sell his licensed exchange to the Patents Company when they attempted to consolidate all of the licensed exchanges under one management. Laemmle and Fox were not alone; there were others who held an early aversion toward the plans of the Patents Company.

Unlicensed exchanges throughout the country tried to maintain their solvency by distributing the product of the unlicensed manufacturing companies: in October, 1909, a total of seven reels per week--compared to around eighteen from the Patents--were available from the independents (Carson Company; Columbia Film Company; Independent Motion Picture Company; Phoenix Company; Powers Company; and World Film Manufacturing Company).[34] Additional independent sources for films were the small number of importers of European product: Cricks and Martin; Hepworth Manufacturing Company; Robert W. Paul; Walter Tyler; William,

---

[32] See notes 15 and 16 above. Most general histories covering this era will focus on Laemmle and Fox as the two leading figures in the independent movement. However, the participation was far more extensive than merely the activities of these two men, as will be shown later in this chapter.

[33] For example, an advertisement in the Moving Picture World, IV (May 1, 1909), 538, read: "Good Morrow! Have you paid $2.00 for a license to pick your teeth this week?"

[34] Moving Picture World, V (November 13, 1909), 681. See Cassady, p. 366.

Brown, and Earle.[35] Less than a dozen exchanges operated openly as unlicensed: Anti-Trust Film Company (Chicago); Chicago Film Exchange (Atlanta, Chicago, Denver, Nashville, Omaha, Salt Lake City, and Washington, D.C.); Eagle Film Exchange (Philadelphia); Eastern Film Exchange (Pittsburgh); Economy Film Service (Pittsburgh); Harstn [sic] and Company (New York); Keystone Film Supply (Scranton, Pennsylvania); Liberty Film Exchange (Philadelphia); New England Film Exchange (Boston); New Jersey Film Rental Company (Jersey City); Unique Film and Construction Company (Chicago).[36] These unlicensed exchanges were in competition with over one hundred licensed agencies. Unlicensed exhibitors in 1909 numbered 2,500 compared to a total of 10,000 to 12,000 licensed theatre operators.[37]

Besides those who decided to risk business operation without Patents' licenses were a few who tried to support the independent cause while still retaining their licensed status. Firms such as Western Film Exchange, organized in 1906 by John R. Freuler and Harry E. Aitken, were licensed by the Trust but also distributed unlicensed films. Another firm, H. and H. Film Exchange, founded by Samuel S. Hutchinson and Charles J. Hite, tried to play both sides of the fence. But such activity did not go unnoticed by the Patents Company. A

---

[35]Cassady, p. 363.

[36]Ibid. See also Moving Picture World, IV (January 23, 1909), advertisements passim.

[37]Conant, p. 19.

letter to Standard Film Exchange of Chicago, dated July 10, 1910, from the Patents Company decreed the following:

> Gentlemen:
> The licenses of the O.T. Crawford Film Exchange Company, St. Louis, Missouri, Western Film Exchange, St. Louis, Missouri, and Kay-Tee Film Exchange, Los Angeles, California, have been cancelled.
>
> We hand you herewith a list of exhibitors served by these exchanges.[38]

Almost half of the over one hundred licenses for film exchanges were revoked during the first two years of the Patents operation.[39] The final controlling move by the Patents Company was the formation of the General Film Company in April, 1910. Within eighteen months, the General Film Company "had purchased fifty-eight [of the sixty-nine licensed] American exchanges, and during the same period the Motion Picture Patents Company cancelled the licenses of ten."[40] The one licensed exchange to hold out against the General Film Company was William Fox, who then joined the other unlicensed exchanges in the battle. For the Patents' partners, the General Film Company was a necessary move; but for the United States Government, this move convinced them the Trust had to be stopped.

---

[38] Cassady, pp. 348-49. 2 Record 1076.

[39] Cassady lists 116 licensed exchanges in early 1909, with forty-two being cancelled by February, 1911 (p. 335).

[40] Cassady, p. 357.

Expansion and Competition, 1910-1917

Most sources cite legal action as the cause for the dissolution of the Patents Company. This explanation has been shown to be far too simple.[41] Edison and Biograph were the only stockholders in the Patents Company; the other members received the privilege of operating under Patents' sanction, while Edison and Biograph received the major share of the machine royalties. There is little doubt that this situation weakened the kind of solidarity which the Company expected of its members. An analysis of the internal decay of Patents' *esprit* reveals a fluidity of personnel-trading from the Patents' members to the independent ranks, a willingness of Patents' companies to aid independent production efforts, and challenges to the Patents' regulations brought by the members themselves.[42]

Of course, outside influences were also felt. There was the growing strength of the independents, led by Carl Laemmle, which undermined the Patents' attempt to control stars' salaries through anonymity,[43] to keep film lengths under three

---

[41] For a well-documented study of the multifarious causes for the Patents' failure, see Jeanne Thomas, "The Decay of the Motion Picture Patents Company," *Cinema Journal*, X (Spring 1971), 34-40.

[42] See Thomas, pp. 39-40.

[43] "Although the star system was not as yet in effect in the motion picture industry in 1909, some players were known to the public by a general designation rather than by specific name. For example, the very popular Florence Lawrence was known as the 'Biograph Girl' by the public even though she remained anonymous" (Cassady, p. 369). See also *Moving Picture World*, V (December 18, 1909), 866, for Laemmle's exploitation of Miss Lawrence after he had stolen her away from Biograph.

reels,[44] and to regulate the amount of product released weekly.[45] Not only did the independents plan to exploit star attraction in their productions, but they also continued to release Trust films after their licenses had been revoked.[46] The Trust replied by legal action, but the time factor between instituting a case and receiving a ruling allowed exchanges to continue along this line until their own production units had built up an adequate supply of films for release.

The independent movement had a number of strong points in its favor: (1) the "trust-breaking" spirit evident in the courts, and in the government, gave the independent's cause a sympathetic appeal for the general public; (2) the independent exchanges could deal on a more regional, and more personal level with exhibitors than could the mammoth General Film Company, the Patents distribution outlet;

---

[44] "George Kleine, importer of Gaumont and Eclipse films, was limited to 3,000 running feet [or three reels] of new subjects per week plus 1,500 running feet of special subjects imported" (Cassady, p. 336).

[45] This aspect, however, should not be overstated. Cassady notes, "While importer-licensees were limited in the footage that they were permitted to release, the manufacturer-licensees were not restricted in the amount of motion picture films they were permitted to produce and sell" (p. 336). At the same time, the actual licensing affected control of the weekly supply. Most historians cite the Patents Company's dogmatic policy in dictating how much film their licensees could produce; the facts don't support this. Instead, the Company's licensing should be seen as an indirect method to regulate the number of companies releasing on the market, thereby controlling somewhat the numbers of reels which would be available.

[46] Announcements by H. and H. Film Service Company (3 Record 1433-34), Laemmle Film Service (1439-40), and Western Film Exchange (1455-56) mention the large supply of licensed film available from them, even after their licenses had been revoked. See Cassady, p. 367.

(3) without the commitments called for by Trust production policies, the independents could release as many--or as few--films as the market would stand, and of varying lengths; (4) the independents could also raid the personnel of Trust companies by offering "star status" to the actors and actresses; and (5) they could vary the price of films without adhering to the Trust scale.

By 1912, the power of the Trust had been weakened sufficiently so that the territory was fairly open. For three long years the independents had grown steadily, resisting the Trust at every move. What resulted from this struggle, however, was not merely the downfall of the Patents Company; in its place were put all the ingredients for new and larger trusts.

As early as 1909, the independents had formed the National Independent Moving Picture Alliance aimed at providing an alternative to the Trust.[47] This organization was replaced in the Spring of 1910 by the Motion Picture Distributing and Sales Company, formed by the heads of IMP (Carl Laemmle) and the New York Motion Picture Company (Adam Kessel and Charles Baumann), with some unofficial backing by Western Film Exchange (John R. Freuler and Harry E. Aitken).[48] The

---

[47] Moving Picture World, V (September 25, 1909), 410.

[48] Moving Picture World, VI (April 16, 1910), 589. Laemmle, Kessel, and Baumann could openly advertise their names as "rebels" because they had severed relationship with the Trust. Others--such as Aitken and Freuler--however, still entertained Trust connections and were forced into a "silent partner" relationship in the organized rebellion. Fear of Patents' censure and repressive court action caused many independents to work undercover.

Sales Company was billed in trade journals as direct competition to General Film. However, within a few weeks after the Sales Company had been organized, a number of independents could see no difference between the licensed and unlicensed distribution agencies: on June 18, 1910, a third exchange organization was announced: the Associated Independent Film Manufacturers combine, composed of Thanhouser, Nestor, Eclair, Actophone, Lux, Electrograph, Centaur, Motograph, and others.[49] With dissension now apparent in the independent camp, fear arose that General Film could not be broken. The Sales Company was supported by IMP, Ambrosio, Cines, Eclair, Great Northern, Itala, and Powers; Associated was made up of independents who announced they would "not sell through any Sales Company."[50] Less than a month later, a compromise between the two independent factions was announced:

> The Motion Picture Distributing and Sales Company was reincorporated under a new charter which gave equal representation to Sales Company and Associated Independent interests.[51]

With this compromise, the independents joined together to wage battle with the General Film Company for the next two years.

The early dissension among the independents, however, was again evident in 1912. In April of that year, the trade journals announced

---

[49] Moving Picture World, VI (June 18, 1910), 1037. This article, entitled "An Open Market and an Open Door," expressed the sentiment that the Sales Company was General Film in a different guise. See Cassady, pp. 371-72.

[50] Ibid.

[51] Cassady, p. 372. See Also "The Dove of Peace," Moving Picture World, VII (July 9, 1910), 74-75.

the formation of Mutual Film Corporation;[52] included in this move was the establishment of the Film Supply Company of America to compete with the Sales Company. Laemmle immediately countered by dissolving the Sales Company and organizing Universal, an amalgamation composed of loyal Sales Company members. The independents were again split into two groups:

> Thanhouser, Gaumont, American, Great Northern, Reliance, Eclair, Solax, Majestic, Lux, [New York Motion Picture,] and Comet... were allied with the Film Supply Company; while...IMP, Powers, Rex, Champion, Republic, and Nestor became part of the Universal organization.[53]

Some explanation for this dissension has been offered by noting the personalities involved. Kalton C. Lahue has suggested that it was dissension between Aitken and Laemmle which resulted in the split between Mutual and Universal.[54] Aitken's brother Roy has also chronicled some of the differences which Harry had with other executives.[55] There were other reasons, too, which suggest that Laemmle's Sales Company in practice was not unlike General Film.[56] The Sales Company attempted on a small scale to regulate the number of films offered to the market by its member independent firms. Because Laemmle

---

[52] Moving Picture World, XII (April 6, 1912), 34.

[53] Cassady, pp. 373-74. See also Moving Picture World, XII (May 25, 1912), 707, 807.

[54] Kalton C. Lahue, Bound and Gagged (New York: Barnes, 1968), p. 76.

[55] See Roy E. Aitken, The Birth of a Nation, as told to Al P. Nelson (Middleburg, Virginia: William W. Denlinger, 1965).

[56] See note 49.

held large interests in certain independent companies, it was conceivable that some films (particularly from IMP, Powers, and Rex) would receive preferential treatment, which would arouse the displeasure of other firms. No one factor can explain the actions of men involved with the industry during this period. As suggested at the outset, this group of individuals can be divided between the "gamblers" and the "conservatives," those who were eager to explore new possibilities in production, distribution and exhibition, and those who found comfort in following the previously proven methods.

During this period, the standard length of films for both licensed and unlicensed manufacturers was the one- or two-reel film. In this area especially there was potential conflict brewing between the "gamblers" and the "conservatives." The one- and two-reel film was an accepted, marketable product; longer films demanded more time, more financing, and a generally increased mode of production. The majority of conservative producers seemed reluctant to consider the importance of a new phenomenon appearing in 1912--the feature film.

The arrival of the feature film from overseas played a large part in the attempts to find new methods for distributing the longer films. Because the majority of theatres in the country were small and built for the short, rapid turnover method of exhibition, features had to be aimed at the larger theatres and for extended runs. Consequently, the limited--conservative--distribution of the Sales Company, no doubt, seemed inadequate for those companies wanting to gamble on a more intense method of distribution to support longer films.

Instead of a central distributing agency, the dissident independents favored the selling of territorial rights to regional distributors, a method known as states right distribution. Under this system, the right to exhibit a film would be sold to a territorial distributor for either a flat rate or on a percentage basis. This method was advantageous in that it showed an immediate return to the original producers of the film; the drawback was that the producers might not share in any extraordinary success at the box office.

The developments of 1912 included not only these changes in distribution instituted by the formation of Universal and Mutual, but also an entry into feature production along two fronts. On one side, George Kleine, a Trust member, and Adolph Zukor began importing foreign features and spectacles. The presentation of Queen Elizabeth by Zukor in 1912 led to the formation of "Famous Players in Famous Plays," an organization founded by Zukor on the principle that the feature film and the "star system" were the directions most promising for the industry. On the other side, William Fox formed the Fox Film Company, immediately beginning plans to produce features. Fox joined a long line of distributors-turned-producers, such as Joseph Engel and William Swanson (Rex, founded 1909), Edwin Thanhouser and Charles J. Hite (Thanhouser, f. 1910), Samuel S. Hutchinson and John R. Freuler (American, f. 1910), Harry Aitken (Majestic, f. 1910). The feature film in America had developed both in the importing end and in the domestic end of the industry.

By 1913, a number of one-time distribution companies had become feature film producers. Warner's Features, first organized in 1912, and Box Office Attractions (eventually to become Fox Film Company) were established specifically to produce feature films and to acquire other features from independents for their own distribution chains.[57] This was also the year in which Zukor's Famous Players instituted its "block-booking" form of distribution, in which the company received a guarantee of acceptance of a number of features from the independent distributors and exhibitors.

> In May of 1914, the trade papers announced the formation of Paramount Pictures Corporation to handle distribution of Famous Players Film Company, Jesse L. Lasky Feature Play Company, and Bosworth, Inc., films.[58]

Mutual's attempt to organize a national chain of distributors was quickly followed by other companies, but with an added ingredient-- the accumulation of theatres. Alco, which was the stimulus for Metro Pictures, allied itself with Loew's Theatre Chain, laying the foundation for the eventual formation of M-G-M; World Film (Selznick) also began acquiring theatres for its distribution interests; Triangle (formed by Aitken with directors Thomas Ince, D. W. Griffith, and Mack Sennett) entered the theatre race by purchasing a few large, metropolitan first-run houses; and even four Patents members, V.S.L.E.

---

[57] Cassady, p. 381

[58] Cassady, p. 382. See also *Moving Picture World*, XX (May 30, 1914), 1268.

(Vitagraph, Selig, Lubin, and Essanay) began theatre acquisition.

The rise of the feature film not only intensified distribution concerns, but also led to the development of "movie palaces." Profit could only be won from large crowds viewing the longer, more expensively produced films, and this fact called for more appealing theatres. Throughout the country, a move began for glamorous showcases of feature films, theatres which would attract larger audiences--and higher prices.[59]

For all areas of the motion picture industry, the period from 1910 through 1916 was marked by eventful developments: the dissolution of Patents' control, the rise of the independents, the struggle for power among the independents, and a change in the scale of film production which demanded financial stability beyond the capabilities of the one- and two-reel manufacturers.

The Second Monopoly, 1917-1921

By the beginning of 1917, the structure and operation of the film industry had changed drastically from the nickelodeon days. The Patents Company had been all but dissolved by the Court and by its own members.[60] The number of producing companies had diminished, with

---

[59] For a chronicle of theatre development, see Ben Hall, *The Best Remaining Seats* (New York: Clarkson-Potter, 1961); also Jobes, pp. 271-73.

[60] The actual legal death-knell was sounded by *United States v. Motion Picture Patents Company*, 225 Fed. 800 (E.D. Pennsylvania 1915) in which the Patents Company was found to be a conspiracy in restraint

the result that only a few large feature-film companies controlled the majority of the industry, unconcerned with and unbothered by the number of short-film manufacturers struggling to maintain solvency.

The year 1917 saw the move by Paramount to incorporate Artcraft, Keystone, Realart, and Hearst's Cosmopolitan studios. The year also saw the formation of Goldwyn Pictures and the organization of First National Exhibitors Circuit by twenty-six leading theatre owners throughout the country. First National immediately engaged in competition with Adolph Zukor for control of the industry; owning far more theatres than Zukor, the First National had the financial backing to steal the two highest priced stars of the industry--Mary Pickford and Charlie Chaplin. For the next four years, the industry was to be shaped by the race for theatre acquisition on one side by First National and on the other by Adolph Zukor.

Such a race called for the strongest of financial support. As early as 1912, Wall Street had shown a willingness to participate in the financial activities of the film industry: Crawford Livingston and Otto Kahn had placed their financial resources behind the formation of Mutual. Most of the major theatre chains had backing from financial wizards, and as production increased both in length and in budget, the same type of backing was necessitated for the stability of studios.[61]

---

60 Continued. of trade. Through appeal, the Patents Company was officially dissolved by Motion Picture Patents Company v. United States, 247 U.S. 524 (1918). See also Conant, p. 21.

[61] Jobes, pp. 191-280, passim.

Early in 1918, the United States entered the European War closing some of the foreign markets for American films. After some early boom in theatre attendance, the year saw the demise of Biograph and Edison (the two stalwarts of the Patents Company), Mutual Film Corporation, Triangle Films, and Thanhouser, among other smaller firms.[62] By the war's end, the stage was set for the major companies who were to control all three areas of the industry for twenty years.

In 1919, United Artists was formed by comedian Charles Chaplin, actor Douglas Fairbanks, director D. W. Griffith, and actress, Mary Pickford. Harry and Jack Cohn, with Joseph Brandt, formed C.B.C. Pictures which, in five years, would become Columbia Pictures. Warner Brothers strengthened its alliance with the Stanley Corporation, assuring the company of its own theatres. Paramount, First National, Goldwyn, and Loew's were all actively procuring theatres to insure their own exhibition markets. In two years, the breakdown would be as follows:

```
First National . . . . . . . . . . . . 3400 theatres
Paramount  . . . . . . . . . . . . . .  303 theatres
Loew's (M-G-M) . . . . . . . . . . . .   70 theatres
Goldwyn . . . . . . . . . . . . . . .    30 theatres
```
[63]

---

[62] For a discussion of the motion picture in America during this era, see Timothy J. Lyons, "Hollywood and World War I: 1914-1918," *Journal* *of* *Popular* *Film*, I (Winter 1972), 15-30.

[63] Conant, p. 25. United Artists, Columbia, Warners, and R-K-O are noticeably absent from this list. UA's acquisition of theatres was slow and short-lived, while Columbia never really got involved in the theatre race. Warners did not acquire a theatre until December, 1924; by 1928, Warners had absorbed Vitagraph and Stanley Corporation, gaining 144 theatres in less than four years. R-K-O absorbed the

This move for gaining theatre control was the final step in the "new monopoly." In 1921, the same court actions which eliminated the power of the Patents' monopoly were begun against Famous-Players-Lasky and Paramount for "unfair competition."[64] The era had come full circle: from chaos to monopoly had come new chaos and then a new monopoly. And in its wake, the wave of business expansion had left behind companies which had helped to build the industry but who were ill-equipped to play for such high stakes.

Summary

The activities of the film industry in its first twenty-six years were complex and somewhat chaotic. The problems of building an industry based on mass entertainment were new ones for the unbusiness-like inventors. This new industry was unlike most business ventures in that it did not begin from a source of raw material to develop through a method of mass manufacturing into a system of mass consumption. Instead, this fledgling industry began mid-stream, founded on the inventions as industrial core, with little initial concern for the other areas of manufacturing necessary for real industrial development. An analogy to this situation would be if the automobile industry had begun with a machine for manufacturing tires; the progression of the film industry was simply unlike that followed by previous industries.

---

63 Continued. Keith-Orpheum Theatre interests, but was not formed until 1927. See Daniel Bertrand, W. D. Evans, and E. L. Blanchard, *The Motion Picture Industry: A Pattern of Control*, Temporary National Economic Committee Monograph no. 43 (Washington: Government Printing Office, 1941), pp. 59-60.

[64] Conant, p. 27.

With the domination of machines, the film industry was destined to stagnate as a supplier of mass entertainment until perceptive minds recognized the importance of two major questions: What kinds of films should be made? and, How do they get to the theatre? It was not until the formation of the Motion Picture Patents Company that these problems had even tenable solutions. With the Patents Company, the three areas of the industry--production, distribution, exhibition-- achieved some semblance of economic structure. However, for the industry to prosper, new challenges had to be made to the monopoly of the Patents Company.

Even though the Patents Company represented the first step toward stability, its formation also raised a new question: What should be the relationship among the three areas? This problem would be the major one facing the industry in its developing years--and one, perhaps, which is still central to the workings of the film industry today. The Patents Company saw the relationship as a vertical one, and its members planned to control each step in the film industrial system. To this the government said, "No." The attempt to control the invention, the process, and the product was in violation of the anti-trust laws.

The independents, however, held no claim to inventions and instead could slowly and carefully integrate the areas of the industry in a way similar to the Patents' but without prior claim to machinery. Both groups--licensed and unlicensed--were moving in the same direction, that of vertical integration. One distinction between the two camps was the interest in machinery controlled by the Patents members; another was the difference between inventors and businessmen. For either group to survive, it was necessary to combine the peculiar roles of "artist" and "businessman." While the Patents Company succeeded in stimulating the development of film as a mass art form, their business practices seemed "conservative" when compared to the majority of the "gambler" independents. The Patents' strength was in its claim over machinery; but the independents, without this claim, demonstrated the liability of the Patents' claims, as did the Court.

The companies which survived the competition from the early years into the 'twenties were ones which had built up strong financial backing, efficient methods of production, a closely allied system of distribution, and an assured marketplace for their product--either through their own theatres or through a system such as "block-booking" which required a theatre-owner to take a number of mediocre films in order to get one or two assured successes. The survivors were not only those who controlled their product from birth to death, collecting residuals along the way, but also ones who were willing to attempt innovative methods within the industry. It may be safe to say that had the Patents Company relied less on its claim to machinery and perhaps more on moving the industry forward, it would have been able to co-exist with those firms which did survive. However, this is mere speculation. What is clear is that the independents moved faster and more bravely than did the Patents Company, and in their gambling the independents won out.

A number of independent companies flourished for a short time then died quietly. Others never quite got started. For the "unlicensed" businessmen, this was a period of business blunders, financial acumen, hairbrained gambling, with tremendous success and equally disastrous failure. While the biggest independent companies took the biggest risks, either winning or losing, a few smaller companies managed to lag a step behind, waiting for others' initiative before venturing forward. These smaller companies, because of their conservatism and their careful practice, are not as widely known as their flamboyant rivals; yet, economically, these lesser firms acted as partners to the budding conglomerates in the development of a mass entertainment industry. The American Film Company was such a company.

CHAPTER III

THE AMERICAN FILM MANUFACTURING COMPANY AS A BUSINESS

Introduction

Previous discussion of the American Film Company as a business is typified by Norman Zierold's discussion of the company's origin in *The Moguls*.[1] Zierold's study can serve not only as an example of the few film business history books written for the general public, but also as a general introduction to the type of investigation to be pursued in this chapter.

Like some of the more recent film historians, Zierold has derived his material primarily from previously written accounts and interviews; his interviews were given by men recalling events of fifty or sixty years past.[2] Disregarding this fact, Zierold seems to have placed complete faith in his subjects' memories.

---

[1] New York: Coward-McCann, 1969. Also published as *The Hollywood Tycoons* (London: Hamish Hamilton, 1969).

[2] Among other historians who utilize interviews in their research are Kalton C. Lahue, Kevin Brownlow, and Peter Bogdanovich. Lahue also relies heavily on trade journals written during the period covered and, although he rarely footnotes his material, he is usually quite accurate. Brownlow, too, uses trade journals to balance the flamboyant recollections of his subjects. Film director Bogdanovich, who periodically concerns himself with film criticism and history, also attempts to verify his interviews by checking the facts involved.

His account of the American Film Manufacturing Company begins with some interview material from Allan Dwan, American's first permanent director (1910-1913). Dwan was in his early eighties at the time of the interview, and Zierold seems to have merely transferred Dwan's remarks to the printed page:

> When George Spoor of the American Film Manufacturing Company became interested in one of [Dwan's] ideas, a mercury vapor arc, Dwan took the occasion to present him with stories he had written for the Notre Dame Scholastic, the school's literary magazine. Spoor, ...to Dwan's surprise, said, "How would you like to be our scenario editor?" ...In 1909 Spoor sent him to California.[3]

This passage is an entertaining anecdote; however, there are a few things historically wrong with it. George Spoor was president of Essanay Film Manufacturing Company, not American; Dwan only became a scenarist for Essanay after working there as an electrician; he left Essanay to be scenario editor for American in 1910; and in 1911, American sent him to California where he became a director.[4]

Zierold continues his account in a consistent manner:

> Dwan was a prolific film maker, and other companies sought his services. Soon he was in a position to accept. His leading man, J. Warren Kerrigan, became angry because he set up a second unit with a second leading man, graciously

---

[3] Zierold, p. 97.

[4] See Peter Bogdanovich, Allan Dwan: The Last Pioneer (New York: Praeger, 1970), pp. 14-17; Brownlow, pp. 95-104; Julian Johnson, "A Brief Memorandum on Alan [sic] Dwan," Photoplay, XI (May 1917), 70-71; Jacques Lourcelles, "Allan Dwan," Presence du Cinéma, no. 22-23 (Fall 1966), 1-51.

> handsome Wallace Reid, a property man turned actor. Kerrigan complained to the company president, and Dwan was fired from a job which was now paying $500 a week.

Dwan then found work with Carl Laemmle at Universal.

> "Can you get the American Film Company people to work with you?" [Laemmle] asked him.... Dwan conveyed the terms to his old associates, who all swarmed to his side. It was the end of the American Film Manufacturing Company.[5]

If this account were accurate, my study would have just ended. However, it is not. For example, American did not fold in 1913 but instead lasted until 1921, and when Dwan left American, he took with him only his wife, Pauline Bush; within two years, perhaps ten actors from American's corps of almost one hundred, had joined Dwan at Universal, including his nemesis, J. Warren Kerrigan.

These brief excerpts should suggest the failure of the few business-oreinted historians to verify facts. As long as the sources are scarce and the period remote, some investigators seem more willing to let the myths about the past persist without new analysis. This feeling, unfortunately, also is found within the industry itself whose members are less concerned with an accurate portrayal of their past than they are with protecting cherished moments. In the research for this study, interviews constantly revealed a gap between objective data and the memories of the respondents, especially in the conversations with Zierold's subject, Allan Dwan.

---

[5]Zierold, pp. 98-99.

Peter Bogdanovich, in interviewing Dwan, attempted to reconcile research done for my study with material he was gathering for a monograph on Dwan:

> BOGDANOVICH: We're having some trouble with dates. You say you started directing for American in 1909. This kid from Santa Barbara[6] says you started in 1911.
>
> DWAN: Well, he's wrong. Where'd he get that information?
>
> BOGDANOVICH: Oh, this guy got them from old records he found, old American Film Manufacturing records, you know, and from reviews in the trade papers--reviews in the trade journals, you know....
>
> DWAN: Well, the early dates will have to be a confusion then. Just settle that any way you like. If 1910 is pleasant, make it 1910.... I wouldn't fuss about it.... They're so close together. If you're in December, 1909, it's 1909. But before you can turn around, it's 1910![7]

Fortunately, Bogdanovich included in his final study enough objective evidence from newspapers and business records to offset to a degree Dwan's occasionally faulty memory.

A separate study could be made of previous works which have either ignored the facts behind events or have been based on sources doubtful in reliability. This, however, cannot be the concern in this

---

[6] Bogdanovich is referring to the author of this study. I had prepared a portion of research on American's early years and provided this information to both Dwan and Bogdanovich. This material was eventually included as an appendix to Allan Dwan: The Last Pioneer, pp. 169-73.

[7] From a transcribed interview with Allan Dwan by Peter Bogdanovich, recorded in the Spring of 1969. Although this interview was the major section of Bogdanovich's book, this particular section was not included for obvious reasons.

chapter. What *is* the intent here is to survey the existing evidence about American's business operations—including a sampling of business records, trade journal articles, scholarly research done by other investigators, and to some extent, interviews—and to provide an interpretation of how and why the business was started, how it was run, and how and why it failed.

The complexity of any motion picture firm's operation is revealed in the workings of the American. A number of midwestern exchangemen became aware of a need for production companies to serve the distributors. American was started to supply as much product as quickly as possible to a market whose demand far outweighed the supply. For two years, this seemed to be the dominant operating motivation for the company. Later the exchanges behind American's formation grouped together not only their distribution agencies but also other fledgling production companies into the giant Mutual Film Corporation, and the production motivation for American became more complex. The direction of American's production policy was forced to change, adapting to the interests of the whole, rather than as an individual, producing films for its own benefit.

Mutual, under the reins of Harry Aitken, was one of the most ambitious ventures the film industry had seen. However, when in 1915 Aitken left Mutual in the hands of his former partner, John R. Freuler, the corporation underwent further changes in structure which were readily reflected in American's operations. And when Mutual finally was taken over by its creditors in 1918, American and other member companies were forced to fend for themselves, distributing their films through any available agency. This final stage placed full responsibility for American's success on the films themselves and the distributors' receptivity to handling American's product. Under this situation, American folded within three years.

The foregoing summary suggests the stages in which American's operation as a business will be discussed:

> The Beginnings: Western Film Exchange and
> The Independent Movement (1906-1910)
>
> The Exchanges Form Production Companies:
> The American Film Manufacturing Company
> (1910-1912)
>
> Harry Aitken's Mutual Film Corporation
> and the American (1912-1915)
>
> John R. Freuler's Mutual and the American
> (1915-1918)
>
> American Distributes Where It Can (1918-1921)

The Beginnings: Western Film Exchange and The Independent Movement (1906-1910)

In 1912, the trade journal *Moving Picture World* surveyed the recent past of film industrial development. In an attempt to explain the mushrooming of exchanges which had occurred around 1906, the editors offered the following interpretation:

> The supply of available films was utterly inadequate to the demand. The exhibitor looked not to the manufacturer but to the exchange man. He did not want to buy but to

rent. Under these conditions, it was natural for the
exchange to occupy a position of great importance in
the industry. Exchanges sprang up like mushrooms all
over the country. It took, however, less than a year
to separate the solid concerns from the weak ones.[8]

Typical of the ways in which many of the exchanges were organized were the events leading to John R. Freuler's entry into the film industry. (Freuler is especially significant to this study since he was later one of the founders of American.) A real estate broker in Milwaukee, Freuler became associated with the film industry when he gained an interest, through a defaulting debtor, in the Comique Theatre, a vaudeville showcase.[9]

Located on Kippinickick Avenue in downtown Milwaukee, Freuler's Comique Theatre was an important member of the Martin Beck Orpheum Circuit. As a theatre manager, Freuler quickly surveyed the situation: within five months, he turned the Comique's vaudeville bill--which had

---

[8] Moving Picture Annual and Yearbook for 1912, p. 36.

[9] Information on these early years is difficult to gather, since the period was one of few business records and rapidly changing organization. Facts about Freuler are taken from Ramsaye, p. 452; Mitry, I, 184-85; Jobes, p. 95; and a letter from historian Clark Wilkinson to this writer, dated April 13, 1969, which included some interview material with Harry Aitken, Freuler's partner. All of these sources show some debt to Ramsaye who, although he does not authenticate his facts, relies very heavily on trade journal reports. Much of the substantiation of factual material in this chapter will be forced to depend somewhat on Ramsaye and Mitry, since their sources were trade journals and fairly reliable; whenever possible, their facts will be corroborated --or disputed--by trade journal reference. Many assertions will be based on the opinions of a number of silent film historians who have arrived at differing interpretations of the scanty evidence available.

featured occasional film showings--into a program composed exclusively of films. After a brief respite, on July 23, 1906, the Comique Theatre reopened as a nickelodeon, one of the first theatres in Milwaukee to devote its entire program to featuring motion pictures.[10] At this time, Freuler also developed a working relationship with Harry E. Aitken, a film exchange representative from Chicago whom Freuler had encountered in booking films for the Comique's new program. Aitken's interest in motion pictures likewise had been accidental, developing out of his family's insurance and real estate business in which he used magic lantern shows as a sales technique.[11]

In July, 1906, Freuler and Aitken went into partnership and opened the first office of Western Film Exchange in Milwaukee.[12] Aitken had quickly convinced Freuler that the business opportunities lay in the distribution of films, and within two years Western Film Exchange had opened additional offices in St. Louis and Joplin, while acquiring interest in a number of other small exchanges. The significance of Freuler's and Aitken's enterprise was in their exploitation of the film rental business in the midwest, which had been largely undeveloped in this distribution area. It also seems significant that, whereas most of the strong firms in the film industry had developed from

---

[10] Ramsaye, p. 452; Mitry, I, p. 185. See also H. Russell Austin, The Wisconsin Story: The Building of a Vanguard State (Milwaukee: Journal, 1964), p. 567, and Bayrd Still, Milwaukee: The History of a City (Madison: State Historical Society of Wisconsin, 1948), p. 403.

[11] Austin, p. 567.

[12] Ramsaye, p. 452; Mitry, I, p. 185.

interests in manufacturing machinery for production and exhibition, the interest which motivated Freuler and Aitken was that of distribution and, to a lesser degree, exhibition. An interest in the third aspect of the industry, i.e., production, was to be a later development for Western Film Exchange.

During this period, Chicago stood as the center of midwestern film activity. Essanay, founded in 1907 by manufacturer George K. Spoor and actor Gilbert W. Anderson, was the major production firm in the area. Although a few producing companies attempted to compete with Essanay, only Selig (founded 1906) and Kleine (1901) were able to develop sufficiently to be on the level of Essanay's competition in the Chicago region. One of the more prosperous exchange endeavors was the Chicago Film Exchange, taken over in February, 1908, by Charles J. Hite.[13] This firm eventually had offices located in Atlanta, Chicago, Denver, Nashville, Omaha, Salt Lake City, and Washington, D.C.,[14] along with an interest in a New Jersey theatre chain.[15] Hite also had an interest in the H. and H. Film Service, founded two years after the Chicago Film Exchange, incorporating the C. J. Hite Film Service with the interests of former Chicago banker, Samuel S. Hutchinson.[16] The H. and H. concern was set up to handle the

---

[13] Mitry, I, 193.

[14] Cassady, p. 363.

[15] Mitry, I, 364.

[16] Hutchinson, born in Wyoming in 1869, had entered the film business initially through the exchange area as president and general

distribution of projectors, while the Chicago Film Exchange was established initially for the purpose of film rental of imported product.

In 1908, the strongest film exchanges in the midwest were Aitken and Freuler's Western Film Exchange, Hutchinson and Hite's Chicago Film Exchange, and Carl Laemmle's Film Service, located in Oshkosh, Wisconsin. Within the next two years, a number of events would involve these five men in the competitive struggles of a developing film industry.

The first of these events was the formation of the Motion Picture Patents Company in September of 1908.[17] This effort to control the film industry subjected the exchanges to the prevailing policies of the ten major film manufacturing companies whose films were essential for the survival of the exchanges. Although under the Patents Company, exchanges were allowed the privilege of handling all licensed product for licensed theatres, they could do so only if they refused to distribute the small amount of unlicensed film being produced by a few

---

16 Continued. manager of Theatre Film Service in Chicago in 1905. Along with his association with Hite and the H. and H. Film Service he also played a contemporary role in the Western operations of Theatre Film, in which he acted as secretary of the San Francisco branch for a few months before his interest was bought out by others. See "Notes from San Francisco," Moving Picture World, VI (January 22, 1910), 94. Also, Motion Picture Studio Directory and Trade Annual, 1921 (New York: Motion Picture News, 1921), p. 373, for a biography of Hutchinson. This source will be referred throughout this study as Directory 1921; others in this series will also be cited in this abbreviated form.

[17]Cassady, p. 329. For a more detailed discussion of the Patents Company, see above, Chapter II.

minor firms. For most exchanges, this seemed an equitable arrangement, one which brought some welcome stability to the amount of product consistently available to the weekly market. But for a few, the Patents' policy was viewed as restrictive.

Charles J. Hite was one who felt the restrictions of the Patents Company should be resisted. Early in 1909, Hite's Chicago Film Exchange entered the film production field on a small scale, joining the few other "independent" production companies: Centaur Film Company, Bayonne, New Jersey; Oklahoma Natural Mutoscene Company, Washington, D.C.; Penn Motion Picture Company, Philadelphia; and World Film Manufacturing Company, Portland, Oregon.[18] For almost two years, Hite's company attempted to survive in a market restricted by the Patents' policies; the road, however, was rough since licensed exhibitors and exchanges were wary of handling unlicensed film lest they would lose their Patents' sanction.

Hite eventually recognized his inability to battle the Patents' power alone. With his associate, Samuel S. Hutchinson, he established an alliance with Freuler and Aitken who had also entertained thoughts of joining the unlicensed producers. Hutchinson had attempted to elude the Patents Company by distributing imported films through the O'Malley and Smith Advertising Company,[19] a dummy firm necessitated by the Patents' strong control over licenses for film importers. Hite,

---

[18] Ibid., p. 363.

[19] Ramsaye, pp. 574-75; Mitry, II, 163.

Hutchinson, Freuler, and Aitken also seemed spurred to action by Carl Laemmle's refusal to join his exchanges to the Patents' movement. Laemmle had also demonstrated his challenge to the Patents by forming the Independent Motion Pictures production firm. He had paved the way for the independent movement when he formed the National Independent Motion Picture Alliance on March 20, 1909, with fellow exchangemen J. J. Murdock, William H. Swanson, Adam Kessel, Charles Baumann, Pat Powers, and Edwin Thanhouser.[20] The Alliance was a further strengthening of the Film Service Association, a group of exchange operators formed before the Patents Company to prevent "duping" of films and to provide some coordination of the diverse exchange practices. The leaders of both the Film Service Association and the National Independent Motion Picture Alliance were those who resisted joining the Patents Company and instead became producers of motion pictures: Laemmle founded IMP in May, 1909; with Edison's former top director, Edwin S. Porter, William Swanson formed Bison Life pictures in the same month, the company eventually becoming Defender, then Rex; Powers formed his own company in October, 1909;[21] Kessel and Baumann joined Fred Balshofer in the formation of Crescent Films, the seed for the New York Motion Picture Company;[22] Edwin Thanhouser began his own production

---

[20] Mitry, I, 332; Cassady, p. 370; *Moving Pictures World*, V (September 25, 1909), 410.

[21] Mitry, I, 332.

[22] See Balshofer and Miller, pp. 14-29 *passim*. Also, *Moving Picture World*, IV (May 8, 1909), 613.

company in March of 1910;[23] and Murdock quickly formed an importing concern, International Film and Projecting Company, in the Spring of 1909.[24]

Within a few months, the Patents Company had established its policies throughout the industry. Hite, Hutchinson, Freuler, and Aitken benefited from the exemplary action of Laemmle and his associates, so that in the Spring of 1910 when the National Independent Alliance became the Motion Picture Sales and Distributing Company, Hite and his allies joined the movement. The situation was now one of two warring camps: in the stronger position was the Patents Company with ten major manufacturers and the majority of exchanges and exhibitors under license;[25] challenging them were the members of the Motion Picture Distributing and Sales Company. Both groups employed similar means to implement their goal, the stabilization of the industry, and both groups had their dissenters.

The Sales Company had been organized not simply as a challenge to the Patents Company but more specifically as an alternative to the Patents' General Film Company, an amalgamation of previously licensed exchanges. General Film, founded in April, 1910,[26] extended a license to John R. Freuler and the Western Film Exchange. As with most of

---

[23] Ramsaye, p. 498.

[24] Ramsaye, p. 495; 2 *Record* 1120.

[25] Cassady, pp. 332-33.

[26] *Ibid.*, p. 350.

General's licenses, this was actually a renewal of license, since the Patents Company had awarded to Freuler on February 20, 1910, an exclusive franchise in states covered by the Western Film Exchange. Freuler's participation in the Sales Company, of course, endangered his licensed status with the Patents' and with General Film; however, the benefits of maintaining a position in both licensed and unlicensed distribution areas must have been strong enough to necessitate some elusive business actions by Freuler and his associates.[27]

During the summer of 1910, Freuler's tenuous position between the Patents' and the Independents' camps became apparent. There was trouble amidst the ranks of the Sales Company with Aitken and others complaining that Laemmle's interests were being served over the other members'.[28] Since at this time Aitken and Freuler were planning three major studios (American and Reliance, both to be announced in October, and Majestic, which began in January, 1911),[29] and since Hite was contemplating the purchase of Thanhouser's studio (November 15, 1910),[30] the concern was strongly for the insurance of a favorable

---

[27] For example, Aitken's name was not publicly associated with Western Film Exchange since he was known by some to be a part of the independent movement, even while he was co-director with Freuler of Western. Also, when Freuler decided to branch out into production, this action was accomplished initially under Hutchinson's dummy firm, O'Malley and Smith, supposedly an "advertising company." See Ramsaye, pp. 574-75.

[28] Kalton C. Lahue, Bound and Gagged, p. 76.

[29] Mitry, II, 85.

[30] Ibid., I, 336.

distribution outlet. Aitken and Freuler threw their support behind the Associated Independent Film Manufacturers (founded by Thanhouser, Nestor, Eclair, Actophone, and others), announcing they would not deal "through any Sales Company."[31]

The dissenters' point was well-taken: Laemmle reorganized the Sales Company with "equal representation to Sales Company and Associated interests."[32]

> Under the terms of the agreement between the [Sales] Company and its members, (a) each manufacturer was required to distribute his goods through the Sales Company, (b) films were to be sold in accordance with a schedule of prices, and (c) a fee was to be levied on each release as a distribution charge to the manufacturers. Thus by concerted activity, reminiscent of "Trust" behavior, the independents consolidated their sales effort, and by so doing enhanced their chances of succeeding against "Trust" opposition.[33]

The situation in the summer of 1910 was one of an uneasy peace among the independents. On one side, the prospects were promising:

> The Motion Picture Distributing and Sales Company program consisted of twenty-seven reels per week from twenty or more domestic and foreign manufacturers [while the Patents' offered approximately thirty reels from ten companies]. They had entered into distribution arrangements with forty-seven non-licensed rental exchanges [compared to the almost seventy licensed exchanges] located in twenty-seven cities in the United States and Canada. These rental exchanges in turn served approximately 4,000 theatres [of the over 10,000 in the country] which by that time were operating without benefit of

---

[31] See Cassady, pp. 371-72. Also, "An Open Market and An Open Door," *Moving Picture World*, VI (June 18, 1910), 1037.

[32] Cassady, p. 332. See also, "The Dove of Peace," *Moving Picture World*, VII (July 9, 1910), 74-75.

[33] *Ibid.*, p. 372.

Patents Company licenses. Thus eighteen months after the
formation of the Patents Company, there was a substantial
and well-organized segment operating independently of
"Trust" control.[34]

Although allied by their struggle against the Patents Company, self-interests were still high among the exchangemen-turned-producers. The independents lacked the machinery interests of the Patents Company which guaranteed a substantial profit to patents holders; instead, they were interested in maintaining as open a field as possible for their exchange activities. Each of the members of the independent Sales Company had also seen the need to enter the production end of the industry. Laemmle and others had demonstrated the possibilities for success; now what remained for the further development of the independent movement was additional production activity. Harry Aitken, John Freuler, Charles Hite, and Samuel Hutchinson were ready for this move with the formation of the American Film Manufacturing Company during the first week of October.

The Exchanges Form Production Companies (1910-1912)

One by one, Freuler's Western Film Exchange licenses received the scrutiny of the Patents Company.[35] On July 19, 1910, the St. Louis

---

[34] Ibid., p. 372-73.

[35] Contrary to the exciting reports of Terry Ramsaye, "The Patents Company...did not have an espionage division for the purpose of detecting violations, but rather relied largely on reports from various licensees for such information" (Cassady, p. 347). On a number of occasions throughout the summer of 1910 and early Fall, licensees who were threatened by Freuler's rapidly growing concerns seemed ready to let the Patents Company know of Freuler's activities.

license was cancelled;[36] and in the next few weeks, other offices of Western had their licenses revoked by the Patents. Freuler, however, attempted to continue business as usual:

> The Western Film Exchange announcement [after its licenses had been cancelled] list[ed] Biograph, Edison, Essanay, Kalem, Lubin, Méliès, Pathé, Selig, and Vitagraph as "...manufacturers whose product we will have to select from."[37]

H. and H. Film Service also continued announcing "the immense stock we have of licensed goods" long after its licenses had been revoked and replevin suits had been filed.[38]

However, the dubious practice of releasing licensed films illegally could not continue indefinitely. With the supply of licensed films shut off, not only did Freuler and Hite have to contend with the legal action brought against them by the Patents Company, but also they were forced to depend upon the small rank of independent producers. The need for their own source of supply was becoming evident.

The first public hint that Freuler and his associates would enter production was a small notice in the trade journal, Moving Picture World, entitled "Chicago Notes":

[36] Cassady, pp. 348-49; 2 Record 1076.

[37] Cassady, p. 367. Cited from 3 Record 1076.

[38] Cassady, p. 367. Cited from 3 Record 1433-34. A replevin suit is "a personal action...brought to recover possession of goods unlawfully taken (generally...applicable to the taking of goods distrained for rent).... The word means a delivery to the owner of the pledges or thing taken in distress." Black's Law Dictionary, pp. 1463-64.

> That the independents are every hopeful for the future of
> the moving picture "game" is proven by the fact that new
> manufacturers are springing up in every corner. The latest
> addition to the already large fraternity of independent
> manufacturers is a new company being launched by Messrs.
> Kennedy & Hamilton, formerly with Essanay Film Mfg. Co.
> If both the gentlemen have profited by their experience
> with the very popular Essanay Films, they will quickly
> make a mark, for the independent market is certainly in
> need of good comedies.[39]

The following week, the same column included another mention of this venture:

> Kennedy and Hamilton, who, we are informed, will operate
> under the firm name of American Film Manufacturing Company,
> have leased the Phoenix plant on Orleans street, while the
> theatre of Lincoln J. Carter on Segwick street will be
> used as their studio.[40]

Significantly, neither Freuler, Aitken, Hutchinson, nor Hite were mentioned in the preliminary announcements, since they were all involved in litigation with the Trust. Instead, the supposed brains behind the new operation were Aubrey M. Kennedy, who had served as Essanay's general manager for three years, and Gilbert P. Hamilton, Essanay's former superintendent of factory and production.[41]

---

[39] Moving Picture World, VII (September 17, 1910), 639.

[40] Moving Picture World, VII (September 24, 1910), 684.

[41] See biographies of both men in Directory 1921, pp. 268 and 265, respectively.

The first actual public announcement of the American Film Manufacturing Company was heralded during the first week of October:[42]

American Film for the American People
Manufactured by the
American Film Manufacturing Company

This is the announcement of something new in the Film World--a new Independent Film Manufacturer. But although we are new, we are already old. A new Film Manufacturer may have much of everything--all that money will buy in the way of plant, equipment and talent--and fail. No NEW concern can have a reputation ahead of its first product unless that reputation shall rest upon the experienced personnel of its organization--EXPERIENCED EMPLOYEES. We therefore respectfully invite your attention to the appended list which composes partially the staff of the American Film Manufacturing Company.

EXECUTIVE
A. M. Kennedy, General Manager
G. P. Hamilton, Superintendent Factory and Studio

PRODUCTION
Thomas Ricketts, Dramatic Producer
Sam Morris, Comedy Producer
Frank Beal, Western Producer

TALENT
J. Warren Kerrigan, Leading Man
David G. Fisher, Juvenile Lead
Harry Clifford, Juvenile Lead
Miss Dott Farley, Character Parts
Miss Josephine Ricketts, Juvenile Leads
Miss Jessie Mosley, Character Parts

---

[42] The actual date of American's founding cannot be determined more specifically. Depending upon the trade journal consulted, the first public announcement was between October 5 and 8. Ramsaye, who depends heavily on The Motion Picture News, cites October 5; The Moving Picture World carried the announcement on October 8. Those few historians who mention American usually cite Ramsaye's date, although previous notices in the journals which mention the company suggest that plans began in August, with the hiring of Kennedy and Hamilton in early September, and the accumulation of a staff during the last week of September, 1910.

PROPERTY
Robert Coffee, Chief Property Man
Nelson Lund, Property Man
Edward R. James, Property Man

SCENARIO
Allan Dewan [sic], Scenario Expert

DEVELOPMENT
Henry Meyer, Asst. Superintendent and Chemist
E. R. Fraks, Foreman
Miss Anna Gallaghan, Forewoman

MECHANICAL
Chas. Ziebarth, Mech. Expert
Otto Hubel, Electrician

NOTE: In addition to the above listed heads of various departments of the American Film Mfg. Co. every employee in our Office, Factory, and Studio has had from two to five years' experience in the manufacture of film for an established manufacturer. There is not an inexperienced man in our employ.

We have eliminated all question of doubt about our first release. We have a modern plant and facilities, brains, money and a combination of know-how. Every man in our organization has had from two to five years experience in film making--all the way from the studio to the screen. They are conscientiously and diligently striving for the highest attainment in film making. WATCH FOR TWO IMPORTANT THINGS--OUR SUBSEQUENT ANNOUNCEMENT AND

OUR FIRST RELEASE

AMERICAN FILM MANUFACTURING COMPANY
BANK FLOOR
ASHLAND BLOCK
CHICAGO, U.S.A.[43]

American's coup was not only a welcome addition to the independent ranks but also a successful depletion of Essanay's staff, alluded to in the announcement as "an established manufacturer." The strongest Patents member in Chicago had supplied--albeit, unwillingly--the

---

[43] Moving Picture World, VII (October 8, 1910), 817.

nucleus for American's production, directing, acting, writing, and technical corps. With the blare of trumpets, John R. Freuler and Harry Aitken had entered the production field.

George K. Spoor was not to take the raid on his staff lightly. The following week, after Trust censure had been extended to most of American's associates, a publicity release from Essanay attempted to counter American's attack. Under the heading, "Essanay Reorganize Their Studio and Plant Staff Extensively," the article avoided any direct reference to American:

> Many changes have been made in both the studio and plant staff of the Essanay Film Manufacturing Company during the past two weeks, which cannot but greatly benefit the releases made by this firm. The production department at the big Chicago studio is in the hands of Harry McCrea Webster, stage director, well known both East and West as a man of unusual originality and ability in the theatrical world. An entire new stock company has also been enlisted and productions will shortly prove that no mistake has been made in this direction. Numerous other employees of the studio were also released and better people have been engaged to fill their positions. The printing, developing and mechanical departments also shared in a general change that cannot be otherwise than highly beneficial to the weekly output of this firm. The management also states that their Western Company has been largely increased, and is in personal charge of G. M. Anderson, and under his direction working in Colorado at the present time, making some very excellent subjects which are shortly to be released.[44]

---

[44] Moving Picture World, VII (October 15, 1910), 864.

It seemed clear to Essanay that American had stolen not only its staff but also the format of its production strength: comedies and Westerns. And this is exactly what the American had in mind.

Three units were immediately established for the "Flying A," called so because of the company's symbol: Thomas Ricketts was to handle the dramas and Sam Morris the comedies, both at work either in the Chicago studio or on location nearby; Frank Beal was given the responsibility for the Western troupe which was sent into the Southwest to mirror the activities of Essanay's "Broncho Billy" Anderson.

The first release announced for American was Romantic Redskins, to be available November 2,[45] starring Essanay's former comedienne, Dot Farley. The release date was subsequently changed to November 14, beginning a schedule of release on Mondays and Thursdays, instead of the Wednesdays and Saturdays originally announced.[46] Regardless of American's shaky beginnings, the anxiety of the trade awaiting the first release was indicated by the weekly notices in the trade journals:

> That loud rumbling sound in the region around Lake Michigan, like the warning that precedes a volcanic eruption, has been traced to the movements of the American Film Manufacturing Company. Ground is being broken for the erection of a new factory to be ready before the close of this year; meanwhile, American comedies are being produced in the plant of the

---

[45] Kalton C. Lahue, World of Laughter: The Motion Picture Comedy Short, 1910-1930 (Norman: University of Oklahoma, 1966), p. 62. See also Ramsaye, pp. 574-75, and Mitry, I, 336.

[46] It also seems fair to speculate that many problems needed to be solved, thereby delaying the first release two weeks.

defunct Phoenix Company, which has been leased for three months, and a company of cowboy actors are setting the natives of Wisconsin talking about their escapades. Truly the American Film Manufacturing Company mean business and we await with interest the appearance of their first release.[47]

The establishment of the American Film Company out in Chicago is an event of the highest significance. Ever since the Independent film manufacturing movement took shape, Chicago was weak in this end of matters. Last year, two or three abortive attempts were made to institute manufacturers there. They failed, because the men at the head of affairs were neither scientifically, commercially or personally capable of handling the situation. At last, in the establishment of the American Film Company, we have a concern worthy of the Independent cause in Chicago.[48]

From November, 1910, to April, 1911, American produced forty-two reels of 1000-foot films, releasing two reels weekly. Their schedule of output was stable, yet contemporary reviews indicate the quality was variable.[49] The films produced during the initial months by American's three companies were made up equally of Western comedies and dramas, and social comedies. Most of these were filmed in and around the Chicago area. With the announcement that their Western company

---

[47]"American Enterprise," *Moving Picture World*, VII (October 15, 1910), 865.

[48]"The American Film Manufacturing Company," *Moving Picture World*, VII (November 19, 1910), 1162.

[49]See *Moving Picture World*, VIII (February 11, 1911), 318-19. In reviewing *Bertie's Bandit* (released January 26), the critic noted the rising level of cinematographic quality: "Earlier releases were frequently criticized by managers as well as patrons because the photography was not what it should be."

was filming along the Santa Fe Trail in New Mexico,[50] the American began to plan for a concentration on their Western product. In April, the company announced their production schedule to be exclusively Western:

> Real Western. Western films made <u>in</u> the West--<u>of</u> the West--<u>by</u> our Western Company. Remember "The Squaw and the Man"--"The Tenderfoot's Roundup"--"Bertie's Bandit"--"In the Land of Cactus"? Two such subjects each week will be released by us from now on. Americans--nothing but Western--commencing week of April 24th. All "Americans" hereafter will be "Western." Two "<u>American Westerns</u>" each week. Mondays and Thursdays.[51]

American's action was not without precedent. Two months earlier, Essanay had made the following statement:

> We do not believe it possible to faithfully reproduce Western pictures--call them cowboy pictures if you will--without going right out into the districts which the film is supposed to portray. The people...insist upon Western films being really Western films, and that the Essanay Company have been successful in their efforts is proved by the fact that their Western films are accepted and approved by Western audiences, who would be the last people in the world to accept substitutions artificially staged in the East.[52]

---

[50] <u>Moving Picture World</u>, VII. (December 3, 1910), 1350; "American Plans in the West," <u>Moving Picture World</u>, VIII (January 7, 1911), 31.

[51] <u>Moving Picture World</u>, VIII (April 8, 1911), 779.

[52] Quoted from "In the Far West," <u>Bioscope</u>, February 9, 1911, in Anthony Slide, <u>Early American Cinema</u> (New York: Barnes, 1970), p. 66. Compare Essanay's statement to the following 1911 publicity release from American: "There is no artificial lighting system in a studio that can approach the perfection of sunlight. There is no scenic artist who has ever been born who could originate and paint scenery that will anywhere equal the stupendous scenic beauties of the Western country. We propose to instill into 'Flying A' Cowboy films the spirit of the West as it

American followed Essanay's lead in denouncing the Westerns being produced on the East Coast, and in doing so, the company placed much of its confidence in its Western troupe, directed by Frank Beal.

This confidence, however, was to be short-lived. Allan Dwan, who was American's scenarist at this time, recalled the situation which existed in April of 1911:

> They'd sent Beal...[out West] with a company.... They said, "How'd you like to go out to California and see what's going on out there with Beal? They claim they have no stories." I said, "It shounds fine."
>
> I went out...and after a long search I finally found our company at San Juan Capistrano in a little hotel. There were about eight actors, a lot of cowboys, some horses, and everyone was sitting there doing nothing. I said, "Why aren't you working?" They said, "Well, our director has been away on a binge for two weeks in Los Angeles, and we don't see him very often, so we haven't made any pictures." It looked like a pretty sad situation and I wired the Chicago office, "I suggest you disband the company. You have no director." They wired back, "You direct."[53]

---

52 Continued. really is, the atmosphere of the West as it really was, and the romance of Western life as everybody, even the Westerners themselves, fondly imagine it had ought to be." Quoted in Slide, p. 82.

[53] Bogdanovich, p. 17. Almost precisely the same story was given by Dwan to Kevin Brownlow (p. 97) and to this writer in a letter dated May 15, 1969. Dwan insisted to Bogdanovich that he joined American in 1909 and was sent out West with Beal, that he received word to disband the company, and that after he paid the company's way back to Chicago, he was fired from American--only to be re-hired after the firm changed hands. His confusion seems to be in the fact that if he did go out West in 1909, it was for Essanay, the studio for which both he and Beal were working at that time, and that his "re-hiring" actually connected with American's raid on Essanay's staff. This explanation justifies the dates Dwan recalls; however, he has repeatedly refused to accept this reasoning, preferring to believe that American was founded in either 1908 or 1909. A number of other factual discrepancies also arise, such as contemporary newspaper reports of American's Western troupe arrival in Santa Barbara, California, on July 6, 1912, while Dwan insisted that he arrived in Santa Barbara in 1910.

So Dwan followed the precedent of accidental involvement which his superiors has experienced and became the principal director for American.

At this stage in American's development, the primary concern was a steady supply of attractive product. The position which American held in the industry was as supplier to the Sales Company whose function was to serve its many distributor members. This concern was to remain the same as long as American was merely a member of the Sales Company supply force. However, developments within the association of Hite, Hutchinson, Freuler, and Aitken, coupled with those which would occur to the production schedule under Dwan's influence, were to change American's position by the next year.

Hite and his associates held interest not only in the production at American but also in similar ventures. Aitken had allied himself to Kessel and Baumann's Reliance Company, founded at the same time as American.[54] Hite purchased Edwin Thanhouser's interest in the Thanhouser studio on November 15, 1910.[55] In addition to his financial backing of American, he was also behind Freuler and Aitken's Majestic Pictures, formed on January 12, 1911.[56] In the summer of 1911, Hite and his associates had interests in the Chicago Film Exchange and the Western Film Exchange, and four independent studios: American,

---

[54]Mitry, II, 84.

[55]Ibid.

[56]Ibid.

Thanhouser, Reliance, and Majestic. By the Spring of 1912, they could survey their position as one of substantial strength, one strong enough to break with the Sales Company.

Before this break could occur, though, sufficient development in production was necessary to convince the backers that the production companies would support a new independent conglomerate based on the Sales Company practices.

Under Allan Dwan's direction, American developed sufficiently to assure its stability. Beginning in April, 1911, the company decreased the activity of its two Chicago companies and placed major responsibility for two reels per week on Dwan's Western troupe. Dwan readily accepted this challenge, filming at first around San Juan Capistrano and then moving to nearby Lakeside, California. Dwan's company produced two reels weekly from Lakeside until, in the summer of 1911, they moved to La Mesa to take advantage of new background settings. Here they remained until July, 1912, when they became permanently located in Santa Barbara, 250 miles to the North.

Dwan's methods of production called heavily upon his scenarist background:

> I'd pile everyone into two buckboards, a ranch wagon for our equipment, the cowboys on their horses--the actors too if they were riding in the picture. On the way out, I'd try to contrive something to do. I'd see a cliff or something of the sort. I had a heavy named Jack Richardson, so we'd send J. Warren Kerrigan, the leading man, up there to struggle with Richardson and throw him off the cliff. Now having made the

last scene of the picture, I had to go backwards and try
to figure out why all this happened.[57]

The films began to follow a set pattern with stories always building to some obligatory fight or discovery scene.[58] Dwan enjoyed not only his employers' approval but also some moderate success in contemporary reviews.[59] In less than two years, American had become a permanent, well-respected member of the independent movement.

Harry Aitken's Mutual and the American (1912-1915)

The first sign of a schism in the independent ranks was the announcement in early April, 1912, that certain manufacturing interests had organized a company, Mutual Film Corporation, for the purpose of acquiring rental exchanges. This was followed shortly by an announcement of the organization of the Film Supply Company of America and the securing by that company of exclusive rights to the product of some of the more important Sales Company manufacturers.[60]

Aitken and Freuler had suffered long enough under the preferential treatment Laemmle had demonstrated toward his own interests through the Sales Company.

---

[57] Bogdanovich, pp. 19-20.

[58] The early Westerns will by analyzed in Chapter V.

[59] Some indication for American's growing success can be found in the progression of its advertising campaign in the trade journals and in the increasing praise in the reviews. See ads and reviews in *Moving Picture World*, 1911-1912. The contemporary critic, Robert Grau, also had praise for the American program: "The American Film Manufacturing Company, in its policy of exploiting the American cowboy, re-enact, with its talented company, such stories as it is able to obtain, pertaining to the early West, teeming with drama and comedy, tragedy and pathos, amid the virginal scenery and backgrounds of the range country." *The Stage in the Twentieth Century* (New York: Broadway, 1912), p. 135.

[60] Cassady, p. 373. See also *Moving Picture World*, XII (April 6, 1912), 34, and XII (May 25, 1912), 807.

When the day came to discuss a renewal contract, Aitken-Freuler withdrew their product. With S. S. Hutchinson, another small producer, and Charles J. Hite, president of Thanhouser,...the midwesterners organized Mutual, a company designed to imitate General Film with a national system of exchanges.[61]

Mutual had the initial advantage of already controlling the large exchange interests of Freuler and his associates. With their already prolific sources for production and distribution, all Mutual needed for its beginnings was a substantial financial backing. This was found in the persons of financiers Crawford Livingston and Otto Kahn, members of Kuhn, Loeb, and Company, Wall Street bankers.[62]

Harry E. Aitken was elected president, Freuler vice-president and general administrator. Felix Kahn, who represented Crawford Livingston, was appointed secretary, and Calvin Brown was in charge of public relations. The representatives of the former Chicago Film Exchange...were placed in charge of regional offices.[63]

The way in which Mutual was formed and structured was similar to General Film and the Sales Company:

It went along quietly, without blare of drums, for several months, buying an exchange here one day and one there the next day. At one stroke it acquired the extensive Gaumont [licensed] exchange interests in Canada.[64]

---

[61] Jobes, p. 95.

[62] Ibid.; Hampton, p. 102; Ramsaye, p. 580.

[63] Mitry, I, 339. My translation.

[64] Grau, *Theatre of Science*, pp. 54-55.

Mutual also inherited the Western Import Company of London, founded by Aitken in 1910, with offices in Paris, Vienna, Brussels, and London,[65] along with Hutchinson's American Company, London, Limited, formed for the European handling of the "Flying A" product.[66]

Over half of the members of the Sales Company flocked to Mutual's side: Thanhouser, Gaumont, American, Great Northern, Reliance, Eclair, Solax, Majestic, Lux, Comet, and two weeks later, New York Motion Picture Company and Bison. Laemmle, however, was not to be outdone. With his own IMP, and Powers, Rex, Champion, Republic, and Nestor, he formed Universal, leaving the Sales Company a mere shell.[67] By June, 1912, Mutual and Universal were as powerful as General Film, all of them with similar business structures.

After almost a year in La Mesa, Allan Dwan and his troupe--geographically oblivious to the changes occurring in their parent companies--began to search about for fresh scenery.

> [Actor Marshall Neilan] was a California and he knew everything around there.... One weekend he wanted to go back to Los Angeles and I said, "Why don't you go a little further and find me a place where I can have the ocean and the mountains and ranches and everything we need to make pictures?" He said, "Well, I'll look for a place." So a few days later I got a phone call from Santa Barbara, and he said, "I've found exactly

---

[65] Grau, *Theatre of Science*, p. 57.

[66] *Directory 1921*, p. 373.

[67] *Moving Picture World*, XII (June 8, 1912), 911. Laemmle announced that, like Mutual, he would withdraw his films from the Sales Company on June 10, 1912.

what you want down here." So I packed up the outfit, put
them on their horses and their wagons and off we went from
La Mesa all the way to Santa Barbara.[68]

The Santa Barbara local newspaper, The Morning Press, announced the arrival: "Film Company Come Tomorrow to Locate in Santa Barbara; Company of Thirty from La Mesa Secures Lease on Former Ostrich Farm."[69] The following day, The Morning Press anticipated the surprise of the community as the "Flying A" marched into town:

> A bunch of typical cowboys can be expected to ride into the city from the south today, but the citizens of this peaceable community should not feel any great concern, as the town will not be shot up.[70]

Dwan located the company at the deserted ostrich farm and set about making plans to begin production.

On July 9, production began in Santa Barbara,[71] with some evidence that the Chicago office was planning to develop the Western troupe further.[72] By November, these plans seemed to be set. In an article entitled, "Permanent Home, 2 Troupes, for American Film Co.

---

[68] Bogdanovich, p. 22.

[69] The Morning Press, July 5, 1912, p. 3.

[70] Ibid., July 6, 1912, p. 3.

[71] Ibid., July 9, 1912, p. 2.

[72] The Morning Press, July 14, 1912, p. 2, reported, "With its two Western companies, one in Santa Barbara and the other in Chicago, the American Film Mfg. Co. announces itself in the market for some good Indian stores of one-reel length. Good prices will be paid for acceptable manuscripts."

Here; Purchase of Suitable Site at Reasonable Figure is Only Question Now," The Morning Press publicized the commitment the company had made to remain in Santa Barbara:

> The Company has rented the store room at 14 East Cota Street, as a temporary developing plant, and after this week all the pictures will be developed before being sent to the Chicago office, where the negatives will be made. The Chicago office will still be maintained for business reasons, it being more convenient to the principal film houses.[73]

The article continued to outline plans for the formation of a second unit, to be announced November 10. The subsequent announcement also stated that "all American plays would be produced in Santa Barbara and...the eastern company would immediately be disbanded and its place filled by the new one."[74]

In two years, American had progressed from an independent company with three shooting units, to a strong member of Mutual with all of its production being done on the West Coast. The new plans required added facilities which were announced on November 28[75] with completion aimed for the Spring of 1913. The new studio would house the two companies, Dwan's continuing to produce two one-reel Westerns per week, and the other company under Wallace Reid producing one "society play"

---

[73] Ibid., November 5, 1912, p. 3. Instead of "negatives," the article should more properly have stated that the film would be sent to Chicago "where the release positives will be made."

[74] Ibid., November 10, 1912, p. 3.

[75] The Morning Press, November 28, 1912, p. 5.

weekly. The architect's plans of J. C. Pool seemed to promise the most impressive studio yet to be built on the Coast:

> Beauty and utility were never better combined then in this plan. There will be a general mission effect. Along Mission Street there will be an eight-foot arched brick or concrete wall, and at the east corner the office building, which will be surmounted by a mission tower. The main entrance will be midway between the east and west corners. After entering the heavy iron gateway two roads will diverge, finally leading to either side of the glass and concrete studio in which interior pictures will be taken. This studio will vary in height from 18 to 26 feet, and be 40 by 60 feet in dimension. The structure will be of steel frame, with three of the sides portable, of sections that may easily be taken out, the purpose being to make easy the adjustment of light. The property and scenic room will be immediately back of the studio.
>
> The administration building, with its mission tower, will be at the corner nearest State Street, while on the south corner, at Chapala Street, will be the lounging room and dressing rooms for the players. This latter building will run back a considerable distance, with sufficient number of dressing rooms so that the players will have every convenience to make-up for plays. There will be running water in every room, and the most modern system of heating for this part of the country.
>
> The development plant, about 30 by 40 feet, will be immediately back of the administration building. The projection room will be in the administration building, thus conveniently located as related to the development department. Every negative is run off before being sent to Chicago.
>
> There will be a garage for five machines, back of the dressing room, and immediately behind it the stables. The carpenter shop, etc., will be located in that part of the ground.[76]

In July, American's production schedule increased to three reels per week, two being supplied by Dwan and one by the Chicago company.

---

[76] "American's Santa Barbara Plant," Moving Picture World, XV (February 8, 1913), 559; reprinted from The Morning Press.

When the Chicago company was disbanded, the second company in Santa Barbara took over their responsibility for a weekly reel of film.

The prospects for American's future seemed promising to Allan Dwan until he became involved in a personality clash with star J. Warren Kerrigan:

> Kerrigan didn't like the second unit idea, he didn't like Wallace Reid being a star...so he put a knock into the company by letter saying I was getting out of hand and that unless I was replaced, he was going to leave the company. So out came Hutchinson.... He talked to Kerrigan and he talked to me and I told him very frankly, "Things are going to be just the way I want them or else they're not going to be at all, as far as I'm concerned." So he left me a note on my desk...: "As of now," it said, "you are no longer with the company."[77]

Dwan left for Universal in May, 1913, taking with him his wife, actress Pauline Bush. By this time, American had placed all of its trust in the Santa Barbara operations and quickly replaced Dwan with experienced directors Lorimer Johnston and Sydney Ayres. The production schedule was not interrupted, and plans continued for the new studio which was finally ready for use during the Summer of 1913.[78]

While American stabilized its production program and ventured into new forms of the photoplay besides their staple of Westerns, Mutual was continuing to grow and to prosper. By the Fall of 1913, Mutual was

---

[77] Bogdanovich, pp. 27-28.

[78] "American Studios at Santa Barbara," *Moving Picture World*, XXI (July 11, 1914), 240. See also G. Vaughn Obern, "The American Film Company: The Flying 'A'," a brief paper provided for use by Obern, University of California at Los Angeles, Motion Picture Division (December 12, 1966), pp. 9-11.

distributing the films of Thanhouser, Princess, Reliance, Komic, Majestic, Kay-Bee, Broncho, Domino, Apollo, Keystone, and American. Aitken had also formed the Continental Feature Film Corporation to handle the features of Reliance and Majestic, especially those directed by Thomas H. Ince and D. W. Griffith. Mutual had "more than fifty distributing offices in the United States and Canada, and offices in several of the large cities in Great Britain and on the Continent."[79] But all was not well within Mutual's ranks.

> Almost from the beginning, Harry [Aitken] had clashed head-on with his old acquaintance and partner, John R. Freuler. As Mutual's chief executive, Aitken was to come under a cloud of suspected favoritism and discrimination soon after his tenure began. Freuler and Samuel S. Hutchison [sic], both of the American Film Manufacturing Company, became very unhappy about the manner in which Mutual handled their product, but they were firmly bound by contract to supply Mutual with a specified quantity of films for distribution and were thus unable to do much more than grumble loudly in an effort to make life as miserable as possible for Aitken.[80]

One of the major disputes was over the length of films to release through Mutual. Hutchinson had strongly upheld the one-reel limit for American since its formation. It was not until the Spring of 1913 that American began to release two-reelers, and then only very occasionally. The number of two-reel films increased slowly during

[79] Grau, Theatre of Science, p. 54.

[80] Kalton C. Lahue, Dreams for Sale: The Rise and Fall of the Triangle Film Corporation (New York: Barnes, 1971), p. 22.

the Fall of 1913, with 1914 showing an even greater dependence upon two- and three-reel films.[81] Features--five reels or more--were not done by American until The Quest, released in March, 1915. Considering that the rest of the industry began thinking seriously about features as early as 1913,[82] Freuler and Hutchinson's attitude can be seen in retrospect as extremely conservative. They had landed upon a formula which was successful and had no desire to "rock the boat." But Harry Aitken's ideas would not slow down.

Maintaining some form of harmony between the progressive Aitken and the cautious Freuler was a job performed by Charles Hite, whose personal qualities enabled him to keep his two partners away from each other. The untimely death of Hite on August 22, 1914,[83] created an even more tense situation.

> Shortly even the occasional meetings between Aitken and Freuler became acrimonious shouting matches. Business arrangements were worked out on a lower executive level, as the top corporate posts were stalemated in every direction.[84]

With Hite gone, Freuler and Hutchinson began to make some changes in American's program, probably more because of the rapidly changing motion picture business than because of Harry Aitken's proddings. Early

---

[81] An analysis of the number and lengths of films produced by American will be found in Chapter V.

[82] Cassady, pp. 375-84. See also the list of features and feature production companies in Moving Picture Annual and Yearbook for 1912, pp. 127-28.

[83] Mitry, II, 87; Ramsaye, p. 666.

[84] Lahue, Dreams for Sale, pp. 22-23.

in 1914, American instituted the "Beauty" brand of films, a series
of light comedies modeled somewhat on the successful Keystone comedies.
The schedule for the first two months of 1914 features two-reel
dramas released on Mondays, one-reel "Beauty" comedies on Wednesdays
and one-reel Westerns on Saturdays. Production was stepped up in March
to include one "Beauty" brand, a Western, and two comedies to be
released weekly; American's product was now available four days a
week. With this increased production--and the new Santa Barbara
studio--came also additional personnel and more care in production
methods.[85] For the next twelve months, American increased the comedy
film production and placed less and less emphasis on the one-reel
Western. Perhaps a major reason for this shift was the developing
feature film movement, the growing sophistication of audiences, and
the general need recognized by producers to develop newer, fresher
forms beyond the Western.[86]

In March, 1915, American released its first feature, The Quest,
an "ambitious film"[87] with Margarita Fischer and her husband,
Harry Pollard, both of them "Beauty" stalwarts, William Garwood,
Lottie Pickford, Charlotte Burton, and directed by Thomas

---

[85] For a discussion of personnel and information on production methods, see Chapter IV.

[86] There does not seem to be any one reason to explain the gradual shift of American from Westerns to light comedies and sentimental dramas. The general trend of the industry was moving in this direction, and perhaps American simply joined this movement. Other developments, however, such as the growing demand for more complex story material and the expansion of American's scenario department, may have contributed toward this shift.

[87] Mitry, I, 344.

Ricketts.[88] While Freuler and Hutchinson were vacationing in Europe, Aitken refused to release the picture, claiming that "it was not up to standard."[89]

> When the American's chiefs returned from Europe, they found that Aitken had left The Quest on the shelf. Meanwhile the Reliance-Majestic, Griffith and Ince features were going to market.[90]

The Quest was to have been American's first "Masterpicture," a term coined by Aitken after the popular reputation of D. W. Griffith as "The Master." Freuler and Hutchinson openly derided the name of the series, "referring contemptuously to the 'Masterpiece' series as 'Griffith-pieces.'"[91] Aitken had already alienated the Mutual directors by his founding of Continental Features to release certain Griffith and Ince films outside the Mutual sources. The tension between Freuler and Aitken was finally to come to a head in May, 1915, at Mutual's Board of Directors meeting:

> By that time, there was much animosity within the corporate offices and most of it was focused on the president. While

---

[88] Ricketts had directed the Chicago company early in American's career but left to join Nestor at its Hollywood studio. See Edwin O. Palmer, History of Hollywood (Hollywood: Cawston, 1937), I, 192-93; also Ricketts' obituary notice in "Early Days in Los Angeles," Los Angeles Herald-Examiner, February 5, 1964, chronicling Ricketts' death at the age of 86. After a brief time with Universal, Ricketts had returned to American in 1913. See Directory 1920, pp. 311-12.

[89] Ramsaye, p. 718.

[90] Ibid., pp. 717-18.

[91] Lahue, Dreams for Sale, p. 23.

Aitken was dividing his time among his many interests, Freuler had feverishly contacted the 700 stockholders to line up sufficient support in his bid to unseat the incumbent president, and as a result the election of the chief officer for the coming year proved to be a cut-and-dried affair, with Freuler winning easily.[92]

Aitken was no longer a member of Mutual,[93] and the tension eased somewhat.

But Mutual would never again regain the position it held under Aitken. Its first two years were "active, progressive and prosperous" with remarkable "vision, courage, financial resources, energy and ability for its time."[94] Benjamin Hampton, himself a producer during this period, suitably characterized not only Aitken the producer but also Mutual Film Corporation during Aitken's tenure:

> Aitken, gifted with unusual personal persuasiveness, was an exceptional promoter and business builder, with rare talent for persuading directors, players, bankers to conform to his plans.[95]

For its next four years, Mutual would gradually suffer the loss of these qualities, a loss that eventually would affect the American Film Manufacturing Company.

---

[92] *Ibid.*, p. 25.

[93] Aitken's career, however, was not over. With Griffith, Ince, and Mack Sennett of Keystone, he formed Triangle; the following year he released Griffith's *The Birth of a Nation*. He never again reached the heights of this period, instead spending the rest of his life dreaming of a remake of *The Birth*. See Roy E. Aitken.

[94] Hampton, p. 102.

[95] *Ibid.*

John R. Freuler's Mutual and the American (1915-1918)

Harry Aitken's departure from Mutual meant the loss of Majestic, Reliance, and Keystone and NYMPC films for Mutual release. Freuler was faced with the problem of decreased production for the Mutual outlets; this factor perhaps more than anything affected the program at American.

Freuler and Hutchinson had formed the North American Film Corporation on January 2, 1915,[96] to explore the possibility of serial production. Hite's Thanhouser had enjoyed enormous success with The Million Dollar Mystery, simultaneously syndicating the serial story in the Chicago Tribune.[97] So American was anxious to follow this success; in selecting Roy L. McCardell's treatment for The Diamond from the Sky, the company entered the serial field. The event also had significance in other areas:

> [American] created a sensation by paying Roy McCardell... $30,000 for the story and editorial supervision of [the] serial.... Until this event writers had been receiving fifty to five hundred dollars for film stories, and no novelist or playwright had hitherto been paid more than a thousand dollars or so for the use of his material. American's fee to McCardell aroused the literary world, and authors and playwrights began to believe that movies might become an important factor in their business affairs.[98]

---

[96] Mitry incorrectly reports this date as 1914 (I, 343); however, Ramsaye, who served as the editor for North American's scenario contest through the Chicago Tribune, cites 1915 (p. 668). This year corresponds with trade journal mention.

[97] See Ramsaye, pp. 663-68.

[98] Hampton, p. 103.

The conservative management of American must have been strongly committed to serial production to offer such a high price for story material. The commitment can also be seen as an avoidance of entering feature production *per se*; instead, under the serial method American could produce a feature and release it gradually, maintaining a backlog of films. Mary Pickford was offered $4,000 a week for the lead role in The Diamond from the Sky:

> Mary refused..[the] offer.... Meanwhile the serial makers insisted on having the valued name of Pickford for their advertising, so Lottie Pickford, sister of Mary, was employed for the leading role.[99]

Plans called for thirty two-reel episodes to be released weekly beginning May 3.[100] The first director was Jacques Jaccard, with the directing chores later taken over by William Desmond Taylor.[101]

American's success with the serial was followed by an offer of $5,000 "for the best idea for a sequel to The Diamond from the Sky."[102]

---

[99] Ramsaye, p. 669.

[100] The release period spanned May 3 through November 22, 1915. See appended filmography.

[101] Both of these men were part of the later developments in the film industry. See Chapter IV.

[102] Lahue, Bound and Gagged, p. 125. It is interesting to note that the author of the four episode sequel (November 25-December 18, 1916) was Terry Ramsaye, who had selected the original McCardell treatment the previous year.

American also entered the war preparedness serial campaign with The Secret of the Submarine (May 22-July 17, 1916).[103]

When scenarist Clifford Howard arrived at American in the Fall of 1915, the studio was one of the most developed on the Coast, second in size only to the new Universal studio in Hollywood.[104] Howard, coming from the small Balboa studio, was impressed with American's activity:

> I here found five or six stages, one of them enclosed and using the Klieg lights which had recently come into use. There were eight separate units working at the studio, turning out a wide range of pictures--single-reel comedies, two-reel Westerns, three- and five-reel dramas, fifteen episode serials, and a periodic super-special of six or seven reels. Also, the scenario department had three readers and a staff of nine writers in addition to the editor.[105]

American had committed itself to releasing one "Mutual Masterpiece" per month; in addition to this obligation, the company was also producing one "Beauty" reel, a two-reel "Flying A" Western, and a one- or two-reel drama. By September, the company had added a three-reel "American Star Feature" which in the following month became the short-lived "Clipper Star Features," and a one- or two-reel Western

---

[103] See Kalton C. Lahue, Continued Next Week, pp. 38-39.

[104] See Grau, Theatre of Science, p. 52; also Photoplay Art, II (August, 1916), 11.

[105] Clifford Howard, "The Cinema in Retrospect," Close Up (London), III (December, 1928), 37.

("Mustang" which absorbed "Flying A"). During the Fall of 1915, American was producing as many as eight and nine films per week.[106]

Clifford Howard's tenure with American also saw a number of improvements:

> There was no film-printing machine at the studio when I first went there, nor any outside laboratory for doing such work. All the cutting was done with the original negative. When that work was completed the negative film was sent to...Chicago, where the positive prints were made for distribution to the exhibitors. We at the studio never knew how our pictures actually looked until after they had been released and shown in the theatres.... However, in the course of a year, we were supplied with a printer, and held a little celebration in honor of our first studio positive.[107]

Howard witnessed the introduction to on-set music for dramatic scenes, and the rise of the developing star system. He worked closely with Mary Miles Minter, Lottie Pickford, Gail Kane, Julia Day, May Allison, Lew Cody, William Russell, Douglas MacLean, and Nigel de Brullier, and directors Henry King and Frank Borzage, among others.[108]

American created a storm of controversy with the screen version of the 1913 stage success of Brieux's play about syphilis, Damaged Goods. Stage star Richard Bennett made his screen debut in the role he played on Broadway. Another sensation of 1915 for American was Howard's scenario for Purity which called for the entire cast to

---

[106] See appended filmography.

[107] Howard, pp. 37-38.

[108] Ibid., pp. 38-39.

cavort in the nude through the classical settings of the millionaire estates in nearby Montecito.

> Audrey Munson...[had] been chosen out of a multitude of models, to pose for the figure on the memorial coin of the World's Fair at San Francisco in 1915. The newpapers took her up and exploited her as the woman with the ideally perfect figure. At the height of this notoriety the president of the American Film Company, with laudable enterprise, secured her signature to a contract to appear in a moving picture, and forthwith proceeded to whet the public appetite with appetizing advance notices regarding the forthcoming super-special film in which this famous artist's model, receiving the enormous salary of five hundred dollars a week, would appear in the unequivocal glory of her profession.
>
> Following which the selection fell upon me to write a scenario that would not only fulfill these promises to the public, but at the same time would also disarm the censors. As a beginning to this end I hit upon the title <u>Purity</u>; and with this as an inspiration I constructed an eight-reel scenario along highly poetic and idealistic lines.[109]

The year 1916 was American's most prolific year in terms of film production, and represented the apex of the firm's career. A breakdown, year by year, of production reveals the following in Table 1. It should be clear from this table that the progression of American's film production moved steadily toward longer, or feature films.[110] And this progression necessitated a larger production staff and also increased facilities. In May, 1916, the studio had been enlarged to accommodate twelve companies,[111] the payroll enlarged from $1,000 weekly

---

[109] Ibid., p. 40.

[110] This table, and the consideration of film quantity and quality, will be treated in more detail in Chapter V.

[111] Robert C. Duncan, "The American Studio," *Picture Play*, IV (May, 1916), 189.

TABLE 1

AMERICAN FILM PRODUCTION: 1910-1921

	number of reels	number of films
1910	14	16
1911	109	130
1912	133	140
1913	173	161
1914	216	167
1915	401	247
1916	596	242
1917	193	54
1918	124	26
1919	88	17
1920	84	15
1921	65	13

in 1912[112] for the Western Company, to $19,000 in 1916.[113] By the peak production year of 1916, the studio had under contract eighteen permanent directors, 75-100 players, 150-500 extras, and 200-300 technical personnel.[114]

Mutual, too, had expanded slightly to fill the void left by Aitken's departure, taking with him his companies. In February, 1916, Freuler signed the top comedian in motion pictures, Charlie Chaplin, to a contract for $670,000.[115] For a short time, there was speculation that Chaplin would be housed at the American studio;[116] however, Mutual gave the comedian his own studio--The Lone Star--located in Hollywood.[117] Mutual also was behind the formation of the Vogue and Signal producing companies, the latter being headed by Hutchinson himself.[118] When Chaplin left Mutual in 1917 for First National, Mutual began its steady decline.

> Freuler was exceedingly aware that Mutual's old line producers were going to let the concern die the same death that was overtaking the General Film, and for the same uninspired reason.

---

[112] *The Morning Press*, August 12, 1912, p. 2.

[113] Duncan, p. 190.

[114] *Ibid.*

[115] Theodore Huff, *Charlie Chaplin* (New York: Pyramid, 1964), p. 53.

[116] Roy E. Aitken, p. 75.

[117] Huff, p. 54.

[118] Duncan, p. 200. See also Lahue, *Bound and Gagged*, p. 283, and the discussion in Chapter IV of Hutchinson and Freuler's business interests.

> If there were to be Mutual pictures Freuler had to get
> them. He wanted [Mary] Pickford.[119]

But Mutual lost "America's Sweetheart"--for the second time--to Famous Players. With Chaplin gone, the Corporation had only a few "box office stars" under contract, and most of these were with American. The move was on for theatre accumulation, a field which Mutual had totally ignored.[120]

American became Mutual's chief source of supply in 1917 and 1918, producing exclusively five-reel features. In an attempt to increase the supply of Mutual films, American also re-released many of the one-reelers which had been produced by Allan Dwan and others during the company's first few years;[121] this practice, however, was discontinued in April, 1917.

It was clear by 1918 that Mutual could no longer compete against such ventures as First National, Warner's, and Famous Players, all of whom had acquired theatres for a guarantee of exhibiting their product. And as Mutual declined, American too began to lose its strength.

American Distributes Where It Can (1918-1921)

In 1918, the motion picture industry in the United States was struggling to appeal to a public too busy working for the Great

---

[119] Ramsaye, p. 743.

[120] See Chapter II. Aitken had begun to gather a few theatres, but these became part of Triangle, the corporation he founded after leaving Mutual.

[121] See appended filmography for the re-releases, usually noted by the brand "Mutual-American."

War to attend the motion picture theatres. For the first part of the year, business had prospered; but by Spring, the boom had ended.[122]

One of those who found the business competition and the changing economy too much to bear was John R. Freuler.

On May 8, 1918, the Central Trust Company of Illinois attached Mutual's funds.[123]

Freuler gradually relinquished his command over Mutual, while retaining his executive position with American. With Mutual insolvent, American was without a parent. Like Mutual's other producing units,

---

[122] See Gertrude Jobes' account of this period, pp. 152-90.

[123] Ibid., p. 170. Mutual did not die a quick death. Instead, under receivership, the corporation attempted to bail itself out for more than a year. In November, 1917, Mutual had filed an injunction against NYMPC and its associates Keystone, Broncho, and Domino--companies which Aitken had withdrawn; this move, however, was denied by the court in February, 1918. In May, Freuler resigned to be replaced by James A. Sheldon, formerly of the Syndicate Film Corporation. Through a number of endeavors, Mutual tried to secure a supply of films for its distribution outlets. On September 6, 1919, they acquired the Affiliated Exhibitors films for release, and on November 12, the name of the corporation changed to Exhibitors-Mutual Film Corporation, after the Affiliated interests had gained control on November 8. Exhibitors-Mutual secured the popular Robertson-Cole films on November 21. Little by little, other exchanges began to buy up the Mutual exchange offices, and in July, Exhibitors-Mutual's only production company, R-C pictures, cancelled its contract charging the company with insolvency. Although the court found in favor of the Exhibitors-Mutual, Hallmark Pictures took over the E-M interests to handle the Mutual-Chaplin re-releases with Robertson-Cole distributing. On January 5, 1921, Robertson-Cole absorbed Hallmark, thus acquiring the Mutual interests. See "The Year in Headlines," Wid's Year Book, 1918; 1919; 1920; 1921 (New York: Wid's Films and Film Folks, 1918; 1919; 1920; 1921).

Vogue and Signal, American either had to find a new distributor, distribute on its own, or fail.

An article in the September, 1918, issue of *Motion Picture Magazine* surveyed American's position in the industry:

> This is one of the studios which has stood the test of hard times, business changes and war encroachments, and at the present writing special dividends are declared. Everything is done conservatively, pictures are turned out in record time, and arrangements are now completed whereby two new companies are to be added to the four already working on the big glass stage.[124]

American had under contract stars Mary Miles Minter--a pale competitor to Mary Pickford, Westerner William Russell, and former "Beauty" star Margarita Fischer. Directing were Lloyd Ingraham, Edward Sloman, and Henry King, all destined to achieve fame in later film work.[125] But although on the surface the prospects for American seemed promising, there was a lack of the traditional hectic activity at the studio. Director Edward Sloman recalled the studio during this period as one of little organization and of somewhat confused business practices:

> [They] had this nasty habit of going down to Los Angeles, engaging someone for one picture, and then letting them go. I guess they hoped by keeping the personnel down they'd save some money. But things didn't get better; they got worse.[126]

---

[124] Ruth Kingston, "At the American Studio," *Motion Picture Magazine*, XVI (September, 1918), 57.

[125] See Chapter IV.

[126] From a recorded interview with Edward Sloman, at his home in Beverly Hills, California, May 10, 1969.

Some of the residents of Santa Barbara also remembered this period as one in which the American employees were refused credit at local stores since the company had become repeatedly late with payments.[127]

At the end of 1919, the company was practically bankrupt. The state of their assets was as follows in Table 2. With material assets valued at $205,600.80, and $73.55 in real cash, the company had actual incurred debts of $35,745.37. In this condition, it was only a matter of time before the company would be forced to liquidate.

In July, 1918, American announced its plan to distribute through Pathé Exchanges on a states-right basis.[128] During 1919, the company released seventeen films; in 1920, the output was fifteen; and in 1921, thirteen films were released, the majority of these either re-releases from the 1916-1917 period or films made by Hutchinson's Signal Company. During the summer of 1920, American indicated in the trade journals that it would make specials only through 1921, implying that the company would cease after this date.[129] This announcement was coupled with a note that "American Film Co. and the Biografia, Central European film companies, form new five million crown company," a development which never again was mentioned in the press.[130] In

---

[127] From an interview with Isaac A. Bonilla, curator of the Santa Barbara Historical Museum, and former stable boy for the "Flying A"; at the Gledhill Library (Santa Barbara), January 21, 1969.

[128] Wid's Year Book, 1918, n.p.

[129] Ibid., 1919-20, n.p.

[130] Ibid., 1920, p. 101.

TABLE 2

RECAPITULATION OF INVENTORY: DECEMBER 31, 1919[a]

Real Estate	$15,163.75
Building	86,373.33
Live Stock	150.00
Automobiles	16,530.00
Props	22,117.84
Wardrobe	4,480.85
Furniture and Fixtures	4,472.21
Equipment	56,212.82
Accounts Receivable	1,362.62
Accounts Payable	4,433.72
Notes Payable	21,036.00
Balance in Bank	73.55
Work in Process-- Pict. A-168--Actual Cost	9,275.65

[a]From the collection of American Film Company papers held by Joel Conway, Santa Barbara, California.

December, American announced it would "states-right films made by [the] <u>Chicago Tribune</u> in Ireland,"[131] again a promise which saw no fulfillment.

When in February, 1921, Margarita Fischer signed with Independent Films Association and director George Cox moved to Universal,[132] American lost the last key production personnel on its payroll. A fitting obituary for American was anticipated in a local guide written for tourists:

> The company believe in using brains in the business, and catering to what the public wants, not what they think is wanted; so in marking time occasionally and not making films, they wait until the public taste has been ascertained, then make films to suit that taste.[133]

American had been a part of a rapidly developing industry and had prospered in its activities. But the company had failed to gamble as successfully as others; it had failed to see beyond the value in controlling distribution and production to that third area of the industry which was attracting the major companies' interest, i.e., exhibition. Without its own theatres, and having lost its exchanges, American ceased production in 1921. After re-releasing some of its more successful features, the studio became a mere shell for others' use.

---

[131] <u>Ibid.</u>, <u>1921</u>, p. 93.

[132] <u>Ibid.</u>, p. 99.

[133] John R. Southworth, <u>Santa Barbara and Montecito</u> (Santa Barbara, California: Orena-Schauer, 1920), p. 185.

95

CHAPTER IV

AMERICAN'S PERSONNEL

Introduction

The importance of a film production company's personnel goes beyong the type of nostalgia being written today as "film history." Any complete coverage of an historical event must entail discussion of the many causal factors which shape this event. From the previous chapter, it should be clear that the pervading business structure of a film company influences the events to a large degree. The policies of the company can also be seen in the types of personnel employed, the reasons for their employment, and their subsequent careers.

Not all investigation into the personnel of silent film companies has to be relegated to the rank of "recollection," or "nostalgia for nostalgia's sake." Instead, this area of examination can aim to elucidate the human contribution to a business enterprise. Such information can be derived from trade journal annual biographies and general biofilmographies which list the career data of individuals involved in the motion picture industry.[1] This chapter on American's personnel will attempt

---

[1] Such sources vary more in quality than availability. The more reliable for the silent film are the Motion Picture Studio Directories, published by The Motion Picture News beginning in 1918, and Wid's (later Film Daily) Yearbook also begun in 1918; these two sources were close to the contemporary activities of the industry and represented a pipeline of information to the trade. Other sources also provide such data: F. C. Justice and Tom R. Smith (ed. and comp.), Who's Who in the Film World (Los Angeles: Film World, 1914); Ruth Wing, Blue Book of the Screen (Hollywood: Blue Book, 1923); and Filmlexicon

to use some of these sources to provide a picture of who American hired and why, how they were used, and where they went.

While there may be confusion between an investigation of personnel and the nostalgic chronical of who-was-where-when, there are notable differences between the approaches and perhaps even areas where they overlap. The personnel investigation of American which will follow begins with the company's three original units formed in 1910, progresses to an examination of the Western Company (1910-13), covers the expanded employment (1914-17), and then charts the eventual decline of the personnel on American's payroll (1918-21). The intent throughout this chapter is to discover what kinds of employees were hired by American, for what general or specific duties, the backgrounds of these individuals, their length of stay with American, and their subsequent employment. The discussion reveals a similar pattern to the chapter on American as a business: as the company declined, so too did the quality and number of personnel.

Nostalgic investigation is not necessarily concerned with such questions. What is at issue in such reporting is the popular appeal held by certain stars during their career, along with off-screen details of their lives. The point at which the personnel investigation becomes "nostalgic," in a sense, is when some understanding of a star's appeal in American films is desired.

---

1 Continued. _degli autori e delle Opera_ (Rome: Bianco e Nero, 1961). It would be impossible in this study to treat each and every one of American's over 5,000 employees. A small number have been selected as representative of others; the entire personnel--those whom information has been located--are listed in Appendix C.

The limited number of personnel selected for this investigation represents the three types of employees working for American: 1) those who remained with American throughout the company's career; 2) personnel who stayed with the company only temporarily and whose career ended after their stay with American; and 3) those who after leaving American achieved success with other firms. The sampling of employees will be discussed according to their level of production responsibilities for American.

The Executive Branch, 1910-1921

In 1917, The Moving Picture World invited prominent film producers to reflect upon the industry's development. American's president, Samuel S. Hutchinson, offered the following remarks:

> It was approximately ten years ago that I launched forth into the motion picture industry--an amusement that everybody at that time considered "but a fad of the moment"--for in those days not even the most farsighted of men suspected that in 1917 the business of producing and distributing film would be ranked as the fifth industry.
>
> It was in the exchange field that I made my start....[I]n partnership with the late Charles J. Hite, I formed what was christened the H. & H. Film Service, and even at that time the exchange was a comparatively small organization. Mr. Hite and I were not only the exchange managers, but also attended to the bookings, the shipment of film, the accounting department and sometimes served as our own stenographers. Today when there are some 3,200 employees in the organizations of which I am an executive [i.e., American, Mutual, Vogue, Signal, and American Projecting companies], it seems almost ridiculous to think back to the time when a real stenographer and an office boy were considered a luxury rather than a necessity.[2]

When Hutchinson founded the American Film Company in 1910, he had not only the assistance of Hite but also that of John R. Freuler, some

---

[2]"American's President Talks of Ten Years," Moving Picture World, XXXI (March 10, 1917), 1502.

unofficial backing by Harry Aitken, and the publicized participation of Gilbert P. Hamilton and Aubrey M. Kennedy. By 1917, of the original founders only Freuler and Hutchinson remained with the American.

For the initial year of American's operation, Hamilton and Kennedy held the executive reins over the company's production, with Hutchinson and his associates remaining in the background. Hamilton brought valuable experience to the new company having entered the film industry through the developing department of the Edison studios. After a brief stint at Biograph as a cameraman, he joined Essanay as superintendent of factory and production, a position he held for four and a half years. When Hamilton joined American in 1910, he occupied the same supervisory position he had held with Essanay.[3]

Aubrey M. Kennedy also had the background necessary for the new company to operate efficiently. Having served Essanay for three years as general manager,[4] Kennedy not only offered valuable experience to American but could also function as a complement to Hamilton with whom he had worked during his tenure at Essanay. This workable arrangement, however, was to be short-lived.

Within a year, Hutchinson lost the support of his superintendent. Taking with him comedienne Dot Farley, Hamilton left the American to

---

[3] Directory 1921, p. 265. It is interesting to note that Hamilton's biography in Directory 1921 does not mention the year he spent with American, although the information is included in the Directory for 1918. Perhaps since American ceased production in 1921, Hamilton did not want to acknowledge publicly his past association with a defunct company.

[4] Directory 1921, p. 268.

organize the St. Louis Motion Picture Company and later the Albuquerque company.[5] His career later developed from general manager of both companies to director for such firms as Century, Metro, and Triangle. With the loss of Hamilton, Hutchinson took a more active part in the daily operations of the company producing units and factory.

Kennedy remained with American through 1912. However, he too soon felt the motion picture wanderlust and left American to form the Santa Barbara Motion Picture Company, with Elmer J. Boeseke, taking with him a number of American personnel. After a few years of prosperity with his Santa Barbara company, and the Navajo, Alhambra, C. K., Crown City, and Kriterion "Star" companies,[6] Kennedy became general manager for Universal, then Goldwyn.

Hamilton and Kennedy had served as valuable executive material to the young American. With their departure, however, Hutchinson was able to step in, readjust the personnel and continue operation. Hutchinson's banking and exchange background no doubt aided him in overseeing the business operations of American. His partner, John R. Freuler, far from possessing the public personality of Hutchinson, remained behind the scenes. Throughout American's career, Freuler acted as secretary and treasurer, even after he has resigned his presidency at Mutual. While Hutchinson allowed his name to be used in

---

[5] _Directory 1918_, p. 172.

[6] See Kennedy's advertisement in H. E. Wildy (comp.), _The Photoplayers, Inc._, 1915 (Los Angeles: Photoplayers, 1915), n.p.

American advertising as the "Master Producer,"[7] Freuler preferred a less public position of involvement. As president of Mutual and chairman of the executive board, Freuler held executive interest not only in American but also in Lone Star, Thanhouser, Majestic-Reliance, New York Motion Picture, Vogue, States Film, North American, and Signal.

From 1912-1918, American's executive branch and personnel structure was intimately connected to the company's association with Mutual, in which both Hutchinson and Freuler had major roles. A company organizational chart for most of American's existence would reveal the following type of "chain of command" shown in Figure 1.[8]

The members of the executive branch, perhaps more than any other area of American's business operation, remained fairly constant throughout the company's career. With Hutchinson as president and Freuler as secretary-treasurer, the high executive ranks did not change in the twelve years of the company's operation. The early executives, Hamilton and Kennedy, had remained for a relatively short time; the other members of the executive branch, however, did not follow suit. American's laboratory superintendent and head of factory operations, Charles A. Ziebarth held this position for twelve years, later becoming an expert with Bell and Howell.[9] The company's general manager, Richard R. Nehls, used his experience from Kleine to perform

---

[7] See Ramsaye, p. 718.

[8] No such chart of Mutual has been found in other sources. Helpful in constructing this one was the organization chart of Paramount-Famous-Lasky, 1929, in Lewis, p. 30.

[9] Directory 1918, p. 264.

101

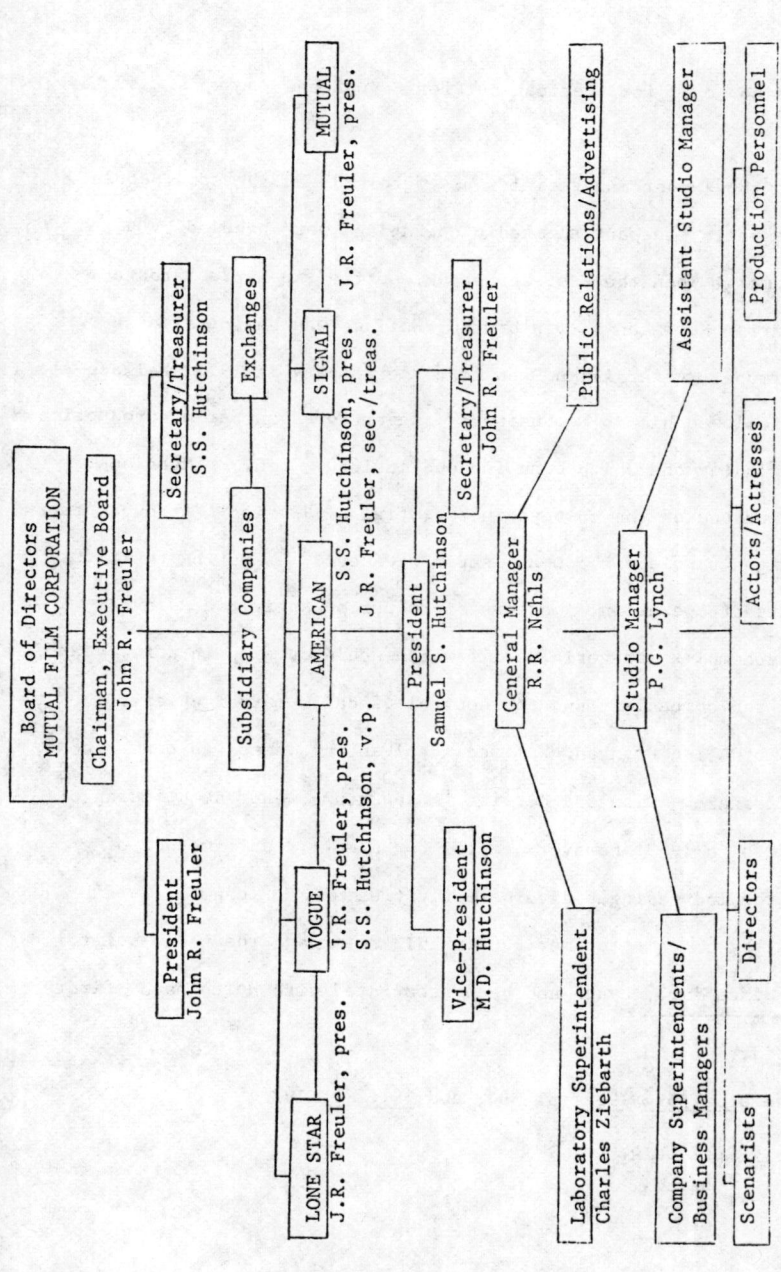

FIGURE 1

ORGANIZATIONAL CHART: MUTUAL FILM CORPORATION

his duties not only for American but for Signal and Vogue as well.[10]

While the upper managerial ranks were held by the same people for twelve years, the actual studio operations were handled by a number of men. When the Western company settled in Santa Barbara, star J. Warren Kerrigan's twin brother Wallace was business manager for the troupe. After Allan Dwan left the company in 1913, Wallace Kerrigan followed him to be business manager for a number of production units, including one which Dwan founded in 1920.[11] C. P. Morrison, who had been one of the cowboys in the original "Flying A" troupe, took over Kerrigan's role as "company superintendent."[12] During the first three years of operation, American's production activities did not demand the complex managerial staff which would develop in a few years. With only two companies, and the control of daily matter chiefly in the hands of Allan Dwan and Wallace Kerrigan, business was conducted on a small scale. Dwan and Kerrigan's departure, and the building of a new studio in 1913, however, called for a more stable method of managing the increasingly diverse activities of American.

P. G. Lynch came to American in 1913 to manage the newly-built studio. Since 1908, Lynch had been associated with Hutchinson, first

---

[10] Ibid., p. 260.

[11] See Directory 1921, p. 384, and 1918, p. 193.

[12] Directory 1918, p. 260.

as manager of the San Francisco booking department of Theatre Film Service and later as manager of Mutual's San Francisco exchange.[13] Like Hutchinson, Lynch had previous experience in banking; he remained with American through 1917, before becoming production manager for Universal.

To replace Lynch, Hutchinson again turned to an associate in the exchange business. J. R. Crone had begun his career as a clerk in General Film's office in San Francisco; he later served as manager of Mutual's San Francisco and Los Angeles exchanges, having been studio manager for Vogue before joining American in the same capacity.[14]

American's executive branch was made-up of three groups: 1) the founders, Hutchinson and Freuler, who with a few employees like Ziebarth and Nehls, held their posts for twelve years; 2) temporary executives, such as Hamilton, Kennedy, and Wallace Kerrigan, who after serving American for a short time, moved on to other ventures; and 3) subsidiary appointments (Lynch and Crone), men who rose through Mutual's ranks to positions of management with American. Although there was a consistency of management provided by Hutchinson and Freuler, other areas of American's personnel were much more diverse, as the discussions below should reveal.

Directors

When American began production in 1910, Thomas Ricketts was engaged from Essanay to produce the new company's dramatic

---

[13] Ibid.

[14] Ibid., p. 254.

offerings.[15] Ricketts was to remain with American only one year, leaving with his wife, Josephine Ditt, to join the Nestor studio in California.[16] His departure coincided with American's gradual shift toward Westerns with an abandonment of the serious dramas and comedies produced by the Chicago company.

However, Ricketts' association with American was not over. After two years with Nestor, Horsley, and Universal, he was again hired by American in the Summer of 1913, as director of the second company. Here he would remain through 1916, handling many of American's feature "Masterpictures."[17] Ricketts' work with American is significant for a number of reasons. In the first few months of operation, American tried to engage in all types of photoplays. During this short period, Ricketts was valuable for his Essanay experience with dramas. After Allan Dwan left the company in 1913, and the heads of American wanted to move toward more diversified forms than the Western, Ricketts rejoined the company as dramatic and comedy director. In 1916, Robert Duncan pictured Ricketts' role at American in the following way:

> Ricketts is the man in charge of the artistic end of the productions...[and] the man to whom credit for American's change from Western style of pictures to those of a general

---

[15] Other directors employed during the first two years of American's operation were William J. Bowman, Frank Beal, and Sam Morris.

[16] See Palmer, I, 192-93.

[17] *Directory 1918*, p. 190. One of Rickett's split-reel comedies, *Courage of Sorts* (released October 13, 1913), will be analyzed below in Chapter V.

> nature really belongs. He has personally directed most
> of its big pictures, including the Mutual Masterpictures
> and such special productions as "Damaged Goods."[18]

After 1915, Ricketts moved to Centaur, leaving American after four years of valuable contributions to the company.

While Ricketts' specialty was the dramatic photoplay, Allan Dwan became a specialist in Westerns.[19] In his three years with American, Dwan directed almost two hundred one-reel Westerns, built on formula plots revolving around the hero (J. Warren Kerrigan) confronting the villain (Jack Richardson) to save the girl (Pauline Bush). Dwan played a valuable role for American, consistently turning out product on schedule, with moderate success. His tenure can be seen as providing the necessary stabilization for the company to venture into new types of photoplays. His stay with American also gave him the experience to pursue a long career of filmmaking, including the direction of Robin Hood (1922) with Douglas Fairbanks, The Iron Mask (1929), Rebecca of Sunnybrook Farm (1938), and Sands of Iwo Jima (1949). Dwan was one of the very few directors at American whose career lasted through the coming of sound: for Allan Dwan, American was a prolific training ground.

Dwan's firing in the Spring of 1913 necessitated hiring new directors. Lorimer Johnston, Sidney Ayres, and Thomas Ricketts were

---

[18] Duncan, p. 190.

[19] See above, Chapter III, p. 67 for Dwan's entry into the directing field.

engaged not only to continue Dwan's work but to expand production as well. The newly-built studio offered the opportunities for interior shooting, and also exterior filming could take advantage of the studio structure itself which served as Spanish decor or contemporary backgrounds. At this time, the second company (formed in the Summer of 1912) was producing light comedies and receiving some success. It was not surprising, then, that in the late Fall of 1913, Hutchinson decided the second company should begin releasing under its own name. Johnston was producing spectacles on the Santa Barbara beaches, Ayres and Ricketts were handling the dramas, and the time seemed right to intensify the light comedy production. This was done by the institution of the "Beauty" brand and the hiring of Harry Pollard as star and director.

Pollard had an extremely active career with American. In 1914, he acted in, authored, and directed at least one film a month; when in 1915, Hutchinson wanted a director for The Quest, American's first feature, Pollard was the natural choice. With his wife, actress Margarita Fischer, Pollard then acted in and directed American features for two years, not only at the Santa Barbara studios but at his own studio in San Diego as well.

Pollard brought a number of assets to American. He had been a leading man with Essanay and Rolin-Pathé, and he had also gained directing experience with these two companies.[20] He was also capable

---

[20] Directory 1918, p. 188.

of authoring his own scripts, providing a control over his films from script to direction to acting. Under Pollard's direction, "Beauty" films gained enough popularity to add another company, under the direction of James Douglas, Archer McMackin, and Oral Humphreys.

When Harry Pollard left American to join Goldwyn, the company had changed considerably from its status in 1914. In two years, American had developed three companies devoted to short dramas (Companies #1, #2, and #3), two units filming "Beauty" comedies, two Western companies (Mustang #1 and #2), a unit working on three-reel dramas (Clipper), and a feature film company.[21]

The new Mustang company was initially established for transferring Charles Van Loan's "Buck Parvin" series to the screen. Chosen to direct the series was William Bertram, an actor with American and former assistant to American's directors Thomas Ricketts and Henry Otto. Former properties man, B. Reeves Eason, was later promoted to assist Bertram with producing westerns, eventually being given his own company.[22] In addition to Bertram, another actor at American was given the direction of his own Western company. Frank Borzage, fresh from acting jobs with Universal and Lubin, was given the lead and direction of Western films for American in 1916. Together with Anna

---

[21] Duncan, p. 191.

[22] Eason gained fame later as a second unit director, renowned for his staging of the chariot race in Ben Hur (1926), the burning of Atlanta in Gone with the Wind (1939), and the battle sequences in Sergeant York (1941). See Goodman, pp. 289-293.

Little, his leading lady, Borzage directed and appeared in a number of Westerns during his six months with American.[23]

A number of other directors worked for American in 1915 and 1916, for short periods. Jacques Jaccard began the initial episodes of the serial The Diamond from the Sky, with directing chores taken over later by William Desmond Taylor.[24] Al Santell directed the Billy Van Densen series for the "Beauty" brand along with writing and directing the features starring comedians Kolb and Dill.[25] "Mustang" films had the assistance of not only Bertram, Eason, and Borzage, but also C. Rea Berger, Frank Cooley, Warren Ellsworth, John Prescott, and Murdock MacQuarrie.[26]

By 1917, American had a half dozen directors under contract and had use of the services of a number of others for short periods. The permanent staff directors were those whose work was devoted specifically to features. Lloyd Ingraham was one of the first directors hired by American to supervise features, specifically those of Mary Miles Minter.

---

[23] Borzage's subsequent career as a director included Humoresque (1920), Seventh Heaven (1927), A Farewell to Arms (1932), and The Big Fisherman (1959).

[24] Jaccard began as a cameraman, then joined fellow cameraman, George Marshall, directing serials for Universal. Taylor became a successful director for Famous-Players; his murder in 1923 involved stars Mary Miles Minter and Mabel Normand in a scandal Hollywood could never forget.

[25] Directory 1918, p. 190. T. N. Heffron is also credited with one of the Kolb and Dill features, Peck of Pickles, released in November, 1916. See Directory 1921, pp. 266-67.

[26] For information on these directors, see Directory 1918, pp. 158, 164, 188, and 184, respectively.

Ingraham had been an actor and director with Reliance-Majestic, Essanay, and Fine Arts before joining American, and remained with the company from 1917-1919.[27] Almost all of the Mary Miles Minter films were under his direction, a number which included over a dozen features.

Henry King joined American in 1917, after an acting career with Lubin and Balboa. At American, King directed almost twenty Westerns, beginning a distinguished career in this genre which culminated with The Gunfighter (1950). King's work for American revealed a keen sense for handling the western story of character rather than action,[28] a sensitivity which was strongly praised in his later work, notably Tol'able David (1921).

While King's work for American was merely the beginning of his directorial credits, Edward Sloman's career reached its high point at American. Although he continued directing until 1939, Sloman found American the scene for the majority of his work. Here he refined his directorial training from Lubin, Balboa, and Universal, and was responsible for over a dozen feature released from 1918 to 1921. This corpus included all types of films for American: sentimental melodramas with Mary Miles Minter (The Ghost of Rosy Taylor), high-action westerns with William Russell (Slam-Bang Jim), and romantic comedies featuring Margarita Fischer (Put Up Your Hands). His versatility was an asset to a company devoting all its efforts to feature films.

---

[27] Directory 1921, p. 267. Chapter V contains an analysis of Ingraham's The Eyes of Julia Deep.

[28] See Chapter V for a discussion of one King Western feature, Six Feet Four.

After he left American, Sloman directed a feature Western for Benjamin B. Hampton, a few films for J. L. Frothingham, and additional films as an independent.[29]

When Sloman left American in 1920--leaving two of his features to be released during the following year--American was faced with a growing dilemma. In 1918 and 1919, the company did not have enough work to keep directors under a regular contract; Sloman, King, Rollin Sturgeon, and Roy William Neill were forced to direct for other companies during American's slack periods. As directors proved their worth to other companies, offers of higher salaries were not surprising--nor turned down. Slowly, American began losing its more successful directors and in their place hired others on short-term contracts.

Despite the capability of the replacements, American had lost the repertory *esprit* which it had maintained to some degree through 1917. Emmett J. Flynn, Burton George, Rupert Julian, and George L. Cox directed at American for a few months each but soon gravitated to bigger offerings.[30]

---

[29] For a discussion of Sloman's career, see Brownlow, pp. 154-63. Brownlow's evaluation of Sloman as a director seems a little high--as it does for most of his subjects. The contemporary trade journals do not tout Sloman as a director quite as much as Brownlow implies, although the evaluation may be based on Brownlow's delight in discovering "the lost work of Edward Sloman."

[30] For biographies, see *Directory 1921*, pp. 263 (Flynn), 170 (George), 268 (Julian), and 260 (Cox). None of these men seem to have pursued a vigorous career after 1921. Flynn continued directing into the 1930's; George ceased his film work in 1921; Julian had some success in the 1920's with Universal horror films; and Cox stopped directing in 1921.

One of the strongest attractions to working for American's repertory companies had been the Santa Barbara locale. Free from the hectic atmosphere of a growing Hollywood, American's personnel could perform filmmaking activities while enjoying the idyllic setting on the California coast. As the industry developed into an efficiently organized business, the jobs clearly were elsewhere. Those who wanted to continue work at higher salaries were forced to join the rat race one hundred miles to the South. Those who did not, merely retired to the Santa Barbara community either finding other employment or making occasional trips southward when work demanded.

In all areas of production, this loss of a "family atmosphere" to the filmmaking activities was a contributing cause for American's decline. During the early years of the industry, the company could offer not only permanent employment but also an atmosphere more congenial to some than the Hollywood scene. By 1917, all the major companies were busily at work in Hollywood. And for directors who were in demand, the place to be was Hollywood, not Santa Barbara.

Scenarists

From 1910-1913, Allan Dwan handled the majority of scenarios for American, retaining this responsibility even after he became a director in 1911. Early scenario writing for Dwan represented more a commedia dell'arte story outline method than a complete "script to screen" treatment.[31] In 1913, however, more attention was suddenly

---

[31] See Dwan's comments above, Chapter III.

given to script material. Richard Washburn Child's "Her Big Story" was selected for American production in May, 1913, and began an increasing dependence upon published short stores and scenarios submitted by free-lance writers.

One reason for this change in policy was Dwan's departure; another may simply be the growing sophistication of American's filmmaking. A breakdown of the scenarios of films released from August through December, 1913, reveals this change in American's scenario policy. Information on this period is detailed in Table 3 to follow.

Free-lance writers submitted their material either through an agency (e.g., Photoplay Clearing House) or on their own; others, such as Richard Washburn Child, allowed short stories to be adapted by the American company. During this period, the staff of American also contributed scenarios, with offerings coming from directors Dwan and Johnston, actor J. Warren Kerrigan, actress Louise Lester, and publicity director, O. F. Doud. Others, such as Clarence and Theodosia Harris, J. H. Hungerford, Jacques Jaccard, Flora B. Snyder, and Chet Whitney, later joined American as permanent staff members.

Besides free-lance writers and staff contributions, American also explored an area which would later become an important source for story material. In 1912, Chattauqua comedian Opie Read adapted his novel and play The Starbucks for American's Chicago cameras. Published in 1902, The Starbucks had been a popular work and

TABLE 3

AMERICAN SCENARIOS--AUGUST 18-DECEMBER 18, 1913

Release Date	Title	Author	How Acquired
August			
18	A Tide in the Affairs of Men	Photoplay Clearing House	free-lance
21	The Golden Heart	George S. Cantwell	free-lance
23	Flesh of His Flesh	information not available	
25	For the Flag	Lorimer Johnston	director
28	From the Portals of Despair	Billie West	free-lance
30	Jack Meets His Waterloo	J. Warren Kerrigan	actor
September			
1	Where There's Life	information not available	
4	A Poisoned Chop	Alice A. Methley	free-lance
6	The Mysterious Eyes	Mary F. Lonsdale	free-lance
8	For the Crown	Lorimer Johnston	director
11	Through the Neighbor's Window	information not available	

TABLE 3 (Cont'd.)

Release Date	Title	Author	How Acquired
September			
13	Red Sweeney's Defeat	information not available	
15	Calamity Anne, Heroine	Louise Lester	actress
18	A Fall Into Luck	R. S. Schrumon	free-lance
20	Jim Takes A Chance	Photoplay Clearing House	free-lance
22	The Ghost of the Hacienda	Pearl Gaddis	free-lance
25	Mrs. Carter's Campaign	A. H. Giehler	free-lance
27	Master of Himself	Louis N. Levin	free-lance
29	The Flirt and The Bandit	Edward Gordon	free-lance
October			
2	Badge of Honor	Max Goldberg	free-lance
4	Crooks and Credulous	Charlotte M. Brush	free-lance
6	A Pitfall of the Installment Plan	William H. Osborne	free-lance
9	Taming A Cowboy	Hilma Attwool	free-lance

TABLE 3 (Cont'd.)

Release Date	Title	Author	How Acquired
October			
11	Calamity Anne's Sacrifice	Louise Lester	actress
13	Courage of Sorts	Information not available	
16	The End of Black Bart, or The Duel in the Mountains	A. Bruce Campbell	free-lance
18	The Making of A Woman	Information not available	
20	Hidden Treasure Ranch	T. H. Bridson	free-lance
23	The Step Brothers	George M. Riesener	free-lance
25	In the Mountains of Virginia	T. E. McAuliffe	free-lance
27	In the Days of Trajan	Lorimer Johnston	director
30	In Three Hours	Gordon V. May	free-lance
November			
1	Follies of A Day and Night, or The Mishaps of E. Z. Smithers	Frank E. Smith	free-lance
3	The Girl and The Greaser	J. H. Hungerford	free-lance

TABLE 3 (Cont'd.)

Release Date	Title	Author	How Acquired
November			
6	What Her Diary Told	Margaret Kennedy	free-lance
8	The Haunted House	M. B. Harvey	free-lance
10	Martha's Decision	information not available	
13	An Assisted Proposal, or The Difficulties of A Bashful Cowboy	Chester Whitney	free-lance
15	The Drummer's Honeymoon	H. M. Sutton	free-lance
17	The Trail of The Lost Chord	Clarence J. Harvis	free-lance
20	The Tale of the Ticker	Francis M. Wright	free-lance
22	Calamity Anne's Dream	Louise Lester	actress
24	The Occult	Charles D. Myers	free-lance
27	A Spartan Girl of the West	Theodosia Harris	free-lance
29	At Midnight	Gordon V. May	free-lance

TABLE 3 (Cont'd.)

Release Date	Title	Author	How Acquired
December			
1	American Born	F. A. Heiskell	free-lance
6	A Divorce Scandal	O. F. Doud	publicity director
8	Trapped in a Forest Fire	Jacques Jaccard	free-lance
11	His First Cake	J. W. Sayre	free-lance
13	Armed Intervention	Flora B. Snyder	free-lance
15	Where the Road Forks	Anna I. Lockwood	free-lance
18	Personal Magnetism	O. A. Nelson	free-lance

Information based on copyright records of the Library of Congress and trade bio-bibliographies of scenarists. The general film industry during this period relied greatly on free-lance contribution; the larger studios, however, were beginning to acquire permanent scenario departments early in 1912.

an equally successful stage play.[32] For the film, Read played the role of the leading character Jasper Starbuck, a philosophizing rustic.[33] American's success in this venture, however, was not repeated until 1915 when the entire Broadway production of Edmund Brieux's Damaged Goods was brought to the screen.

The years 1914 and 1915 showed American still dependent upon free-lance writers and previously published sources. However, during this period a scenario staff was instituted with resident writers housed at the studio. Over fifteen writers worked for American during this two year period, some staying for the entire time, others for merely a few months.

Writers were hired--like directors--for specific companies; James Edward Hungerford, Marc Edmund Jones, and M. R. McKinstry wrote solely for the "Beauty" brand, 1914-15; Clarence and Theodosia Harris handled "Mustang" and other Westerns; and Catherine Carr was hired specifically as scenario editor of The Diamond from the Sky. The dependence, however was still primarily on free-lance writers at least for the original story material; much of the staff responsibilities were more in adaptation than actual script writing.

The staff writers of 1916 became more integral to the production activities as the company enlarged and features became the major product.

---

[32]Robert L. Morris, Opie Read: American Humorist, 1852-1939 (New York: Helios, 1965), p. 181.

[33]Harry P. Harrison, Culture Under Canvas: The Story of Tent Chautauqua (New York: Hastings House, 1958), p. 169.

C. B. "Pop" Hoadley, his son Harold, Clifford Howard, Karl Coolidge, Anthony W. Coldewey, and Arthur Henry Gooden shared a background of newspaper work. As resident scenarists during 1916 and 1917, these six men maintained the major responsibility for American's feature films. The shorter films (such as "Beauty" and "Mustang") continued to be "written" by free-lancers and temporary staff writers.

Of the six staff writers during this period, only Coldewey extended his career into the 1930's. Howard ended his career in film after serving as associate editor of C. B. DeMille's King of Kings (1927); Gooden wrote his last film in 1925; Coolidge stopped writing in 1924 at Universal; and the two Hoadleys ceased their scenarist careers in 1921.

The year 1917 represented the apex of resident writing for American. As with the directors, American's hiring after this point was for short-term scenarists, either for one picture or for one particular director. Jules Furthman was one writer to have a relatively long stay with American. From October, 1918, through March, 1920, Furthman wrote scenarios for Henry King and Edward Sloman.[34] Here he wrote twelve scenarios, most of these Westerns starring William Russell. Furthman's career then developed as screenwriter for Josef von Sternberg and Howard Hawks, his career culminating with Rio Bravo (1959).

---

[34] Furthman's stay with American co-incided with the First World War; therefore, he was forced to use the alias of Stephen Fox "due to the too-Germanic tone of his own name." See Richard Koszarski, "Jules Furthman," Film Comment, IV (Winter 1970-71), 26-31.

Another writer, Daniel F. Whitcomb, mirrored Furthman's career with American. Whitcomb came to American with experience at Fox, Keystone, Ince, and Balboa, and wrote seven scenarios while at the Santa Barbara studio. These included a Mary Miles Minter vehicle (<u>Rosemary Climbs the Heights</u>), a Western melodrama (<u>Sunset Jones</u>), and a Margarita Fischer feature (<u>The Dangerous Talent</u>). Whitcomb remained with American through its closing years. Unlike Furthman, however, his career ended in 1924 after three years of writing Westerns for small companies.

American's scenario policy had come full-circle. Beginning with Allan Dwan as its sole scenarist, the company later grew to depend on free-lance contributions and material written by actors, directors, and other personnel. From this point, American engaged a permanent staff of scenarists only to lose them one by one until in the final year of the existence, the company had only one writer under contract.

<u>Actors and Actresses</u>

For the first year of American's production, star quality was not a consideration. Not until 1912 when concentration was put on the Western troupe did American have actors and actresses who appeared in similar roles for film after film. The Western company was originally made up of J. Warren Kerrigan, male lead; Pauline Bush, female lead; Marshall Neilan, juvenile; Jack Richardson and George Periolat, heavies; Charlotte Burton, female heavy; Jessalyn Van Trump, ingenue; Louise Lester, comedienne; and miscellaneous cowboys, such as the Morrison brothers, Charles, Pete, and Carl.

Of the original Western company, only Richardson, Lester (Mrs. Richardson), and George Periolat remained for more than six years.[35] Kerrigan remained through 1913, before joining Universal for a career climaxed by his performance in James Cruze's The Covered Wagon (1923). His career with American began in comedy roles, but he soon found his niche as the hero of the "Flying A" Westerns. Kerrigan was a "handsome, boyish"[36] figure who was usually called upon to "use his brain rather than brawn in overcoming adversity."[37] Unlike "Broncho Billy" Anderson, he failed to evolve a character of any depth or identifiable personality beyond his good looks. Instead, Kerrigan was used in formula plots in which he accomplished similar goals through similar means in each successive film. American's accent was on patterned plots in which Kerrigan repeatedly "won out in the end."

The formation of the second company in 1912 suggested a change in plot emphasis and character development in American's films. Leading man Wallace Reid was more handsome than Kerrigan, without the pidgeon-chested physique which Kerrigan possessed. The plots of the "society plays" produced by the second company called for attractive, upper-class appearing personalities devoid of the ruggedness of Kerrigan, Richardson, and Periolat. In appearance, Reid, Eugene Pallette, and Edward Coxen

---

[35] Mr. and Mrs. Richardson remained through 1916, Periolat until 1918. See Directory 1921, pp. 197, 229, 195, respectively.

[36] Kalton C. Lahue, Winners of the West (New York: Barnes, 1971), p. 210.

[37] Ibid.

fulfilled this requirement.³⁸ With the second company, American began an increasingly attentive attitude toward plot development and attractive "stars," two aspects not emphasized in the premiere company's films.

With the instituting of the "Beauty" brand in 1914, from the members of the second company, American brought in new talent competent in light comedy. Margarita Fischer had worked for Selig, Imp, Universal, Rex, Nestor, and Bison before coming to American with her husband, director Harry Pollard.³⁹ For American, Miss Fischer appeared in over two dozen films from 1914 to 1921, before joining her husband at Universal. As an actress she demonstrated an admirable range, being able to portray both innocent ingenues and sophisticated women of the world.⁴⁰

Versatility, however, was not the strong point of all of American's stars. Charlotte (Lottie) Pickford, hired in 1915 for The Diamond from the Sky, appeared in only a few films for American, with little

---

[38] Reid was with American only a short time, leaving to join Vitagraph and Griffith; Reid eventually became a box office idol for Paramount until his death from narcotics addiction on January 18, 1923. See Wing, pp. 224-25. Pallette soon outgrew his youthful romantic leads and became a popular character actor, his gravel voice providing a transition into sound films such as Shanghai Express (1932), The Adventures of Robin Hood (1938) in which he played Friar Tuck, and The Mark of Zorro (1940), before his death in 1954. Coxen left American in 1916 to join Goldwyn and Universal for a career lasting into the 1930's.

[39] Directory 1918, p. 96; 1921, p. 220.

[40] For an example of Margarita Fischer's acting talents, see the discussion in Chapter V of The Pearl of Paradise (1916).

subsequent career,[41] a pattern followed by many of her co-stars in the serial. One of the actors hired for this serial who did prosper with American was William Russell. With experience at Biograph, Thanhouser, and Famous Players, Russell joined American in 1915 and remained for over five years playing the lead in (and co-directing with John Prescott) over thirty films, most of these Westerns. Russell was a tall, rugged cowboy whose good looks and brawn were exploited in American films.[42] After leaving the company, he formed his own independent unit to produce Westerns and melodramas into the early 1930's.

The year 1915 was also the date of American's film version of the controversial Broadway success, Damaged Goods, based on Edmund Brieux's play about the dangers of syphilis. Richard Bennett's hesitancy to join the motion picture industry was typical of many prosperous stage personalities:

> He regarded the business of film-making as on a par with treason, dope peddling and matricide, and once told his stage manager, "Whenever you think there are movie scouts out front, let me know and I'll stay home sick."
>
> However, it was no longer possible to ignore the growing business of silent movie-making. Although he had complete control of the highly successful movie version, since he wrote the script, directed the film and recreated the role of Brignac, it began a long disaffection with the industry.[43]

---

[41] Directory 1921, p. 235.

[42] See the analysis of Six Feet Four (1919) in Chapter V, a William Russell-Henry King feature.

[43] Joan Bennett and Lois Kibbee, The Bennett Playbill: Five Generations of the Famous Theatre Family (New York: Holt, Rinehart and Winston, 1970), pp. 51-52. Thomas Ricketts is credited with the direction of Damaged Goods, although the temperamental Bennett may have been a strong influence on whatever Ricketts attempted to do.

Bennett acted in American films from 1915 to 1916 (And the Law Says, The Valley of Decision, Gilded Youth), before returning to the stage. For American, Bennett's hiring was a significant coup, the company's first real effort in "famous plays with famous players" since The Starbucks in 1912. But for Bennett, the engagement could not end soon enough:

> When pictures went to Hollywood and began to talk, he enjoyed them somewhat more, but neither he nor Mother ever regarded them with anything but polite tolerance and contempt.[44]

Bennett appeared in a few films after being with American, ending his career in The Magnificent Ambersons (1942) and Journey Into Fear (1943) before his death on October 22, 1944.[45]

An actor who was the antithesis to Bennett's personality was cowboy Art Acord, engaged for the title role in the "Buck Parvin" series. The popular Saturday Evening Post serialization of Charles Van Loan's stories brought Acord to American from a career with Bison, Selig, and Universal. A successful stunt rider and rodeo competitor, Acord remained with American until he joined the U. S. Forces in World War I, winning the croix-de-guerre at Verdun. For the "Mustang" films at American, Acord typified the quiet, restless cowboy who was more at home on a horse than in an elegant sitting room. Acord's success with

---

[44] Ibid., p. 52.

[45] Ibid., p. 289.

American was not followed after the War: for five years he appeared in "B" Westerns before joining a Western troupe touring South America. He died in Mexico in 1931.[46]

In 1916, American followed its policy begun a year earlier with The Diamond from the Sky in hiring a special cast for the war-preparedness serial, The Secret of the Submarine. Juanita Hansen starred with support from Hugh Bennett, Thomas Chatterton, Harry Edmundson, Lamar Johnstone, Hylda Hollis (Mrs. Edward Sloman), and George Webb. Miss Hansen was American's answer to Pearl White who had received such success in The Perils of Pauline series. Through a series of adventures, The Secret of the Submarine had Juanita Hansen triumph over invading spies. Her career after American was similar to that of Wallace Reid: from the pinnacle of success as a serial queen, she fell to the depths, a victim of cocaine and heroine addiction. From 1928 until her death in 1961, she was unable to participate actively in filmmaking activities.[47]

Of the original cast for The Secret of the Submarine, only George Clancy, Hylda Hollis, and George Webb remained with American to appear in a few additional films. This period was American's "star" period, and supporting actors and actresses were replaced almost as quickly as they were hired. Instead, stars such as Gail Kane, Winnifred Greenwood, Audrey Munson, Kolb and Dill, Ashton Dearholt, Anna Little, Rhea

---

[46] For a capsule history of Acord's career, see Lahue, Winners of the West, pp. 15-24.

[47] See Lahue, Continued Next Week, pp. 78-81.

Mitchell, Vivian Rich, Franklin Ritchie, Alan Forrest, Julliette Day, and Milton Sills were brought to American to be featured in special photoplays of five reels or more. Perhaps the most shining of these stars was Mary Miles Minter who joined American in May, 1916.[48]

Having begun on the stage as a child actress, Miss Minter came to American from success with Powers and Metro, billed as a top contender to Mary Pickford for the role of "America's Sweetheart." Edward Wagenknecht, in recalling his boyhood viewing of Miss Minter's films, provided a clear assessment of her screen personality:

> How good an actress Mary Miles Minter was during her years of screen fame it would not be hard to say. The saccharine vehicles in which she was generally presented all too seldom afforded opportunities for acting. She herself was not saccharine, however; she was a golden, peaches-and-cream kind of girl, in whom all the sweet, innocent charms of youth were embodied as irresistably as in any human being this generation has seen, and those who did not like her might quite reasonably have gone on to declare that they did not like sunshine either.[49]

---

[48] Information about Miss Minter comes from a variety of sources. DeWitt Bodeen, her erstwhile biographer, supplied much of the information, including some perspective to that which already existed in print. In addition to Bodeen's counsel, three interviews were conducted with Miss Minter (now Mrs. Brandon O'Hilderbrandt) yielding some perspective to her career at American. Since she was involved in the scandal surrounding William Desmond Taylor's murder in 1922, much of the information about her is of dubious value, and accounts for moments of unwillingness to discuss her career at times during the interviews, conducted during the Spring, 1969, at her home in Santa Monica, California.

[49] Edward Wagenknecht, The Movies in the Age of Innocence (Norman: University of Oklahoma, 1962), pp. 233-34.

Wagenknecht's assessment was based strictly on Miss Minter's screen personality: others were only too eager to point out her off-screen contradictions to the roles she played.[50]

Through twenty-six films, Miss Minter was featured as the charming ingenue whose courageous spirit saved the day from despair.[51] In 1919, she replaced Mary Pickford at Adolph Zukor's Realart company, appearing in similar vehicles until her forced retirement from the screen in 1923. For American, Mary Miles Minter represented a successful property, one whom they exploited through features stressing her Pickford-like resemblance. Perhaps the job was too well done, for she was soon in demand by producers more able to offer the high salary and benefits she desired.

Miss Minter was American's last big star. Although Margarita Fischer remained with the company through it waning two years, American was never again to recapture the appeal of the Minter features. As throughout American's career, other producers kept a watchful eye on American's development of a star. When the time was right, the stars were "spirit[ed] away in the dead of night with an offer too attractive to refuse."[52]

---

[50] Edward Sloman, for example, who directed her in a number of features, found Miss Minter a "spoiled brat" and a "lousy actress." From the Sloman interview; see also Brownlow, p. 161.

[51] An analysis of one of these features, The Eyes of Julia Deep, appears below in Chapter V.

[52] Lahue, Winners of the West, p. 213.

Production Personnel

Rounding out American's staff were the numerous production personnel who supported the filmmaking activities. American's development in this area followed the pattern seen in other personnel segments. The original companies had only the minimum of support--property head, cameraman, live-stock supervisor--until the new studio was built in 1913, which consequently demanded more specialized and diverse types of technical assistance.

Roy F. Overbaugh was American's cameraman with the Western Company. Assisted by Roger Dale Armstrong, Overbaugh photographed most of the American offerings from 1910-1913, working with the company intermittently as chief cinematographer throughout most of American's career.[53] Overbaugh's career continued into the 1930's, filming scenes for First National and Universal, including Henry King's Fury (1923) and other features starring Richard Barthelmess. Other cameramen quickly found new opportunities elsewhere, such as George Marshall, later a director, who photographed the first few episodes of The Diamond from the Sky.[54]

American saw the need for assistant directors beginning in 1914 when production activity increased to a number of units operating simultaneously in the studio. Assistant directors served as right-hand

---

[53] See "Movie Capital," an interview with Overbaugh in the Santa Barbara News-Press, August 10, 1958, E 10-11; also Directory 1923-24, p. 197.

[54] Directory 1918, p. 184. Marshall has had an extremely long-lasting career. Beginning in film as a cameraman in 1913, he has directed over four hundred features, including You Can't Cheat An Honest Man (1939), The Ghost Breakers (1940), and one part of the trilogy How

men to the chief directors of features, with some of these such as William Bertram eventually being given their own directorial assignments. F. Harmon Weight typified the assistant directors employed by American. With little previous experience, Weight joined the company in 1916 to remain one year before becoming an assistant director for Paralta, then receiving directorial assignments with Selznick and Distinctive, his career lasting through 1924.[55]

As studio production expanded, so too did the production personnel. In 1916, over two hundred stage carpenters, utility workmen, and other personnel were responsible for mounting American's productions.[56] This number slowly decreased through the next five years until American's production personnel were hired from the Hollywood corps on a day-to-day basis.

Summary

The policies for personnel hiring did not cause American's downfall. Instead, American's employment practice was intimately connected to the general operations of the company. When more and longer films were produced, more people were hired; as production decreased so too did the personnel list.

American went through a number of stages in its hiring policies. The first employees (1910-1913) had a minimum of experience, mostly

---

54 Continued. the West Was Won (1962). Most recently he has directed Bob Hope-Phyllis Diller films, and "The Lucy Show" for television.

[55] Directory 1923-24, p. 191.

[56] Duncan, p. 190.

with Trust manufacturing companies. The second period (1914-17) required people from more diversified companies, hired for their special strengths in production activities. And the third period (1917-21) required only enough people to produce the small number of features released by American. As the company developed, so did the background experience of the majority of personnel. This factor, however, may be attributed more to a developing industry with more opportunities for apprenticeship than to merely a sophistication of American's employment practices per se.

Within the large number of personnel which came to American for a short time, then moved on to other opportunities, was a substantial core who remained with American throughout the company's career. These people--directors, scenarists, actors and actresses, production personnel--provided a backbone for the consistency of management represented by Hutchinson and his associates. In the first three years of operation, American had fostered a repertory or "stock" company method in which the "family" of personnel gathered together daily to produce films.

The physical set-up of the early operations cannot be overlooked. The Western Company especially promoted a communal relationship in their activities: personnel lived in quarters nearby the studio, often taking their meals together under one roof. This spirit, however, began to break down as the company enlarged, as e and more personnel were employed, and as hiring was done on a short-term basis.

The climate and locale of Santa Barbara no doubt also influenced this collective enterprise. The small city allowed not only a closeness of personnel to the studio but also an integration with the community. Rural Hollywood had little of the benefits which Santa Barbara had to offer, except one--more employment opportunities.

When the studio ceased production in 1921, over five thousand members of the industry could claim some part of American's twelve years of production. Of this number, perhaps ten per cent are known today. The remainder either faded away during future work or merely abdicated their place in the industry, preferring to remain in Santa Barbara.

It is also clear that American as an employer was similar to a number of small companies in their inability to retain high-quality personnel. American constantly favored the star while losing the director, which was a short-sighted attitude on the company's part. With less financial backing behind them, the American executives watched many of their prized-personnel be successfully tempted to leave the company for Universal or other firms whose offers American could not match. Although American did not retain those whose careers blossomed in later work, the company can be seen as a "training ground" offering valuable apprenticeship to members of the motion picture industry. This repertory function was a valuable one for the industry, as was the continual supply of films, the topic for discussion in the chapter to follow.

CHAPTER V

AMERICAN'S FILMS

Introduction

During twelve years of operation, the American Film Company produced 1,228 films. Of this number, the company registered less than half, or 534, with the Library of Congress. Today, even amidst a renewed interest in preserving older films, only a small number of American films can be located for study.

American's output was not unusual for a company of its size operating during this period. Also, its failure to copyright even half of its films was not unique in a period when most companies simply disregarded such protection. What is significant is the small percentage of American's released films which are extant today.

The move toward restoration of this country's film heritage has been a slow one. Most contemporary historical evaluation of American is based solely on the films which have survived; only recently have historians begun to reinvestigate the possibilities that some excellent films are ones which have been lost.

As the restoration movement increases, the product of major studios is rapidly being rediscovered. The films of Biograph, Universal, Paramount, and Warners have been uncovered, with the availability of the total corpus for these studios finally becoming a possibility. But

American was not a major studio, and like the smaller, equally prodigious firms of Kalem (a successful independent, 1905-1917), Monogram (producing and distributing Westerns in the 1930's and 1940's), and American-International (a "horror film" company releasing since the mid-1950's), American and its films have received little attention from the archivists.

Of the extant films from American, the largest number are held by the National Film Archive in London,[1] and these are unavailable for study except within the Archive's facilities. Film Classic Exchange, a Los Angeles rental company, has eight American films for rental or purchase, some of these incomplete. And Blackhawk Films, specializing in 8mm and Super 8 sale out of Davenport, Iowa, features three American films among its vast collection.[2] Other sources include private collectors[3] and the Library of Congress-American Film Institute holdings.[4]

---

[1] The British Film Institute's *National Film Catalogue, Part III: Silent Films, 1895-1930* (London: B.F.I., 1966) lists fourteen films made by American, most of these incomplete.

[2] The eleven films to be discussed in this chapter were made available through Film Classic and Blackhawk Films.

[3] Of the numerous collectors in the country contacted for this study, only a small number had any of American's films, and these were ones already available from Film Classic and Blackhawk.

[4] The Library of Congress paper print collection contains hundreds of American's films; however, these have proven to be relatively useless. The paper prints submitted by American contained only stills from various scenes, mostly in an illogical order, possibly the order in which they were developed. These can serve only to offer some idea of the "look" of the films rather than any analytical possibilities. The Library's paper print rolls were consulted for this study but failed to offer any revealing conclusions for mention here.

For the historian interested in the early films of any one company, his research is beset with difficulties of availability,[5] the poor quality of the extant prints,[6] and the lack of reliability or completeness of these remaining films.[7] These difficulties, however, are not without solution, although the compromises involved may be less than ideal. While the films are unavailable, trade journals of the period report each and every film, its content and length, with some critical evaluation. This criticism also reveals some estimation of the cinematographic qualities of the films. The same sources can be used to evaluate the completeness of existing prints.

Given the difficulties and the suggested remedies for studying a company's total output of films, this investigation has found six major types of films produced by American: 1) Western Comedy, 2) Western Drama, 3) Contemporary Social Comedy, 4) Contemporary Social

---

[5]For example, I would suggest that the films of Biograph are more available today than those of other companies specifically because of Mary Pickford's and D. W. Griffith's career with this company.

[6]Often historians have based their judgments of film quality on the existing prints, rather than considering the aging process of the celluloid. One investigator who has attempted to compensate for this historical myopia is Kevin Brownlow whose critical evaluations may be excessive in the other extreme.

[7]Films deposited for copyright, for example, were often not the same as the final release version. There are numerous examples of historical evaluation of films based on the daily rushes or stills housed in the Library of Congress. See, for example, George Pratt, "A Myth Is as Good as a Milestone," Image (Rochester), November 1957, p. 210.

Drama, 5) Period Drama, and 6) Documentary.[8] The types were determined not only by the dominant locale featured in the individual films but also by the major tone of the plot, comic or serious, and the nature of the action and consequences.

A compiling of information about the number of films in each type is revealed in Table 4. Another aspect, the lengths of the films, is revealed in Table 5. This breakdown shows how films produced by American steadily increased in length while after 1915, they decreased in number, as the company moved into feature production devoting more time to longer films.

From this information, a number of aspects of the films must be investigated. What is the nature of the plot, and how does the plot relate to the types of films produced by American? What role does the camera play in the films, in terms of positioning and movement?[9] How is editing structured?[10] What function do the titles serve in the

---

[8] Information about the few documentaries produced by American is included here, although these will not be part of the discussion to follow.

[9] For the purposes of this discussion, "shots" are defined as uninterrupted images, seemingly recorded within a complete running of the camera. "Camera set-ups" will denote an unchanging positioning of the camera at a given distance from the subject.

[10] In discussing editing, the term "cut" will refer to a direct change of "shot" without any intervening transition; "fade" will mean a gradual darkening of the image to black (fade-out) or a gradual lightening from black (fade-in). A "dissolve" will denote the simultaneous fading out of one shot over the fading in of another; an "iris" will refer to a darkened circle framing the image, this circle's position changing as the image is "irised-in" (opening of the circle) or "irised-out" (closing of the circle).

TABLE 4[a]

FILM TYPES RELEASED BY AMERICAN, 1910-1921

	1910	1911	1912	1913	1914	1915	1916	1917	1918	1919	1920	1921	Totals	(%)
WESTERN COMEDY	2	34	25	28	4	11	12	6	2	1	0	0	125	10.2%
WESTERN DRAMA	2	60	90	45	5	30	33	6	6	6	4	9	296	24.1%
CONTEMPORARY SOCIAL COMEDY	9	28	11	43	54	83	79	11	5	6	3	2	334	27.2%
CONTEMPORARY SOCIAL DRAMA	3	4	7	32	96	115	105	28	11	4	7	2	414	33.7%
PERIOD DRAMA	0	0	0	4	8	8	13	3	2	0	1	0	39	3.2%
DOCUMENTARY	0	4	7	9	0	0	0	0	0	0	0	0	20	1.6%
Totals	16	130	140	161	167	247	242	54	26	17	15	13	1228	

[a] In context of the rest of the industry, American's choice of film types indicates a conservative approach. The general movement was toward longer serious and comic films, with Westerns remaining a consistently produced commodity. Spectacle films grew in popularity after 1915, a movement which American failed to reflect because of the large financial investment such films demanded. This table of film types should indicate, in general, American's desire to produce films in the types which had proven their popularity through the work of other more innovative companies.

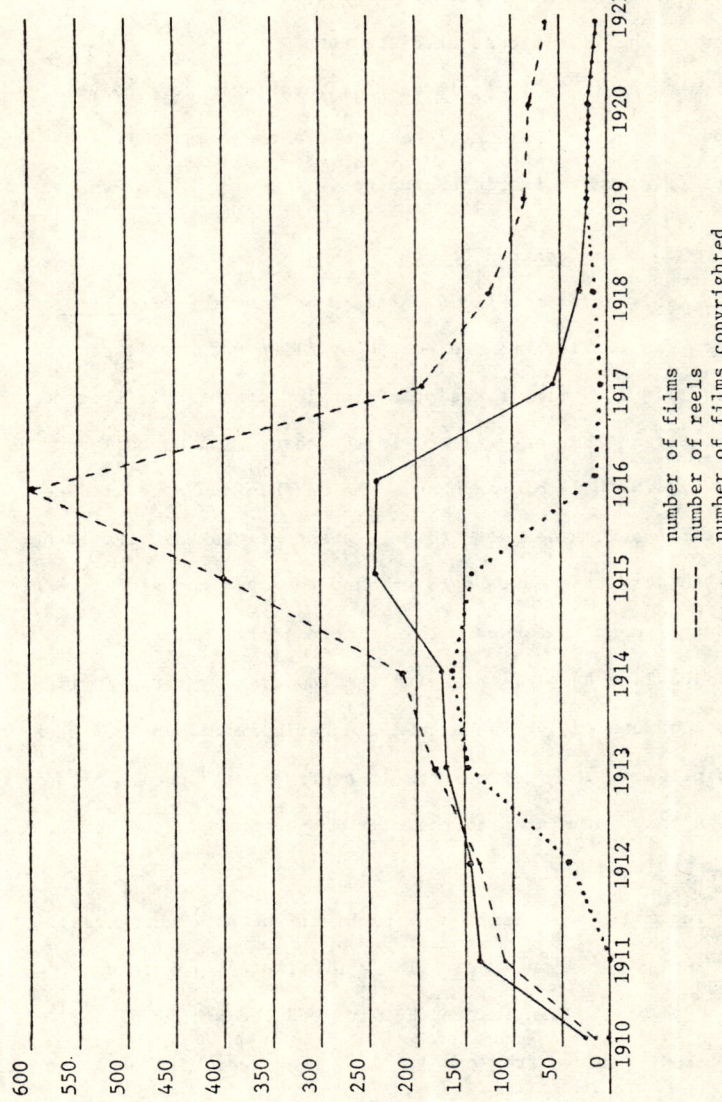

FIGURE 2

AMERICAN FILMS, 1910-1921
NUMBER OF FILMS, REELS, AND COPYRIGHT

film? How does the lighting contribute? And what types of acting are exemplified by the film's cast of characters?

In the discussion to follow, eleven films available for analysis will be treated in view of the questions raised above to give an idea of the types of films which American produced.

Western Comedy

One of the earliest of the films released by American was <u>Three Million Dollars</u>, the fortieth film directed by Allan Dwan (released September 7, 1911). The film is a simple plotting of a father's attempt to wed his daughter so that she will collect a three million dollar inheritance. With the help of ranchhands, he has his daughter kidnaped, leaving her tied up near a handsome cowboy; when she awakens, the father plans to have the Justice-of-the-Peace on hand to marry the girl to "her hero." An added element is found in this simple story: at the beginning, the girl (Pauline Bush) flirts with the cowboy (J. Warren Kerrigan), much to the displeasure of her father (George Periolat); when the ranchhands kidnap a prospective bidegroom, their captive turns out to be Kerrigan. While the manipulator of the plot is the father, the real winners are the girl and her beau.

<u>Three Million Dollars</u> is made up of eighteen shots, each lasting less than one minute. This one-reel film (approximately fourteen minutes) has no editing within scenes, but instead the progression of the narrative merely follows from one locale to another with each shot revealing a different camera set-up. Only twice in the film is the

same set-up used, and each of these times the action in the shot has changed considerably from its previous use.

Over half of the eight titles in the films serve to announce the action to follow. The opening title establishes what becomes the comic thrust of the film:

> The Girl Makes A Hit
> With the Storekeeper---
> But Father Disapproves.[11]

In the following scene, a letter from the executor of the uncle's will is announced by "Three Million Dollars." A later scene is prefaced by a summary:

> The Girl Refuses To Get
> Married Because Nobody
> Loves Her.

Two other titles serve to name one scene as "The Abduction" and another to announce the willingness of the Justice-of-the-Peace (Jack Richardson) to comply with the father's plan: "Sold."

The three remaining titles report the dialogue within a scene. As the father meets the ranchhands, he says, "A Thousand Dollars A Piece If You Help Me Get My Daughter Married." After Kerrigan and Bush escape, they determine that the kidnapping was actually to their advantage: "Let's Go Back and Get Married." And when the father arrives

---

[11] As far as possible, the citation of titles throughout this chapter will follow the original capitalization and the general division of lines.

with the Justice-of-the-Peace to find the two young people gone, he confronts the ranchhands: "What Did You Do With My Daughter?"

For 1911, Three Million Dollars appears technically and dramatically below average. The story is simple, with the titles merely reinforcing the action, rather than adding any new dimension. The camera remains stationary through each shot, and the exterior locales eliminate any studio considerations such as light and shadow. The reliance upon natural scenery, moreover, works as a credit to the film, matching well the naturalistic style of acting.

A later film, also directed by Allan Dwan, was Calamity Anne's Trust (released April 26, 1913; re-released March 2, 1917). Peter Bogdanovich viewed this film as proof of D. W. Griffith's influence on Dwan:

> A year and a half--and almost two hundred shorts [after Three Million Dollars], Calamity Anne's Trust (1913) reveals Griffith's impact. The camera is much closer to the action now, there is cutting within scenes, greater flexibility, the compositions are no longer merely functional, and the acting has some charm.[12]

Calamity Anne's Trust also differs from Three Million Dollars in its emphasis on character. Calamity Anne (Louise Lester) is a Ma Kettle-type of character who lords it over the cowboys, smoking a corn-cob pipe, unconcerned with feminine graces. This film was the sixth in a series featuring this particular character; the popularity is indicated by the number of films American released in the series (thirteen) and the fact that three of these were later re-released.

---

[12]Bogdanovich, p. 6.

<u>Calamity Anne's Trust</u> begins with the title character discovering a note on the dead body of Sad-Eyed O'Brien:

> Tell my little girl it was an
> accident. Take good care of
> her. God will judge you.

Despite the taunts of the cowboys (including J. Warren Kerrigan), Calamity protects the girl (Pauline Bush) from the cowboys' flirtations and finally marries her off to a millionaire's son (J. A. Harrison). The film's plot is grounded in Calamity Anne's fulfillment of her "trust"; a subplot treats the millionaire (George Periolat) in search of his son. Periolat and Harrison are interesting in that their roles as "dudes" offer ample comic material in the hands of the cowboys.

This film contains a total of thirty-nine shots, over twice the number in <u>Three Million Dollars</u>, both films being the same length. Of the thirty-nine shots, only sixteen are different camera set-ups. In terms of camera positioning, the film does not differ substantially from the earlier example; the editing, however, is far advanced, with scenes including a number of viewpoints and reactions to the action. The shots are either long (full-length of the actors) or medium-long in camera positioning, a variety lacking in the full shots of <u>Three Million Dollars</u>.

Titles in <u>Calamity Anne's Trust</u> continue to function on the level of those in the earlier film. These titles introduce sequences, such as "Sad-Eyed O'Brien's Daughter," "Calamity Guards the Girl," "The

Elopement," "The Great Millionaire," and "Calamity's Trust Fulfilled." Only one title reveals dialogue: the Millionaire asks Kerrigan "Have You Seen My Boy?" Again, in this film, the natural settings (all exterior) and the natural acting style take the burden of the narrative away from the titles.

A film of the same length, released October 13, 1913, is Courage of Sorts, with Thomas Ricketts directing members of the second company. The film is the same in shot number as Calamity Anne's Trust (thirty-nine), but it demonstrates a more active attention to plot and camera while losing some of the character interest represented by Calamity Anne.

The old cattleman's daughter (Winnifred Greenwood) wants her father's permission to marry young Dr. Winton (Edward Coxen), but "the brave lion" must have some assurance of his prospective son-in-law's courage. The father requires Winton to "Spend a Night in the Haunted House and She is Yours." After Winton has agreed, the daughter sees her father put on a sheet to play a "ghostly" trick on the young suitor. She and Winton get to the house early, string up a skeleton, and after frightening "the brave lion," they receive his blessings.

Of the thirty-nine shots, ten are different camera set ups, indicating a stronger dependence on editing than demonstrated in the two earlier films. Two shots reveal slight camera movement to follow an action, and one set-up is used for interior scenes. The two factors of movement and interior shooting may at first seem quite an advance in technique; however, the movement of the camera is only functional, without any interpretive motive, and the interior setting is naturally lighted, revealing not only sunlight on the character's faces but also a rippling of the tablecloth from a breeze.

Titles in <u>Courage of Sorts</u> continue the minimal "narrative signpost" function: "The Old Cattleman Boasts of his Bravery," "His Daughter," "Young Dr. Winton," "The Haunted Cabin--Afternoon," with only two of the ten titles reporting dialogue. The interesting aspects of this film are the amount of editing of the scenes into at least three segments each and one camera trick which is exploited four times. As the father runs from the "other ghost," he reaches a cornfield and in one jump, he gets from one side of the field to the other, a distance perhaps of two hundred feet. The trick here is derived from stopped-action: as he reaches the field, he jumps--the camera is stopped and the father makes his way to the other side; then he jumps up, and the camera is started again, thus giving the impression of the father's ability to leap over the cornfield in a single bound. The same trick is repeated in the same shot as the Doctor (with a sheet over his head) performs the same feat. When the father reaches a toll gate across the road, again he performs his jumping "skill" as does the Doctor in his chase. In the three examples discussed so far, this camera trick-element represents the first use of editing (within the camera) for a comic effect. The device was innovative, though, only to American; filmmakers had been aware of this trick since the turn-of-the-century work of Georges Méliès.

The final example of Western comedy to be discussed is <u>The Deacon's Card</u>, a "Beauty" film released May 14, 1916. This film represents a blending between the "comedies of manner" which were "Beauty's" trademark and the type of Western comedy represented by the three previous examples. Set in a rural Western town, the plot like <u>Courage of Sorts</u> features the attempts of two young people to be married against the desires of the girl's father, the Deacon. As leader of the Anti-Gambling League, the Deacon upholds the group's slogan: "Down with Card Players and Gamblers!" When Tom (Joe Massey) and Nora (Jo Taylor) are met by the Deacon, Tom inadvertently drops a few cards from his handerchief pocket. The remainder of the story is taken up with Tom and Nora's elopement and the Deacon's error in putting the cards into his pocket and receiving the wrath of the League when, like Tom, he pulls out his handkerchief. All is explained in the end of this one-reel film, with Tom signing an oath promising "never again to gamble or to indulge in any game of chance."

The plot of <u>The Deacon's Card</u> is a standard one, similar to the time-worn tradition of children <u>vs</u>. unreasonable parents in comedy since the Romans. The film is technically advanced from the previous examples in the number of shots (seventy-two) and the number of camera set-ups (forty-six), revealing some dependence on editing in the structuring of the narrative. Also significant is the fact that the film has three dissolves and two iris-framed sequences, both devices functionally indicating a change of scene and time. Irised shots are also used to introduce characters.

Only five titles are used in the film either to introduce a sequence or to report dialogue:

> The Anti-Gambling League
> Committee Calls on the
> Deacon to Discuss the
> forthcoming Crusade.
>
> Down with the Card-players
> and Gamblers!
>
> "Wait! My daughter will
> explain."
>
> Denouncing the Deacon for
> a Card-playing
> Hypocrite, the Committee threatens to
> have him Expelled from
> the Church.
>
> The Committee calls on the
> Parson to Expose the
> Deacon's Hypocrisy.

Given the basic plot of the film, the titles seem to add nothing which was not already apparent from the action.

These four Western comedies indicate a wide range of approaches to the genre. What is common to both Three Million Dollars and Calamity Anne's Trust is a reliance on the Western setting and characters. Courage of Sorts and The Deacon's Card retain some of the setting characteristics while updating both the characters and the situations into a "Western/contemporary social comedy" mixture.

Cinematic elements of these films are not stressed as much as might be expected for this period. What seems to be the major preoccupation in these four fil --and the majority of others in this type, 1910-19--is the situation itself, usually of the "comedy of errors" sort, with some dependence on stock comic characterization.

The genre of Western comedy was popular with American, especially with the Calamity Anne series. As Table 4 has indicated, from 1911-13 the company produced eighty-seven films in this type, almost 25% of the total output during the three year period. When American began production, the Western comedies resembled the Snakeville comedies produced for Essanay by G. M. Anderson in Niles, California. By 1914, however, American had branched out into other forms, leaving the Western comedies to be produced by other firms.

Western Drama

Only one example of this type of film released by American is available for analysis in this study and this example, Six Feet Four, comes late in the company's history (1919). However, the trade journal reports and the archival synopses of the earlier Western dramas can be utilized to reveal how the plots of this type of film developed into the longer, more impressive Six Feet Four.

One of the earliest of American's Western dramas, filmed outside of Chicago, was The Squaw and the Man (released December 29, 1910). Like a number of the Westerns to follow, The Squaw and the Man begins with an Easterner traveling West to escape a false accusation. The Easterner rescues an Indian maiden from the advances of a medicine man and marries her. They settle and have a child only to be visited by the man's mother and his girlfriend who take the half-breed child back

East, leaving the squaw to commit suicide and the man "to die of a broken heart."[13]

This film typifies one of the most peculiarly Western elements in American's dramas. Flight from the East to West is common in these films, with the East representing a stifling world of pressure contrasted with the freedom of the Western environment. The Mother and Girlfriend, as distinctly Eastern characters, disrupt the harmony which the Man had found in the West. Their "civilized" concerns are shown through the need to return the child to the East for "proper education," a move which destroys both the squaw and the man.

When Allan Dwan took over the direction of the Western company, the films began to take on more complex plots, though these still revealed the formulaic nature of the Western genre. An example, The Hermit's Gold, (released June 22, 1911), is a complex tale of two men vying for the love of an avaricious young maiden. Charles and George love Clara but neither has the fortune she requires. While George remains on the ranch, Charles seeks gold in the mountains where he is hurt and then nursed back to health by a wealthy hermit. Having stolen the hermit's gold, Charles confesses to George who then cares for the hermit until the old man, gone insane from the blow on the head he received from Charles, finally dies. Clara then rejects Charles for George who gives her the money but leaves the ranch without her.[14]

---

[13] Moving Picture World, VIII (January 14, 1911), 97.

[14] Ibid., VIII (June 17, 1911), 1394.

The plot of this film is similar to a number made by Dwan in which men are challenged to some feat in order to win the affections of a woman. The role of mountains appears over and over again in these Westerns as a microcosm of the Western setting, in which men can discover fortunes in gold--and also lose their lives.

Another film by Dwan reveals a preoccupation with the violence wrought from greed. The Fear (released September 16, 1912) tells the story of an old smuggler (George Periolat) whose hiding place is discovered by two cowboys (J. Warren Kerrigan and Jack Richardson). Kerrigan fancies the smuggler's daughter (Pauline Bush), arousing Richardson's jealousy. When Richardson tells the smuggler that Kerrigan is going to reveal the hiding place of the stolen goods, the old man tries to kill Kerrigan. In the struggle, Richardson is shot, the girl interferes, and the old man promises to reform and to give his daughter's hand in marriage to Kerrigan.[15]

The added element here is the smuggling plot which made use of Santa Barbara's beaches and caves. The plot also sounds very similar to a number of Dwan Westerns produced for American in which Kerrigan wants the girl, Richardson stands in the way, and all is well in the end.

Another plot repeated through the early Western dramas was one in which a Mexican villain threatens the livelihood of the townspeople. In Unwritten Law of the West (released June 19, 1913), Kerrigan stumbles over the dead body of Pedro who has been stabbed by his wife, Anita.

---

[15] National Film Archive Catalogue, III, 186.

After Kerrigan has been accused of Pedro's murder and run out of town, his girlfriend Helen overhears Anita confess to her father that she killed Pedro because of his brutal assault on her. Kerrigan is cleared of the murder, and the townspeople refuse to prosecute "the unfortunate Anita."[16]

The early one- and two-reel Western dramas depended on plots such as the ones described above, making use of the natural settings provided by the Santa Barbara landscape. By 1915, more care and time was given to the Western dramas, with the "Mustang" company devoting their efforts to two- and three-reel Westerns.

One "Mustang" offering, directed by and starring Frank Borzage, was *The Pitch of Chance*, a two-reel drama released December 24, 1915. In this film, Kentuck (Jack Richardson) and Scott (Borzage) gamble heavily with Scott the winner. In an effort to recover his losses, Kentuck offers his girlfriend Nan (Helene Rosson) as the stakes; Scott, however, wins the card game and rides out of town with Nan. After Scott agrees not to molest Nan, they return to the town where Kentuck engages him in a gunfight. With Kentuck severely wounded, Scott returns the cash winnings, and he and Nan declare their new-found love for each other.[17]

The "Mustang" films represented an added dimension to the Westerns released by American: the strong hero who succumbs to the love of a

---

[16] Ibid., 206.

[17] Ibid., 231.

pretty lady. Previous Westerns stressed the situation over character development. Although many of the early Westerns included a love interest between hero and heroine, the accent seemed to be more on the action necessary for the two to "settle down." The Pitch of Chance reflects a switch to a stronger focus on this love interest: almost half of the film is spent with Nan and Scott falling in love. Through the Westerns to follow, 1916-19, increased length and dependence on "stars" would bring the concentration on character and motivation into more dominant focus.

Six Feet Four (released in September, 1919) is a six-reel (eighty-five minutes) Western drama which demonstrates the culmination of American's work in this genre. Directed by Henry King, the film's scenario was written by Stephen Fox (Jules Furthman), based on a novel by Jackson Gregory. The story deals with Buck Thornton (William Russell) who stands six-feet-four "in his stocking feet." Thornton is being framed by a group of crafty businessmen so that they can gain control of his ranch. Through a series of adventures, Thornton discovers the plot and eliminates his adversaries.

While the main plot is concerned with Thornton's establishing his innocence, a number of sub-plots increase the complexity of the action. The first of these sub-plots develops the love interest between Buck and Winifred Waverly (Vola Vale), who has returned "from a two-year absence in the East to her uncle's ranch near Drytown." This sub-plot is enriched by the fact that Winifred's uncle is Henry Pollard (Charles K. French), the leader of Thornton's enemies. Another complication to the main plot is the unrest among the enemies themselves: Pollard, Broderick, and Ed Bedloe decide to eliminate Ed's brother, Kid Bedloe (Jack Brammall), from their plans.

Early in the film, Buck shows Winifred a wanted posted with a picture of Jimmie Clayton (John Gough), escaped convict; Buck tells her that Clayton once saved his life. Finding Clayton unconscious, Buck then takes the convict to his cabin to nurse his wounds. Since Kid Bedloe is Clayton's best friend, Buck and the Kid form an alliance against Pollard and his men, thereby connecting the sub-plots. An additional thread of the story deals with William Comstock (Harvey Clarke), an undercover marshall who helps Thornton clear himself.

The resolution of the plot complications almost always depends on chance. When Broderick disguises himself as Buck to rob Winifred of the money she is taking to the ranch, he accidentally loses a spur at the cabin, providing Buck with the clue he needed. Also, Buck's height proves to Winifred that he didn't rob her: he cannot get through the doorway without bumping his head, while Broderick cleared the doorway with no problem.

<u>Six Feet Four</u> continues the Western tradition of hale and hardy men. An opening title, attributed to Theodore Roosevelt, sets the atmosphere for the Western setting to follow:

> We knew toil and hardship and
> hunger and thirst, and we saw
> men die violent deaths as they
> worked among the horses and cattle or
> fought out feuds with one another, but

> we felt the beat of hardy life in our
> veins, and ours was the glory of work
> and the joy of living.

While less than half the scenes of the film occur in the "wide-open spaces," the interior sequences reveal a rustic, authentically Western atmosphere which later became Henry King's trademark.[18] Perhaps the most interesting setting is the hotel lobby with the hearth and bar, a place where "the same group always foregathers to await the arrival of the night stage." The heavy-beamed ceiling predominates throughout these shots, giving an oppressive perspective to the hotel sequences.

A total of 461 shots constitute the film with almost half this number (205) representing differing set-ups. From this information, we can gather that the structuring of the narrative depended somewhat on the editing of parallel lines of action within the sub-plots, but the amount of differing angles and distances from which to view the action was not much more advanced than the early Western comedies.

An interesting use of titles highlights <u>Six Feet Four</u>. Of the ninety-nine titles, less than a dozen serve to introduce either characters of locales. The majority report dialogue between characters, often with pictorial comments on the words spoken. For example, after Comstock provides Buck with an alibi, thus ruining the Sheriff's plan

---

[18] Critic Robert Warshow noted: "In <u>The Gunfighter</u> [directed by King in 1951],...the landscape has virtually disappeared. Most of the action takes place indoors, in a cheerless saloon,...in cold, quiet tones of gray,...suggesting those dim photographs of the nineteenth-century West." "Movie Chronicle: The Westerner," <u>The Immediate Experience</u> (New York: Doubleday, 1962), p. 144.

to arrest Buck for robbery, Comstock passes by the Sheriff's office; the Sheriff points him out to Broderick and Ed:

> There's the jasper
> who crabbed our game
> last night.

The title card depicts a large bag, with the word "BEANS" imprinted on it, spilling its contents onto the letters of the reported dialogue. At another point, Comstock tells Buck of the evil plot against him:

> I'm after the men who've
> been trying to make you the
> scapegoat for their own
> crimes.

The title card features a perplexed goat staring at the words being reported.

Aside from the comic embellishments of the titles, the number of verbal reports (averaging thirty-four per reel) indicates a far greater dependence on literal explanation than any of the other films discussed. With the addition of sub-plots, the increasing complexity of character relationship and motivation, the film displays a stronger need for these titles.

For the first few years, the Western drama and comedy were the staple product from American. <u>Six Feet Four</u> suggests how the Western drama was used by the company in later years. During the twelve years of American's production, almost 35% of the films released were Westerns. A major reason for this fact can be found in the popularity of the Western tradition throughout the silent era of filmmaking; another reason points out the environment surrounding the Santa Barbara studio, with the mountains, ranches, and plains necessary to provide "authentic" backgrounds.

With the building of the new studio in 1913, and the subsequent branching out into newer forms of the photoplay, American's number of Westerns decreased until the company's waning years. The Western had provided a firm base for the company's production activities, but as the company developed, new types took the place of the reliable Western.

Contemporary Social Comedy

The early social comedies consisted of a central situation, brought about by some misunderstanding, in which for one reel characters try to restore some order to the social scene. An example is The Borrowed Flat (released January 12, 1911), a split-reel comedy released only a month after American's production began.

Built on the mishaps surrounding April Fools' Day, The Borrowed Flat features Percy Pidgeon (J. Warren Kerrigan) contemplating a visit from his wealthy Aunt Mathilda. When Bobby borrows Percy's apartment for a rendezvous with his fiancee, Percy readdresses Bobby's love note and sends it to the washlady instead. To get even, Bobby impersonates Percy's aunt, with everything clarified once the real Aunt Mathilda arrives.

With a total of fifteen shots (in approximately eight minutes), the film shows only two camera set-ups: a long shot of the apartment, framed like the proscenium arch of the stage, and a close-up position for the inserts of letters, notes, and calling cards. The five titles announce the fragmented gag-episodes: "April First," "Bobby Borrows Percy's Room to Meet His Fiancee," "Ye Gods and Little Fishes--Bridget the Washlady," "With Old Masquerade Clothes, Bobby impersonates Percy's Aunt," and "Percy Discovers Bobby's Joke." The comic business is crude and often peripheral to the main thread of the stoy: when Percy enters, he discovers a sign on his back reading, "Please Kick Me."

The Borrowed Flat shows little of the adeptness which American's comedies would develop in the next few years. When the "Beauty" brand was announced in January, 1914, American had gained a strong reputation for comedy in the films of the second company. The "Beauty" films continued the concentration on "comedy of errors" social situations but with more attention to complexity of story complications and characterizations.

By 1916, the "Beauty" films had been functioning consistently for two years. Ella Wanted to Elope, directed by James S. Douglas and released February 16, 1916, is a good example of the type of story material and film technique represented by the "Beauty" films of this period.

Although Ella (Neva Gerber) has won the affections of Young Jack (Dick Rosson), she holds a schoolgirl crush on her mother's lawyer, Reginald Rosson (William Carroll), much to the displeasure of her mother (Lucille Ward). To cure Ella, the lawyer proposes to her, and they elope. He deserts her at the hotel, where Jack--who had been following them--has Reginald arrested. While the mother and the lawyer try to explain the mix-up to the judge, Jack and Ella sneak away to be married.

This one-reel film has seventy-six shots, forty-three of them different camera set-ups. The major concentration throughout the scenes is on Ella, who is characterized by the titles, representing pages from her diary:

> If pas and mas and other folks
> So fussy wouldn't be,
> How pleasanter and cheerfuller
> This world would be for me!
>
> At sweet sixteen, faint heart doth seem
> An ailment most annoying,
> But boyish pleas the fair to tease
> Are not for her enjoying.

Ella is revealed both through her actions and the ninetten titles as infatuated more with the idea of love than with any one man. Except for her character development, the other personages in the film are fairly stock types: the domineering mother, the innocent schoolboy, and the sophisticated man-of-the-world.

While the one-reel length permitted only a stock comic situation to be explored, the eventual move into feature films for American did not reveal an intensifying of comic situations as might be expected. Instead, after 1916, the accent was on social dramas with some comedy and happy endings embellishing the serious direction of the plot. For American, the feature film--except for those of comedians Kolb and Dill, 1915-16--demanded a more serious plot than the earlier comedies had provided.

Contemporary Social Drama

Over one-third of American's films fall into the category of contemporary social drama, representing films of a serious nature dealing with crisis situations in the daily lives of recognizably contemporary human beings. American's entry into production of this type was slow as long as the Western provided the serious or even melodramatic offerings. By 1914, over half the films released were of a contemporary dramatic nature; the ratio remained approximately the same for the company's final years of production, until the Western reappeared as the staple product in American's releases for 1921.

The years 1913-16 offered a number of dramatic offerings in which such topics as marital discord provided a crisis situation from which the characters struggled for two reels to free themselves. What Her Diary Told (released November 6, 1913) finds Janet Warren faced with two proposals, one from the wealthy and prominent John Weldon, and the other from the man she loves, Harold. Her acceptance of John brings torment to them both.

The plot of What Her Diary Told can be seen in five formal parts:

I. Janet accepts the proposal of John "for his wealth and social position."

II. Wedding plans are announced.

III. On her wedding day, Janet confesses to her diary: "This is my wedding-day. I have married John, knowing that I loved Harold. I will try to do my part, but oh: Diary, my heart is breaking."

IV. After the honeymoon, John reads the wedding day entry in the diary and leaves the house. At his lawyer's office, he arranges for Janet to receive all of his wealth, while he decides to disappear from the scene.

V. Heartbroken, Janet is sent out West to a sanitarium. On a trip into the country, she discovers John who has been hurt in a farming accident. She confesses her realized love and nurses her husband back to health.

The story has a happy ending after both the major characters have suffered the rejection of each other.

Having a total of thirty shots, this one-reel drama includes fourteen camera set-ups, and fades act as transitional devices between the segments. Over half the shots are interior settings, elegant drawing rooms and boudoirs, lighted to provide a natural feeling to the rooms. Although the production style and acting throughout are natural, the main thrust of the plot relies on the discovery of an inanimate object: the page in the diary. Like so many of the films which preceded and followed What Her Diary Told, the plot turnings depended on chance meetings, misinterpreted notes, etc., devices which move the plot without any internal logic of character motivation. As the company developed, more sophistication was apparent in the construction of longer, less contrived dramas.

By 1918, American had put its trust strongly into the social dramas. Especially with the films of Mary Miles Minter, Marguerita Fischer, and Gail Kane, the films contained situations built around characters rather than vice versa. The Eyes of Julia Deep, directed by Lloyd Ingraham and starring Miss Minter in the title role, was released in September, 1918, and represented the dramas which depended upon the title character and her peculiar qualities.

Julia Deep is "the little princess at the Exchange desk" of a large department store. Her passion for books introduces her to the profligate, Terry Hartridge (Alan Forrest) whose library lies dormant while he "blaze[s] a trail across the white lights of the city." Julia helps Terry reform his ways, but the department store manager, Timothy Black (George Periolat), discharges Julia, fearing that "an affair with a shopgirl would ruin [Terry's] career." Despite the pleadings of Julia's most admired customer, the widow Sarah Lowe (Eugenie Besserer), Black does not reconsider. When Julia meets Terry's old flame, actress Lottie Driscoll (Alice Wilson), Lottie stages a dramatic scene in which she attempts suicide because Julia has stolen the man she loves. Julia promises to leave Terry and then accepts Sarah's offer to become the widow's private secretary. Terry finally convinces Julia that Lottie was doing "a bit of offstage acting," and they leave the Lowe household to be married. When Black and Sarah pursue them, the two oldsters decide to make it a double wedding, and all ends happily.

The Eyes of Julia Deep is a sentimental drama with obstacles continually being placed along the road to happiness for Julia and Terry. What distinguishes this film from others produced by American in this type is the power of persuasion which Julia possesses. Whenever the plot necessitates a reversal, the image of Julia's eyes is shown in close-up. An example of this cinematic device is when Julia convinces the Sheriff of Plummetsville not to lock up Terry, Black, and Sarah in the jail for disturbing the peace. The following shot analysis from the film demonstrates how this device is used:

255. SAME AS #253
BLACK and SARAH run up to JULIA, TERRY, and the SHERIFF. SARAH pleads with JULIA.

TITLE: "My child, you've been lured away by this abductor."

BLACK disagrees.

TITLE: "Abductor! She lured him away."

BLACK and SARAH argue until the SHERIFF intervenes.

TITLE: "I'm the sheriff-- what's all this about?"

SARAH explains.

TITLE: "Sheriff, arrest that young man!"

BLACK again interrupts.

TITLE: "Nonsense! Arrest that old woman."

SHERIFF PLUMMET is confused.

TITLE: "Well--you're making so many charges, I guess I'll take you all in."

He does so.

TITLE: The Plummetsville Gaol

256. L.S. INT. JAIL

PLUMMET gestures to the deputy to put all
four in cells, but JULIA interrupts.

TITLE: "Sheriff, you wouldn't lock
us up in cells--
would you?"

257. M.S. OF JULIA

258. M.S. OF PLUMMET

259. E.C.U. OF EYES (SAME AS #151)
[The frame is bordered by black at the top
and bottom.]

260. SAME AS #257

261. SAME AS #258

PLUMMET is won over.

262. SAME AS #256

SHERIFF PLUMMET ushers the four into an
adjoining room.[19]

The device is used at two other points in the film when Julia overcomes a dominant attitude of one of the characters.

Another extremely interesting aspect of the plot development is Julia's solution to Terry's prodigal life. After spending the evening reading in Terry's room, Julia hides behind a curtain to prevent Terry's

---

[19] This example is from the shot analyses done for each of the eleven films discussed at length in this chapter. Abbreviations and terms used are "SAME AS" (referring to the exact same camera set-up as a previous shot), L.S. (long shot), M.S. (medium shot), and E.C.U. (extreme close-up).

discovery of her. Terry, dejected over his financial squanderings, pulls a gun from the desk drawer. Julia prevents his suicide attempt by jumping out from behind the curtain:

    103. SAME AS #101

        JULIA says to TERRY:

        TITLE: "If you don't want your life, then give it to me."

    104. SAME AS #102

        TERRY is confused.

        TITLE: "What would you do with it?".

    105. SAME AS #101

        JULIA explains.

        TITLE: "I'd put you to work and make you earn a profit."

Julia then goes on to explain her idea of forming "a co-operative to pool our earnings." With her as business manager and Terry as workman, they plan to share their wages, arguing that both would have a larger buying capital. The theme is not developed much beyond this point, but the venture into a discussion of profit-making and co-operative living in this 1918 film makes the plot somewhat unusual for its date.

    The five-reel (70 minutes) film contains 429 shots and 238 different camera set-ups, revealing an extended use of editing within scenes, notably in the number of reaction shots. With 172 titles, The Eyes of Julia Deep depends much more on verbal interchange than on action to develop the story line: over 90% of the titles report dialogue.

Almost three-fourths of the scenes are interior ones, a marked difference from the early films which, shot before American had a studio, depended on the exterior scenery for background. The interior scenes are carefully lighted with a notable use of shadow and compositional lighting for dramatic scenes.

What is distinctive about The Eyes of Julia Deep is the development of characters within a framework of dramatic and comic moments. The characters are motivated by their own well-drawn personalities rather than simply by the turns of the plot. The film shows a strong dependence on the studio scenery and reveals a high degree of dialogue through the titles. This sentimental drama represented an important point for American, not only as a vehicle for its top star attraction, Mary Miles Minter, but also as a well-written story blending the sentimental drama with moments of comedy. Miss Minter plays her role in total consistency, portraying the young, naive waif whose "mission in life" is to make everyone happy.

Period Drama

The "period dramas" produced by American were of two types: allegorical dramas and romance-adventures. In addition to their customary duties for turning out social comedies, the "Beauty" companies also attempted a few allegorical photoplays in which characters embodying specific virtues or vices cavort through a scenario of moralistic fervor.[20] Everyheart, released September 21, 1915, is an example of this type of film where the remote setting and characters take on a didactic tone.

Before Everyheart journeys to Earth, he is given bags of "faith," "freedom," and "kindness" to carry with him. A devil figure tries to trade these for bundles of "money," "power," and "passion," but an angel saves Everyheart from the temptation. With the angel as his wife, Everyheart then transmogrifies into earthly form, and the couple enjoys years of spiritual and marital bliss. But Everyheart is careless and uses up his gifts, succumbing to jealousy when his wife receives the attentions of another man. His "Spirit of Jealousy" and "Selfishness" steal his remaining bags of virtue, and he embarks on a hellish journey through a netherland, the "Vale of Sorrows" where he repents and is forgiven. Returning home, he greets his distressed wife with a newly-earned quantity of "kindness," and happiness returns to the couple.

The film seems to be executed in all seriousness, although it is difficult to accept some of the techniques in this vein. Everyheart's storage place for his bags of virtue is a large heart-shaped purse draped over his left shoulder which he fills as he travels through the "Garden of Gifts" early in the film. The opening shot sets the tone to follow in the "Garden" scenes: a huge world revolves above a misty

---

[20] See, for example, the comments on Purity by Clifford Howard in Chapter III.

surface; Everyheart walks toward the globe before dissolving into the "Garden."

Technically, the film makes use of a number of photographic devices. Early in the film, an angel is superimposed above Everyheart saying, "Give me greatly of Kindness, for in the world, Everyheart shall need this gift abundantly." The same angel appears over the gates with the words, "Warning! Every unused gift shall be taken away" emblazened in the sky. Again, this angel mysteriously materializes in the "Vale of Sorrows" in which she transforms a cherub into a starving beggar boy to test Everyheart's sincerity. The film is filled with superimposed spirits crawling out of Everyheart's sleeping body; allegorical figures such as the man in the "Vale of Sorrows" who stumbles from the burden of a large bundle marked, "$"; and dissolves from one locale to another while Everyheart maintains his position in the frame throughout the transition.

This one-reel film contains forty-one shots, with twenty-five camera set-ups. The accent is on the palacial settings of the first sequence and the cinematic tricks that move the plot along. Titles announce various chapters in the life of Everyheart, revealing no dialogue between the characters.

Perhaps the major stimulus to American's brief excursion into this type of photoplay was the availability of the Grecian settings in the nearby millionaire estates of Montecito, located only a few miles south of Santa Barbara. Here films could be devised to encompass temples, ornately designed colonnades surrounding swimming pools, and classical mansions. As early as 1913, director Lorimer Johnston had made use of the Montecito estates in his film, *In the Days of Trajan*, as did the filming of *Purity* in 1915 and *Valley of Decision* in 1916.

Exploitation of setting was also predominant in Harry Pollard's production of *The Pearl of Paradise* (released November 2, 1916). In this South Sea island romance, based on the novel by Andrew Sinclair, the "pearl of Paradise Island" is Yulita (Margarita Fischer) whose uninhibited, child-like manner in seclusion from civilization includes a number of nude scenes along the San Diego, California coastline. With her father, Gomez (Joseph Harris), Yulita nurses back to health a ship-wrecked Navy Lieutenant, the three finally leaving the island to escape a wicked sea captain bent on revenge for Yulita's rejection of him.

This skeletal summary hardly does justice to a complex tale of intrigue and adventure. When Lt. John Weldon (Harry Pollard) recovers, Gomez explains how he and Yulita happen to be on Paradise Island, and at this point the film takes on both narrative and cinematic significance. In the flashback tale, the characters of the story proper adopt the roles of Gomez's past: Yulita becomes her mother, Alice; Weldon becomes Alice's first husband; and the sea captain, Van Dekken (J. Gordon Russell) portrays the villain who makes advances toward Alice. Gomez loved Alice, but the maiden was forced to marry a man of her father's choosing. When Gomez discovers that Alice's husband has become a hopeless alcoholic, allowing himself to be cuckolded by his "friend,"[21] Gomez kills both men and with Alice, flees to the South Sea Island. Away from civilization, Yulita is born and shortly thereafter, Alice dies, leaving Gomez to raise the girl with only the help of the natives. By casting the same actors from the main story into the flashback, Pollard has added foreshadowing to the conclusion of the film in which Weldon rescues Yulita from the attacks of Van Dekken, returning both Yulita and Gomez to civilization.

The five-reel adventure contains 340 shots, with less than a third of these (108) different camera set-ups. The majority of shots are exterior ones, utilizing the sea coast and the surroundings for the island scenes and the Spanish buildings of San Diego's Balboa Park for the flashbacks. Seventy-two titles are included in the film, over half of these reporting dialogue. The film is distinguished, though, by high action rather than by talky transitions.

The Pearl of Paradise is a good example of the type of romantic photoplay utilized by American. Pollard's treatment of plot, subtle acting by all the characters, and close attention to lighting and composition seem, however, to set the film apart from American's other

---

[21] Interesting at this point in the flashback story is the cut to Yulita sitting in a boat immediately after Gomez has completed telling Weldon about the cuckolding episode. Yulita is seated in a row boat with both a goat and a monkey. The shot brings to mind the moments in Shakespeare's Othello, first when Iago baits the Moor by referring to Desdemona's "affair" with Cassio "as prime as goats, as hot as monkeys" (III, iii, 403), and when Othello repeats the idea, railing at Cassio, "Goats and monkeys!" (IV, i, 267). Whether director Pollard was attempting a literary allusion at this point cannot be determined; the parallel between the two episodes, however, is too striking to pass without comment.

offerings as a film advanced beyond the standard fare released from the American studios.

Summary

The majority of American's film plots were built on contrivance of action, with few dealing with character motivation or development. Almost all of the films depended on the particular scenic surroundings of the Santa Barbara area, with the mountains, ranches, seashore, and classical estates offering scenes to complement the interior scenes shot in the big glass studio. Throughout even the later films, the early beginnings with the Western can be seen in the rural landscapes which serve as locale for most of the action in these films.

The Western was perhaps American's most dependable form of the photoplay. With the advantage of realistic backgrounds, films of this type exploited the qualities of the popular Western tradition: strong figures in clearly-cut situations upholding "the Code of the West," usually against threats from black-hearted villains.

While American's production activities began and ended with the Western, excursions into other genres seem to have yielded some success. Contemporary social comedies and dramas made up over half of the films released by American; most of these were well-made plots in which contrivance superceded character development.

The elements of technique in American's films reveal a developing sophistication. From the initial period in which stationary, single set-ups provided the camera's view, the films develop to an increased dependence on editing and multiple viewpoint. The use of titles also grew steadily, until with the final films the titles became the verbal transcription to stories which needed dialogue more than action to sustain themselves.

Table 5 to follow charts American's development in technique, based on the eleven films analyzed in this study. This table reveals an increasing number of shots, together with a growing use of multiple camera set-ups. By 1918, films were using not only more variations of viewpoints to a scene but also almost as many titles as camera set-ups. Only the Western remained fairly laconic in its use of dialogue, as Six Feet Four has demonstrated.

A number of reasons for American's eventual fall can be seen from the films analyzed here. In the realm of plot, American failed to develop very significantly beyond the standard well-made play structure and the Western formula. While others in the industry ventured into the area of spectacles (Intolerance, 1916; The Ten Commandments, 1923; The Hunchback of Notre Dame, 1923; and Ben Hur, 1927), American failed to do much more than dabble in this type of photoplay. While the individual comedians were developing at other studios (Chaplin, Lloyd, Langdon, Keaton), American failed to produce a strong comic personality. The venture into historical melodrama, such as The Birth of a Nation (1915) and The Coward (1916) was not followed by American. And while many in the industry devoted their

TABLE 5

ELEMENTS OF AMERICAN'S FILMMAKING

Title of Film	Average no. of shots per reel	Average no. of set-ups per reel	Average no. of titles per reel	Percentage of locales: Interior / Exterior	
THE BORROWED FLAT (1911)	15	2	5	100%	0%
THREE MILLION DOLLARS (1911)	18	16	8	0%	100%
CALAMITY ANNE'S TRUST (1912)	39	16	8	0%	100%
COURAGE OF SORTS (1912)	39	10	10	25%	75%
WHAT HER DIARY TOLD (1913)	30	14	19	60%	40%
THE DEACON'S CARD (1914)	79	46	5	90%	10%
EVERYHEART (1915)	41	25	14	50%	50%
ELLA WANTED TO ELOPE (1916)	76	43	19	75%	25%
THE PEARL OF PARADISE (1916)	70	22	25	10%	90%
THE EYES OF JULIA DEEP (1918)	86	48	37	75%	25%
SIX FEET FOUR (1919)	77	34	17	50%	50%

efforts toward exploring new techniques, American lagged behind. Except for a few unusual films, such as <u>Damaged Goods</u>, <u>Purity</u>, and <u>The Pearl of Paradise</u>, American's offerings seem more useful as an index to what the lesser companies were producing, while the innovative "gamblers" passed the conservatives by.

CHAPTER VI

CONCLUSIONS

"The Silent Partner" is a fitting metaphor for the American Film Company. In common usage, the term usually refers to someone who has invested money in a business but does not actively participate in its management or its affairs. American invested _films_ and _trained personnel_ in the industry itself (and in Mutual Film Corporation specifically), but the company failed to enjoy an active participation in the future affairs of the industry.[1]

This study of an independent silent film company has been an attempt not just to survey an isolated event in history--i.e., the operation of the American Film Manufacturing Company, 1910-1921--but moreover to delineate the levels of causation at work in such an event. From a general coverage of the industry during American's existence, the study has explored the layers of the company: the business structure, the employees, and the product of the company's efforts--the films themselves. What has been attempted is a complete history in general terms, and specifically a history which uses business and industry as its primary focus.

---

[1]"Silent partner" is also used for this study as a conundrum: "silent" determines the nature of the films produced by American and the period of film history in which the company operated; "partner" suggests the Western film, a genre in which American placed much of its strength.

When American was founded in 1910, the motion picture industry was under the stranglehold of a combine based on manufacturing patents. This "cartel of inventors," the Motion Picture Patents Company, was the industry's response to an era of "almost perfect competition,"[2] in which companies operated independently of each other. The period from 1896 to 1908 was also one in which the film developed from a one-minute curiosity to a fourteen-minute narrative format; yet, further development both artistically and industrially was improbable in the hands of manufacturers whose first interests were in machines and equipment.

By 1910, the Patents Company was being challenged by film producers independent of their control. Carl Laemmle, perhaps the major figure in the early battle against the Trust, had demonstrated the viability of operating outside the Patents claims over machinery. His Independent Moving Picture Company served as an example to other distributors and exhibitors.

The American Film Company's formation reflected the beginnings of most of the independent film companies. Unlike the manufacturers behind the Patents Company, the independents were men who had entered the film industry motivated by an interest in real estate; to intensify profits from their land and buildings, the entrepreneurs became "exhibitors." This background gave the independents an edge over the Patents Company; their experience as theatre operators with constant contact with

---

[2] William F. Hellmuth, Jr., "The Motion Picture Industry," in Walter Adams (ed.), The Structure of American Industry (New York: Macmillan, 1950), p. 269.

filmgoers allowed them to grasp more precisely "what the public wanted" than the manufacturers did.[3]

Mae Huettig's analysis of this period is a concise estimation of how the film itself was utilized under this situation:

> From the beginning the film has often been exploited not primarily as a thing profitable in itself but as a means of profiting from the exploitation of related merchandise, i.e., equipment, real estate, etc.[4]

John R. Freuler and Harry E. Aitken, both of them founders of the American Film Company, had developed an interest in the film industry through their real estate dealings. Like Carl Laemmle, they moved from being exhibitors into the distribution field. From 1906 to 1910, their efforts were strictly in the area of distribution, with their Western Film Exchange becoming a prominent part of the midwestern film activity. When Freuler and Aitken broke from the Patents Company, again following Laemmle's lead, they formed production companies to

---

[3] Terry Ramsaye makes another distinction between the heads of the Patents Company and the independents. Noting that nine of the ten Patents Company members were Gentile, Ramsaye suggests that 90% of the independents were Jewish: "There was an unrecorded but freely expressed determination to maintain a Gentile control of the industry. In consequence enterprises with Jewish personnel and control were forced into high pressure initiative in order to achieve a foothold in the industry" (Annals of the American Academy of Political and Social Science, CXXVIII [November, 1926], 16). I have purposely avoided Ramsaye's remarks on this topic throughout the body of this study, even though his conclusion might explain why the Gentile-led American Film Company failed under the competition from Jewish Carl Laemmle and Adolph Zukor. Rather than perpetuate Ramsaye's chauvinist generalization, I would instead stress the fact that the majority of the independents were European immigrants who were forced to engage in vigorous activity if they were to compete with the entrenched members of the Patents Company.

[4] Huettig, p. 4.

insure the solvency of their distribution business. The founding of the American Film Company brought Freuler and Aitken into an association with Charles J. Hite and Samuel S. Hutchinson, two other distributors who wished a stronger control over the product they handled.

The stronghold of the Patents members actually worked in favor of the independents:

> [It] demonstrated that control rested with distribution and distribution had to be on a national basis to obtain maximum earnings on films. The strategic element in distribution worked in two directions: exhibitors were dependent upon distributors for films; producers were equally dependent upon them for outlets.[5]

Throughout American's career, the dominanting motivation of the company's executives was to supply films to their distribution outlets. As Huettig has suggested, this concern was predominant throughout the industry: the Patents Company needed a steady supply of film to support their camera and projector interests and their licensed exchanges; Carl Laemmle also needed assurance that his chain of exchanges would have a continual source of product to distribute.

At this point in the industry's development, the stress was on furnishing complete programs to the theatres, with "packages" including a Western, a comedy, perhaps a documentary, and a drama. The strength of distribution companies was in their being a central source for exhibitors to rent an entire package of films rather than dealing with three or four different manufacturers directly.

---

[5] Ibid., p. 17.

The "program method" was quickly recognized as an asset by the independent producers. As they formed production companies, they did so with the idea of having at least one company each producing the various types of films necessary to offer complete programs to the exhibitors. Laemmle depended upon his own company for dramas, with support from Powers, Rex, Champion, Republic, and Nestor film companies, each specializing in either dramas, comedies, or Westerns. Aitken and Freuler were also aware of the necessity for specialization: Westerns were produced for their exchanges by American, serials by Thanhouser and Gaumont, with comedies and dramas by Great Northern, Reliance, Eclair, Majestic, Solax, Lux, and Comet. These independents were totally dependent on the needs of the parent company. Without autonomy, such studios were subject to the changing demands brought about by the development of a complex industry.

American continued its service to the exchanges controlled by Freuler and Aitken throughout its first two years of operation. When Mutual Film Corporation was instituted in 1912, Freuler and Aitken had extended the program method of distribution nationwide. Under Mutual's control, American offered comedies ("Beauty" brand), Westerns ("Flying A" and "Mustang"), and dramas ("Clipper"), while some of the other Mutual companies specialized in individual types (e.g., Keystone in "slapstick comedies" and Ince in Westerns). During 1915 and 1916, American existed as a microcosm of Mutual with independent companies specializing in either comedies, dramas, Westerns, or "Mutual Masterpictures." Harry Aitken's withdrawal from Mutual in 1915 meant also the departure of directors D. W. Griffith (Majestic-Reliance dramas), Thomas Ince (William S. Hart Westerns), and Mack Sennett (Keystone comedies). With John R. Freuler at the helm, Mutual's reliance on American for all types of the photoplays, including serials, was intensified. Under this situation, American was at the height of its prosperity.

From 1914 to 1917, the American film industry enjoyed a home market free from European competition. Before this period, such events as the spectacle and the feature film had kept the American producers one step behind European innovation. However, the World War closed the markets in Europe, shutting off perhaps one-fifth of the U.S. outlets for export, but allowing competition to flourish at home. By this time, the developing mass audience was substantial enough to accommodate the tremendous output of companies which, like American, were releasing five and six films per week, and at least one feature per month.

In slightly more than seven years, the American Film Company had grown from a production company with three small units to a large, complex studio operation with fifteen producing groups working under its banner. But in 1917, American began to feel the ill-effects of the strongly competitive market. While American had remained in Santa Barbara, California, Hollywood had become the film production center of the country. Feature films were the dominant product from Hollywood, and the production system there was ripe for the utilization of a vast corps of personnel. In Hollywood, a director could work for two or three companies in a single week and enjoy a constant "moonlighting" type of employment. The personnel who remained with American did so under the risk of cutting themselves off from the majority of production activity in Hollywood. The risk became even greater as American slowly decreased the number of films produced.

Arthur Knight saw this period as one in which the smaller companies were outdistanced by the majors:

> The numerous small, independent studios that owned neither exchanges nor theatres by 1920 found themselves with their backs against the wall. Some few were absorbed into the larger companies: the others quietly expired.[6]

When American ceased production in 1921, the industry had formulated the road it would travel into the 1940's, that of vertical integration. The larger companies had swallowed up their former allies: Universal now stood where once were the studios of Nestor, Christie, Powers, and others; Paramount was made up of what had been Famous Players, Lasky, Bosworth, Artcraft, Realart, and Keystone; the four top salaried film personalities--Chaplin, Fairbanks, Griffith, and Pickford--were now United Artists; and Metro-Goldwyn-Mayer and Twentieth Century-Fox were future developments to consolidate even further the many small companies which had once been the backbone of the industry. In 1921, all the major companies either owned their own distribution agencies and theatres or were strongly allied with interests in these areas. Only a few producing companies, like Columbia Pictures, could exist as suppliers of films to fill out the majors' programs.

American had begun as a program source for exchanges. The company functioned as supplier, in much the same way that a parts manufacturer serves a major industry. Without the component elements, the final

---

[6] Knight, p. 54.

product could not be made; without American's films, Freuler's and Aitken's Western Film Exchange "programs" could not be distributed. Mutual was a further concentration of these policies; but when Mutual ceased to function in 1918, American became a supplier without a client. The larger companies had developed their own subsidiary groups and had no need for a supplier of duplicate types of films. Instead, American had to release its films on an independent, states right basis, dealing directly with non-allied distributors and theatres. These sources, however, were decreasing rapidly as the majors consolidated the three aspects of the industry through the process of vertical integration. By 1921, it was apparent that American had served well its role as "silent partner" to distributing chains, but the company was unable to prosper on its own. American had been dominated by its "partner" interests for so long that the company had failed to recognize either the innovations in narrative and cinematic techniques being developed throughout the industry, or the business integration which was occurring.

American's short-sighted attitude cannot be blamed exclusively on its supplier function and its failure to develop autonomously. Other factors contributed to the company's eventual decline and fall. American had been one of the first companies to locate permanently on the West Coast, taking advantage of the idyllic Santa Barbara setting. The landscape and seashore were both assets _and_ debits to the company. A multiplicity of production values were available for the films, with the repertory company and a type of communal production the resultant mode of American's filmmaking activity; but at the same time, the comfort of this situation worked against the progressive and competitive atmosphere which was present on the Hollywood scene. Removed from the arena of the majority of film production activity, American lost its perspective.

In many ways, the films produced by American reflected the major trends in silent film. Westerns, social comedies and drama, and period films were produced by the company with particular types chosen according to what was most popular with audiences at any given time. Technically, the films from American never reached the level achieved by other producers; yet, the company maintained a reputation for polished, consistent product. The strength of the early films from American was in their audience appeal. As the company developed, however, the producers failed to meet the desires of an increasingly sophisticated audience.

At the time American was founded, the former exhibitors behind the company's formation had been in close contact with the public's wants and needs. But American and Mutual divested themselves of exhibitor interests by their failure to acquire theatres. With Mutual's distributor interest gone, American was merely a producer, twice removed from the public tastes. The experience of the Patents Company and General Film had not provided the American Film and Mutual executives with a meaningful perspective.

Investigation into this seemingly remote period of film history too often loses sight of the present. Maintaining that their attitude is one of objectivity, some historians bathe in the past oblivious to current events. This, however, should not be the case. Objectivity in history is certainly an honest goal, but a difficult one when we consider any historian's personal consciousness. The study of history cannot be merely an escapist occupation, but it must be an investigation of the past in the present state of mind. My particular study has attempted, on at least one level, to bare the facts behind the operation of a single independent silent film company. But this cannot be the final purpose of the study. Isolated information can only be worthwhile when brought into the open, confronting the tensions of the present. The overriding question implied throughout this study has been, "How did the film industry develop to its present state?" This investigation of the American Film Company is only a partial answer to the question. What must be asked now is a new question: "What can the past tell us about the present and the future?" Confronted with similar kinds of questions, Mae Huettig noted a basic fact of film history, one which was observable not only during American's career, but also in the industry's subsequent development and perhaps even in the future:

> As has been the case in other industries and in the history of nations, pioneers and rebels on achieving success often revert to the pattern of behavior of those whom they have overthrown.[7]

The larger companies could prosper through the 1940's precisely because their theatre interests kept a link between them and the public.

---

[7] Huettig, p. 31.

Through their ownership of theatres and exchanges, companies like Paramount not only could feel the pulse of the moviegoing public but they could alter it. Not until the Supreme Court forced vertical integration out of the film industry did the situation change. When in the early 1950's television began to take over the function of mass entertainment, the former exhibitor film producers felt they still "understood" the wants of the mass audience. And industrially, the American film began to falter. Faddish attempts, such as 3-D, supplanted the more earnest efforts to develop the filmmaking art; drive-ins tried to be the television screen to the automobile's "living room"; and the money behind the film was placed strongly in favor of the "blockbuster" spectacle.

> Left to their own devices the producing companies went on making gaudy, studio bound films as though audiences were still guaranteed by the theatres monopolies of pre-war days. They continued to think of films as "show business"--the "business" of churning out "shows" for mass audience.[8]

The situation in the early 1960's was like that in which the film industry--and the American Film Company--found itself in the immediate post-World War I period. In both eras, the major question was, "What should be the relationship among production, distribution, and exhibition?" During the earlier period, it took the innovative move of accumulating theatres to answer the industry's question. In the 1960's, the answer was the entrance of the conglomerates.

---

[8]"Is There Any Future In Hollywood?" *Economist*, CCXXXIV (February 28, 1970), 52.

Like the early exhibitor-distributors who became producers, the motives of the big businessmen were not purely embodied in the film itself as a profit-making device:

> Managers of conglomerates, who collect unrelated undertakings because they are potential money makers, have been going into the film business at a time when none of the industry's indicators have been good.[9]

The conglomerates were similar to the early independents in that both saw other potentials in the film industry: Avco Corporation could see a source for its television interests in controlling Embassy Pictures; Las Vegas investor Kirk Kerkorian could speculate on an entertainment coalition with his own Tracy Investment, Inc., and Metro-Goldwyn-Mayer; Gulf-Western could expand its real estate holdings by acquiring Paramount; Kinney National Services, whose interests include parking lots, saw a connection between its concerns and Warners-Seven Arts, as did Music Corporation of America with Universal and TransAmerica Corporation with United Artists. The businessmen have once again moved into the position of power.

For the conglomerates, the answer was a business-like spotting of audience segments which would support specific types of films. As was the case with the independents, specialization and audience "analysis" were two of the conglomerates' solutions.

The situation today is not totally unlike the period in which the American Film Company was born. The factors which led to American's prosperity, and failure, are also apparent. Today the majority of

---
[9]Ibid.

production responsibility has been given to the independent units receiving "sponsorship" from the conglomerate-controlled studios whose concerns are partially in their own tangential interests and television at a lower investment ratio. The days of <u>Doctor Dolittle</u>, <u>Star</u>, <u>Zabriskie Point</u>, <u>Paint Your Wagon</u>, and <u>Tora, Tora, Tora</u>--films which averaged $10-15 million in cost--may be over for Hollywood, and the "low cost box office winners" may be the only films on which the conglomerates will gamble.

A question which remains is, "What will happen to the film <u>quality</u> under this situation?" Perhaps the experience of the American Film Company can offer an answer. Under a similar system of specialization and saturation, American lost sight of the audience taste it was specifically aiming to satisfy. Formula became the dominant method of filmmaking, with innovation left for the more progressive "Griffiths" of the industry. Under a strict taste-fulfilling mission, the motion picture industry in America is destined to progress at a slow pace. With complex conglomerate interests superseding those of the "artist-filmmakers," it is difficult to predict a real burgeoning in film quality or social benefit. With an oil company controlling a major film company, will any of their films seriously confront the issue of gasoline's pollution of the air? With television a major outlet for most film companies, will any of these companies risk offending potential sponsors?

The past has too often been misused to predict the future. The example of the American Film Company does not determine that like-companies today will strangle themselves under the policy of specialization. What the example does tell us is what occurred in an analogous

situation, giving us signs which we can be watchful for as we view the
present and the future. We can only hope for the sake of our society's
cultural well-being that the "silent partners" of today will actively
participate in the shaping of the industry's management and affairs
to insure a progressive influence on our daily lives.

BIBLIOGRAPHY

BIBLIOGRAPHY

Books

Adams, Walter, ed. The Structure of American Industry. New York: Macmillan, 1950.

Aitken, Roy E. The Birth of a Nation Story. Middleburg, Virginia: William W. Denlinger, 1965.

Austin, H. Russell. The Wisconsin Story: The Building of a Vanguard State. Milwaukee: The Journal Company, 1964.

Balshofer, Fred J., and Miller, Arthur C. One Reel a Week. Berkeley: University of California, 1967.

Bardeche, Maurice, and Brassilach, Robert. History of the Film. Translated by Iris Barry. London: Allen and Unwin, 1945.

Bennett, Joan, and Kibbee, Lois. The Bennett Playbill: Five Generations of the Famous Theatre Family. New York: Holt, Rinehart, and Winston, 1970.

Bernique, Jean. Motion Picture Acting for Professionals and Amateurs: A Technical Treatise on Make-up, Costumes and Expression; Containing Full Directions for the Use of Cosmetics before the Camera, the Costume Requirements and Color Schemes necessary to get the Proper Effect, together with 191 Posed Photographs of Motion Picture Stars, Showing 499 Different Expressions and Emotions. Chicago: Producers Service, 1916.

Bertrand, Daniel; Evans, W. D.; and Blanchard, E. L. The Motion Picture Industry: A Pattern of Control. Temporary National Economic Committee Monograph No. 43. Washington: Government Printing Office, 1941.

Blum, Daniel. A Pictoral History of the Silent Film. New York: Putnam, 1953.

Bogdanovich, Peter. Allan Dwan: The Last Pioneer. New York: Praeger, 1970.

Brownlow, Kevin. *The Parade's Gone By*. New York: Knopf, 1968.

Cassady, Ralph, Jr., and Cassady, Ralph, III. *The Private Antitrust Suit in American Business Competition: A Motion-Picture Industry Case Analysis*. Los Angeles: Bureau of Business and Economic Research, University of California, 1964.

Ceram, C. W. *Archaeology of the Cinema*. New York: Harcourt, Brace, and World, 1965.

Conant, Michael. *Antitrust in the Motion Picture Industry*. Berkeley: University of California, 1960.

Crowther, Bosley. *The Lion's Share: The Story of an Entertainment Empire*. New York: Dutton, 1957.

Drinkwater, John. *The Life and Adventures of Carl Laemmle*. New York: Putnam, 1931.

Fielding, Raymond, ed. *A Technological History of Motion Pictures and Television*. Berkeley: University of California, 1967.

Film Lexicon Degli Autori e Della Opere. Rome: Bianco e Nero, 1958-1967.

French, Philip. *The Movie Moguls*. London: Regnery, 1969.

Glover, J. G., and Cornell, W. B., eds. *The Development of American Industries*. New York: Simmons-Boardman, 1932.

Goodman, Ezra. *The Fifty-Year Decline and Fall of Hollywood*. New York: Simon and Schuster, 1961.

Grau, Robert. *The Business Man in the Amusement World*. New York: Broadway, 1910.

_____. *The Stage in the Twentieth Century*. New York: Broadway, 1912.

_____. *The Theatre of Science: A Volume of Progress and Achievement in the Motion Picture Industry*. New York: Broadway, 1914.

Guback, Thomas. *The International Film Industry*. Bloomington: Indiana University, 1969.

Hall, Ben. *The Best Remaining Seats*. New York: Clarkson-Potter, 1961.

Halliwell, Leslie. *The Filmgoer's Companion: From Nickelodeon to New Wave*. New York: Hill and Wang, 1967.

Hampton, Benjamin B. *History of the American Film Industry*. New York: Dover, 1969.

Harley, John. *World-Wide Influences on the Cinema*. Los Angeles: University of Southern California, 1960.

Harrison, Harry P. *Culture Under Canvas: The Story of Tent Chautauqua*. New York: Hastings House, 1958.

Hendricks, Gordon. *The Edison Motion Picture Myth*. Berkeley: University of California, 1961.

Huaco, George A. *The Sociology of Film Art*. New York: Basic Books, 1965.

Huettig, Mae D. *Economic Control of the Motion Picture Industry*. Philadelphia: University of Pennsylvania, 1944.

Jacobs, Lewis. *The Rise of the American Film*. New York: Harcourt, Brace, 1939.

Jarvie, Ian. *Movies and Society*. New York: Basic Books, 1969.

Jobes, Gertrude. *Motion Picture Empire*. Hamden, Connecticut: Archon, 1966.

Justice, Fred C., and Smith, Tom R., comps. *Who's Who in the Film World*. Los Angeles: Film World, 1914.

Kerrigan, Jack W. *How I Became a Successful Moving Picture Star*. Los Angeles: Kellow and Brown, 1914.

Klingender, F. D., and Legg, Stuart. *Money Behind the Screen*. London: Lawrence and Wishart, 1937.

Knight, Arthur. *The Liveliest Art: A Panoramic History of the Movies*. New York: Macmillan, 1957.

Lahue, Kalton C. *Bound and Gagged: The Story of the Silent Serials*. New York: Barnes, 1968.

_____. *Continued Next Week: A History of the Moving Picture Serial*. Norman: University of Oklahoma, 1964.

_____. *Dreams for Sale: The Rise and Fall of the Triangle Film Corporation*. New York: Barnes, 1971.

_____. *Ladies in Distress*. New York: Barnes, 1970.

_____. *Winners of the West*. New York: Barnes, 1970.

_____. *World of Laughter: The Motion Picture Comedy Short, 1910-1930*. Norman: University of Oklahoma, 1966.

_____, and Brewer, Terry. *Kops and Custards: The Legend of Keystone Films*. Norman: University of Oklahoma, 1968.

Lawson, John Howard. *Film: The Creative Process*. New York: Hill and Wang, 1967.

Leprohon, Pierre. *Histoire du Cinéma*. Volume I: Vie et Mort Cinématographe (1895-1930). Paris: Editions du Cerf, 1961.

Lewis, Howard T. *Cases on the Motion Picture Industry*. Harvard Business Reports, No. 8. New York: McGraw-Hill, 1930.

_____. *The Motion Picture Industry*. New York: Van Nostrand, 1933.

Lovell, Hugh, and Carter, Tasile. *Collective Bargaining in the Motion Picture Industry: A Struggle for Stability*. Berkeley: University of California Institute of Industrial Relations, 1955.

MacGowan, Kenneth. *Behind the Screen: The History and Technique of the Motion Picture*. New York: Delacorte, 1965.

Mayer, Arthur. *Merely Colossal: The Story of the Movies from the Long Chase to the Chaise Lounge*. New York: Simon and Schuster, 1953.

Miller, Virgil E. *Splinters from Hollywood Tripods: Memoires of a Cameraman*. New York: Exposition Press, 1964.

Mitry, Jean. *Dictionnaire du Cinéma*. Paris: Librarie Larousse, 1963.

_____. *Histoire du Cinéma*. Volumes I and II. Paris: Editions Universitaires, 1967-60.

Morris, Robert L. *Opie Read: American Humorist, 1852-1939*. New York: Helios, 1965.

National Film Catalogue. Part III: *The Silent Film, 1895-1930*. London: British Film Institute, 1966.

Niver, Kemp. *Motion Pictures from the Paper Print Collection of the Library of Congress. 1894-1912*. Edited by Bebe Bergsten. Berkeley: University of California, 1967.

Palmer, Edwin O. *History of Hollywood*. Volumes I and II. Hollywood: Arthur H. Cawston, 1937.

Ramsaye, Terry. *A Million and One Nights: A History of the Motion Picture*. New York: Simon and Schuster, 1926.

Sadoul, George. *Histoire du Cinéma mondial*. Paris: Flammarion, 1949.

_____. *Histoire Générale du Cinéma*. Volumes I-III. Paris: Denöel, 1952.

Sarris, Andrew. *The American Cinema: Directors and Directions 1929-1968*. New York: Dutton, 1968.

Schickel, Richard. *Movies: The History of an Art and an Institution*. New York: Basic Books, 1964.

Schuster, Mel. *Motion Picture Performers: A Bibliography of Magazine and Periodical Articles, 1900-1969*. Metuchen, New Jersey: Scarecrow, 1971.

Seldes, Gilbert. *The Movies Come from America*. New York: Scribner, 1937.

Sinclair, Upton. *Upton Sinclair Presents William Fox*. Los Angeles: By the Author, 1933.

Slide, Anthony. *Early American Cinema*. New York: Barnes, 1970.

Smith, Albert E., and Koury, Phil. *Two Reels and a Crank*. New York: Doubleday, 1952.

Southern California Writers' Project of the Works Projects Administration. *Santa Barbara: A Guide to the Channel City and Its Environs*. New York: Hastings House, 1941.

Southworth, John R. *Santa Barbara and Montecito*. Santa Barbara: Orena Studios (Schauer Printing Company), 1920.

Still, Bayrd. *Milwaukee: The History of a City*. Madison: State Historical Society of Wisconsin, 1948.

Storke, Thomas More. *California Editor*. Los Angeles: Westernlore Press, 1958.

Tompkins, Walker A. *Santa Barbara Yesterdays*. Santa Barbara: McNally and Loftin, 1962.

United States Copyright Office. *Motion Pictures, 1912-1939*. Washington: Library of Congress, 1951.

United States Work Projects Administration. *The Film Index*. Volume I: The Film as Art. New York: Museum of Modern Art and H. W. Wilson, 1941.

Van Loan, Charles. *Buck Parvin and the Movies*. New York: Doran, 1919.

Vaughan, F. L. *Economics of Our Patents System*. New York: Macmillan, 1926.

Wagenknecht, Edward. *The Movies in the Age of Innocence*. Norman: University of Oklahoma, 1963.

Walls, Howard Lamarr. *Motion Pictures, 1894-1912, Identified from the Records of the United States Copyright Office*. Washington: Library of Congress, 1953.

Warshow, Robert. *The Immediate Experience*. New York: Doubleday, 1962.

Wing, Ruth. *Blue Book of the Screen*. Hollywood: Blue Book, 1923.

Zierold, Norman. *The Moguls*. New York: Coward-McCann, 1969.

Articles and Periodicals

Barry, Robert H. "Harry Pollard: Writer, Director, Actor." *Photoplay*, VI (June, 1914), 80-2.

Cohn, Alfred A. "Director 'Mickey' [Neilan]." *Photoplay*, XII (September, 1917), 67-70.

Duncan, Robert C. "The American Studio." *Picture Play*, IV (May, 1916), 187-200.

Cassady, Ralph, Jr. "Monopoly in Motion Picture Production and Distribution: 1908-1915." *Southern California Law Review*, XXXII (Summer 1959), 325-390.

Evans, Delight. "Henry King, Virginian." *Photoplay*, XXIII (December, 1922), 34, 112.

Exhibitor's Trade Review (New York). 1916-1923.

Film Daily Yearbook (New York), 1922-1924.

Guinle, Pierre. "Filmographie de Allan Dwan." Presence du Cinéma, 22-23 (Fall, 1966), 25-51.

Harrison, Louis Reeves. "Big Changes Taking Place." Moving Picture World, XIX (January 3, 1914), 24.

Henry, William M. "The Great God [J. Warren] Kerrigan." Photoplay, IX (February, 1916), 32-6.

Howard, Clifford. "The Cinema in Retrospect." Close Up (London), III (November-December, 1928), 16-41.

"Is There Any Future In Hollywood?" Economist, CCXXXIV (February 28, 1970), 51-54.

Johnson, Julian. "A Brief Memorandum on Alan [sic] Dwan, P.E., D.A.P., E.M. [Professor of Electricity, Doctor of Active Photography and Engineer of Emotions]." Photoplay, XI (May, 1917), 70-1.

Johnson, William A. "The Structure of the Motion Picture Industry." Annals of the American Academy of Political and Social Science, CXXVIII (November, 1926), 20-29.

Kingston, Ruth. "At the American Studio." Motion Picture Magazine, XVI (September, 1918), 57-60, 125.

Koszarski, Richard. "Jules Furthman." Film Comment, IV (Winter 1970-71), 26-31.

Lourcelles, Jacques. "Allan Dwan." Presence du Cinéma, 22-23 (Fall, 1966), 1-11.

Motion Picture News. 1910-1913.

Motion Picture Studio Directory and Trade Annual. 1918-1924.

Moving Picture Annual and Yearbook for 1912.

Moving Picture Weekly. 1910-1923.

Moving Picture World. 1910-1922.

Musson, Bennett, and Grau, Robert. "Fortune in Films: The Romance of Moving Pictures." McClures Magazine, XL (November, 1912), 65-76.

"Mutual Film Corporation Issue." Photoplay Art (Los Angeles), II (August, 1916).

Photoplay Magazine (Chicago). 1911-1922.

Pratt, George. "A Myth Is As Good As A Milestone." Image (Rochester), November, 1957, p. 210.

Ramsaye, Terry. "The Motion Picture." Annals of the American Academy of Political and Social Science, CXXVIII (November, 1926), 1-19.

Santa Barbara News-Press (The Morning Press). July, 1912-December, 1922.

Spears, Jack. "Marshall Neilan Had a Natural Filmmaking Talent and a Character Flaw." Films In Review, XIII (November, 1962), 517-40.

Thomas, Jeanne. "The Decay of the Motion Picture Patents Company." Cinema Journal, X (Spring 1971), 34-40.

Thrall, Carl M. "Queen Mary [Miles Minter]." Photoplay, VIII (November, 1915), 96-7.

Wid's Year Book. 1918-1921.

Wildy, H. E., comp. The Photoplayers, Inc., 1915. Official Souvenir of the Photoplayers' Third Annual Ball.

Willis, Richard. "Dot Farley: Comedienne, Tragedienne, and Photo-playwright." Photoplay, VI (November, 1914), 139-41.

Other Sources

Bodeen, DeWitt. Personal interviews. Motion Picture Academy of Arts and Sciences Library, Beverly Hills, California. April 25, 1969; May 9, 1969.

Bogdanovich, Peter. Letters to the author. Van Nuys, California. February, 1969; September 18, 1969; March 20, 1970.

Bonilla, Isaac A. Personal interview. Santa Barbara Historical Museum, Gledhill Library, Santa Barbara, California. January 21, 1969.

Brownlow, Kevin. Letter to the author. London, England. April 25, 1969.

Conway, Joel. Personal interviews. Santa Barbara, California. June 12, 1969; March 30-31, 1970.

Dwan, Allan. Letters to the author. Van Nuys, California. February 7, 1969; March 15, 1969. Telephone interview, March 27, 1970.

Harold Leonard Film Collection, UCLA. Files on Frank Borzage, Allan Dwan, Reeves Eason, Henry King, George Marshall, Terry Ramsaye, and Wallace Reid.

Joel Conway Film Collection. Papers and Ephemera of the American Film Manufacturing Company. 5460 San Patricio Drive, Santa Barbara, California.

King, Henry. Letters to the author. Beverly Hills, California. March 14, 1969; June 14, 1969.

Lahue, Kalton C. Personal interview. Motion Picture Academy of Arts and Sciences Library, Beverly Hills, California. May 9, 1969.

Lahue, Kalton C. Letters to the author. Hollywood, California. February 20, 1969; April 8, 1969; May 1, 1969.

Lounsbury, Myron O. "The Origins of American Film Criticism, 1909-1939." Unpublished Ph.D. dissertation, University of Pennsylvania, 1966.

Marshall, George. Personal interview. Los Angeles, California. April 26, 1969.

Minter, Mary Miles (Mrs. Brandon O'Hilderbrandt). Personal interviews. Santa Monica, California. May, 1969. With DeWitt Bodeen.

Obern, G. Vaughn. "The American Film Company: The Flying 'A'." Paper presented to the Motion Picture Division, University of California at Los Angeles, December 12, 1966.

Phelan, Leontine (Mrs. Robert V.). Personal interview. Santa Barbara, California. January 29, 1969.

Shibuk, Charles, and Everson, William K. "An Index to the Work of Henry King." A research project of the Theodore Huff Memorial Film Society. New York: Huff Film Society, n/d.

Sloman, Edward. Personal interview. Beverly Hills, California. May 10, 1969.

Williamson, Clark. Letters to the author. Baraboo, Wisconsin. April 13, 1969; May 9, 1969.

Non-Print Sources

The Borrowed Flat. 16mm print of the 1911 film. Film Classic Exchange, Los Angeles, California.

Calamity Anne's Trust. 16mm print of the 1912 film. Film Classic Exchange.

Courage of Sorts. 16mm print of the 1913 film. Blackhawk Films, Davenport, Iowa.

The Deacon's Card. 16mm print of the 1914 film. Film Classic Exchange.

Ella Wanted to Elope. 16mm print of the 1916 film. Film Classic Exchange.

Everyheart. 16mm print of the 1915 film. Film Classic Exchange.

The Eyes of Julia Deep. 8mm print of the 1918 film. Blackhawk Films.

The Pearl of Paradise. 8mm print of the 1916 film. Blackhawk Films.

Six Feet Four. 16mm print of the 1919 film. Film Classic Exchange.

Three Million Dollars. 16mm print of the 1911 film. Film Classic Exchange.

What Her Diary Told. 16mm film of the 1913 film. Film Classic Exchange.

Library of Congress Paper Print Collection. Motion Picture Section, Library of Congress. Washington, D.C.

Photographs in the collection of the Santa Barbara Historical Society. The Gledhill Library, Santa Barbara, California.

Photographs in the collection of Mrs. Robert V. Phelan. Santa Barbara, California.

APPENDICES

APPENDIX A

EXCERPTS FROM <u>PHOTOPLAY ART</u>, II (AUGUST 1916)

APPENDIX A

EXCERPTS FROM PHOTOPLAY ART, II (AUGUST 1916)

The following pages have been reproduced from the only known extant copy of Photoplay Art, a California film magazine located in the collection of Mrs. Leontine Phelan of Santa Barbara, California. The use of these excerpts serves two purposes. First, the magazine is an excellent example of the type of film monthlies which were beginning to flourish during this period. Second, this particular issue was devoted to Mutual Film Corporation, with a special section on the American Film Company. While the stories contained in this issue may supplement information in Chapter IV, there are also valuable photographs included which depict the studio in operation. The "bird's-eye view" on the fourth page gives a reasonable idea of the scope of the studio, covering three city blocks. Stills on the following page show the grounds surrounding the glass studio and a view of six sets erected for simultaneous shooting. Other stills in this section detail the Chicago headquarters and factory, along with a number of scenes of actual production activities.

Samuel S. Hutchinson, Dominating Factor of the Great Film World

A quiet, reserved man, a cool calculating thinker, quick to act when his mind is made up and his plans solved, a genius at organizing and financing, a pleasant gentleman—such is Samuel S. Hutchinson, the president of the American Film Company, Inc., treasurer of the Mutual, president of the Signal Company, managing director of the Vogue and possessor of several other important positions and titles.

Mr. Hutchinson has been identified with the film industry for some years and is known throughout film circles as exceptionally shrewd and capable. A close observer of conditions, bold and enterprising, he plans for the future with the perspicacity of a practical philosopher and carries his ideas to a successful termination.

The success of the Theatre Film Service Company of Chicago and San Francisco can be credited to the judgment and sagacious management of Mr. Hutchinson, as its president and general manager during a period of two years. His business ability was again emphasized as president and general manager of the H & H Film Service at a time when business conditions in the film world, according to accounts, were somewhat puzzling and pernicious.

Mr. Hutchinson voluntarily joined the ranks of the Independents at the same time he undertook the organization of the American Film Company, Incorporated, a corporation with offices in Chicago, Illinois, and London, England, and possessing one of the most attractive and artistically designed studios in the world at Santa Barbara, California. Its radical move was hailed enthusiastically by the Independents as they needed artistic and astute reinforcement to assure success in their struggle for existence.

As president of the American Film Company, Incorporated, Mr. Hutchinson has devoted his time and knowledge to building organization in the motion picture business. His keen insight of general affairs and thorough knowledge of the film business, his appreciation and his personal understanding of the wants and necessities of the exhibitors, coupled with a capable force of department heads, experienced directors and actors of his own selection, and a splendid plant and superb field at his command placed him in an enviable position at home and abroad.

Hutchinson is a good type of American, to head the name his organization bears—tall, spare, well set-up with keen bright eyes, well modeled head on square shoulders, not given to talk, but some listener—he has managed to watch his step and keep well up in the procession. He had a scientific education in another line, but managed to switch successfully into the film business without going through all the drudgery of details that marked the painful path of the progenitors of the motion picture makers. He studied the new art form from a new angle of business and saw its possibilities, first through the service side. Like one who reads and runs, he was wide-awake to the voice of the people, receptive to all sorts of suggestions.

Mr. Hutchinson excels in his grasp of detail. There is very little done which does not actually first pass through his hands, nothing is completed without his O. K. He has the ability to make his people feel they are working for HIM as well as for the companies and the public. He never forgets the "personal touch."

Among other big pictures made by companies controlled by him were three successful serials. "The Diamond From The Sky" made a sensation at the time it was released. It was followed by the most popular railroad stories ever made, "The Girl and the Game," with Helen Holmes as the bright particular star. "The Secret of the Submarine" came next and is still coming out in chapters.

Another of an entirely different character is now in the making. Each of these serial photoplays required special organizing and financing and each has been highly successful.

"Damaged Goods" was another sensational picture made at the American studios. Here is a picture which taught a real lesson and which was made with that idea. It has broken several records for attendance and it will be a long time before any feature will be produced which will have the same appeal or which will do more genuine good.

And so Samuel S. Hutchinson is going ahead, making better pictures, getting better stars, studying the public wants.

Seven Big Feature Companies at Work

Midsummer sees seven big feature companies with prominent stars working at the American studios in Santa Barbara, Calif. Nineteen Sixteen has been a year of tremendous expansion at the American studios and the activities seem to increase with each month.

An ever increasing demand for American Mutual pictures is responsible for the activity which has led to an enlargement of all departments. Among the stars who are being featured are Richard Bennett, Mary Miles Minter, Kolb and Dill, Franklin Ritchie, Winnifred Greenwood, Frank Borzage, Anna Little, William Russell, Charlotte Burton, Edward Coxen, Helene Rosson and Thomas Chatterton. All of these stars are popular favorites with the public and exhibitors. The directors are men of continent wide fame and noted for their artistic productions. They include James Kirkwood who is directing Mary Miles Minter, Rea Berger who puts on the comedies of Kolb and Dill, William Russell directing his own company as does Frank Borzage, William C. Dowlan, George Sargent, directing Richard Bennett and Edward Sloman.

The successes turned out from the American studios have gained a wide vogue among the exhibitors of the country. Since the first of the year the productions that have made a strong appeal to the public include "Soul Mates," "The Bruiser," "Garry Murdock" (The Guide) features in which William Russell was starred; "Lying Lips," "The Inner Struggle" and "Dust" in which Winnifred Greenwood and Franklin Ritchie appear; "The Overcoat" and "The Abandonment," starring Rhea Mitchell and Helene Rosson; "The Courtesan" in which Eugenie Forde has the lead; the great serial, "The Secret of the Submarine" and the two Audrey Munson features, "Purity" and "The Girl O' Dreams," which have attained widespread publicity and popularity. Besides these features were the outputs of two other companies putting on two and three reelers and the two Beauty Comedy and the two Mustang companies.

Among the big features to be released with such stars as Mary Miles Minter, Richard Bennett and Kolb and Dill within the coming month or two are the following:

"Youth's Endearing Charm" and "Dulcie's Adventure," featuring Mary Miles Minter.

"A Million for Maty," "The Three Pals" and "Bluff," in which the famous comedians known to every theater and moving picture goer, Kolb and Dill, are the features.

The big Richard Bennett releases include "The Sable Blessing" and "His Brother's Keeper."

An early release of the big William Russell features will be "The Man Who Would not Die," "The Torch Bearer" and "The Love Hermit."

Other coming releases of big five reelers are "The Shadow," featuring Winnifred Greenwood and Edward Coxen; "The Light," with Franklin Ritchie and Helene Rosson in the leads and "The Land O' Lizards" with a notable cast including Frank Borzage, Anna Little and Jack Richardson.

All of the activities at the American studios go forward under the expert and able direction of Mr. P. G. Lynch, studio manager. In the way of efficiency in the management of motion picture studios, the American ranks with the best on the continent.

Mr. P. G. Lynch is manager of the American Film Company at Santa Barbara and the personal representative of Mr. S. S. Hutchinson, one of the pioneers in the industry.

Edward M. Langley is the technical chief and art director of the studios. Under his management all the work of stage production and settings has been systematized in such a way as to give the greatest efficiency to all of the directors at any time.

Instead of one technical man for each department Mr. Langley maintains a staff of experts in every line pertaining to construction, decoration, furnishings, periods and all else that goes to make up the best scenic effects now being seen in motion pictures. The settings given the scenes of each picture excel in their appointments and perfection to the most minute detail.

The photographic department which is

(Continued on page 11)

PHOTOPLAY ART

John R. Freuler, Master Genius of Films

Influence of Mutual Head Felt Wherever Motion Pictures are Produced

John R. Freuler is president and guiding genius of the great Mutual Corporation. To him more than any other individual is due the credit for having taken motion pictures from the rut of indifference and standardizing them. As is known throughout the film world the Mutual is committed to a policy of all-star productions.

In addition to being president of the Mutual, Mr. Freuler is also chairman of the executive board. He is heavily interested in the American Film Co. Inc., of Santa Barbara, Chicago, New York and London and the Lone Star Corporation, which makes Charlie Chaplin Mutual-Special, Thanhouser, Majestic-Reliance, New York Motion Picture Corporation, Vogue, Inc., States Film Corporation, North American Film Corporation and Signal Film Corporation.

Mr. Freuler's influence is felt wherever motion pictures are produced. His name is a household word among the rank and file of those who labor in the films. There is probably only one thing that keeps Mr. Freuler in the East and that is the fact that the Mutual's headquarters are in Chicago. It is generally known among his close friends and acquaintances that he would like to locate in California was such a move logical. The executive head of the great film organization recently found among old papers a faded photograph which he humorously titled the "Mutual Grandfather;" it was the now dark and forgotten Comique theatre, on Kinnickinnic avenue, in Milwaukee.

It was in this little store front theatre, opened in the early half of the last decade, that Mr. Freuler was first introduced to the motion picture business. It was the initial step that subsequently resulted in the establishment by him of the Western Film Exchange of Milwaukee, which grew into a system of exchanges under that name; and which in turn grew into the Mutual Film Corporation.

Mr. Freuler, chatting with a friend, told the story of the Comique with many a smile, recently:

"I was well established in business in Milwaukee and with no concern at all about the pictures," said Mr. Freuler, "when I got pulled into the film business. It happened just as those things always do, by a chance circumstance.

"A man owed me a sum of money, which he found it difficult to repay. He felt greatly obligated and anxious to do me a good turn. This chap had a friend who was traveling with one of those old-fashioned portable picture outfits and a few reels of film. This traveling picture showman wanted to establish a theatre. My debtor friend thought it was a chance for me. He introduced the showman to me at my office in Milwaukee one day. I was induced to put up $480 in cash against this showman's equipment— which by the way was worth, I expect, about $125 then. So we became partners in a 'theatre.' The showman established the theatre—a 'store front show'—and I watched my little investment from afar.

"It was not very important to me and frankly, I was not exactly proud of my share in the picture business then. I used to motor by the place with my family and I always kept my head turned the other way, lest the folks discover by my eyes I was interested in the 'Comique'—the nickel picture show. I felt someway that my position as a partner in a picture show would not make a hit in our 'set.' I used to slip down the street and drop my nickel and duck into the theatre to see the show at night.

"Of course the 'Comique' prospered, but my partner always somehow had enough relatives to put on the payroll to keep the earnings from becoming profits. In the end I had to buy him out to save my $480. Then I had to supervise the running of the theatre. I got interested in selecting pictures. That gave me a peek at the exchange business. The man who gave me 'Comique' also served wanted me to go on his bond so he could get more film to distribute on his circuit. I had to investigate the business. That gave me a notion I would like to be into it from that the Western Film Exchange was born. The rest of the story is more recent history known to everybody.

"I am prouder of the business now than I was the day I became a partner in the 'Comique.'"

JOHN R. FREULER

Bird's-Eye View of the Studio of the American Film Co., Inc., at Santa Barbara, Cal.

P. G. Lynch Best Posted Man in Films

General Manager of American Studio at Santa Barbara, Cal., Scores Great Success in Producing End of Business

"The best posted man in the film business"—This distinction is credited to P. G. Lynch, gen. mgr. of the American Film Company's studio at Santa Barbara.

Three years ago Mr. Lynch took the helm at "Flying A." For five years previous he had been an exchange manager at San Francisco.

Before entering the motion picture industry, Mr. Lynch gained wide experience in business affairs as a banker and mining operator.

When Mr. Lynch first became identified with the Santa Barbara studio of the American Film Company no more than two companies had ever been at work at one time. Since his incumbency there has been as many as fourteen companies all making pictures.

His efficient management has been one of the biggest factors in the rapid growth of the studio, the present magnificent plant having been built since he became identified with the company. There is no angle of motion picture production or managerial details with which he is not acquainted.

Mr. Lynch was born in Nevada in 1878. He is a man of strong character, thoughtful, congenial and kind hearted. His democratic spirit has made him the friend of "extra" and star alike.

Able Assistant

R. E. Stebbins is General Manager Lynch's Right-Hand Man.

R. E. Stebbins, assistant manager of the American Film Company, was prominent as an exhibitor and lecturer in the early days of motion pictures. He became identified with the industry when it was in its infancy.

When motion pictures were but little known he was an exhibitor in Wallace, Idaho, and Spokane, Wash. Mr. Stebbins achieved considerable prominence later as an exhibitor in Stockton, and San Jose, Calif. His next move was in the exchange branch of the business. He was identified with the Mutual exchanges for many years, and helped to establish the Board of Trade Film Exchange, of San Francisco, the first successful organization of its kind in the United States. He was also an officer of this body.

Mr. Stebbins joined the American Film Company at Santa Barbara in February of this year. He is uniquely fitted for the work, having served in all branches. The assistant manager has seen the

Mr. P. G. LYNCH
General Manager of American Film Company, Santa Barbara Studio

Panoramic View of American Studio showing Beautiful and Spacious Grounds

Six years ago the American Film Company made a rather inconspicuous entrance into the film industry with a little studio located at San Juan Capistrano, their first producing company including Jack Richardson and Louise Lester who are still members of the stock company. The company soon discovered that their facilities were inadequate, and a few months later moved the studio to an ostrich farm in Lakeside near Hollywood. This plant, too, was soon outgrown, and in 1912 the company moved to Santa Barbara. A stage twenty feet square was built, and four sets of scenery were quite sufficient for their one producing company, which was making Western subjects only and required few interiors. When a second company was added to the line-up it became necessary to move and enlarge again, and in July, 1913, the first buildings of the now immense plant were put up on the present site on the outskirts of the city. These buildings included a glass studio, executive offices and what is now the main dressing room building. To this original group five outdoor stages and a number of property rooms and shops were added from time to time as the company steadily grew. The latest addition, a huge glass studio, was built last winter and is the largest of its kind on the coast, with a stage area of 80 x 150 feet. The present studio is the second largest in America, and improvements and enlargements are steadily being made.

R. E. STEBBINS
Assistant Manager of American Studio

motion picture business in all its stages of development and has taken an important part in much of the progress achieved, particularly in the West. Through his joining the "Flying A" forces, Mr. Stebbins has come directly in contact with the production end of the film industry.

Seven Big Feature Companies
(Continued from page 8)

presided over by C. H. Heimerl now has nine camera men and the department is one of the best equipped in the industry. Added to this is the fact that the clear air of Santa Barbara gives photographic results declared to be unequalled at any point on the continent.

A large scenario department is maintained with a large staff of writers.

American Mutual publicity is distributed from New York and Chicago. To

Remarkable view of big glass studio taken from second property floor, showing six sets in use at one time

supply this publicity there is a well equipped publicity department maintained at the studios.

The improvements during the year which have grown apace with the growth of the studios include new executive offices, a large row of director's offices handsomely appointed, larger accounting offices, a new telephone exchange, a new building housing the technical department, a photographic studio and the completion of the big glass studio in which ten good sized sets can be put up at any one time. It is the second largest on the coast.

The stars are all provided with spacious dressing rooms and not the least of the attractions on the grounds is the handsome Green Room provided for the use of the actors.

Another big improvement and one that occupies a large amount of space is the relocating of a full sized town, adjacent to the main lot. This town, which is built on the unit system, can be moved about to provide any kind of a village and is two blocks long.

Not the least of the factors which go to make up the popularity of the scenic effects of American pictures is the matter of outside locations in which Santa Barbara and its environments excel. In Santa Barbara there is a combination of city and town, mountain and seashore,

"Close-ups" of Mutual Headquarters, Chicago, Ill., Showing also Building of American Film Company, Inc., Strongest Unit of Great Exchange, and Developing and Drying Rooms of their Immense Laboratories

1. Plaza; 2. Back from Location; 3. Stage Where Western Interiors Are Made; 4. In Glass Studio; 5. Carpenter Shop; 6. Supply Room.

ranching Channel Islands, thirty miles out in the Pacific and bits of Italy, France and Spain in the millionaires residences in Montecito. There are magnificent homes of many multi-millionaires of world wide reputation which in nearly every instance are thrown open to the use of the company.

The method of choosing these locations is left to the location man. He, learning a director's wants, can fit the pictures expertly into the atmosphere required. The magnificent climatic conditions always furnish good light effects and the truthful portrayal of the scenes, backed by nature's beauty adds immensely to the scenic beauties of American Mutual pictures. At Santa Barbara the mountains come down to the Pacific, which is an unusually fortunate condition. Nowhere else can be found the combination of mountains and ocean as found in the Santa Barbara country.

Most Liked Star

Richard Bennett of Stage Fame Triumphs in Pictures

Richard Bennett, the famed stage star, needs no introduction to the theatregoers throughout the country. For a number of years he has been counted among the most popular stars of New York and other leading cities. His remarkable work during the past three or four years has been enough in itself to establish him among the leading actors of the day.

Nearly every adult person in New York saw and marvelled at his wonderfully dramatic acting in "Damaged Goods," a preachment play which caused a greater sensation than any other the theatergoer has ever known. Realizing the immense good that could be accomplished by putting this powerful production into pictures, The American Company induced Mr. Bennett to present the play before the camera, and the film version of "Damaged Goods" is doing wonderful in booking itself to the most popular moving picture in among recent features.

Mr. Bennett, following his work in "Damaged Goods," appeared in the great and "Rosemary" was his last feature "Rio Grande" which enjoyed a successful

PHOTOPLAY ART

run during the winter. So insistent was the demand made by the picture public for more of Richard Bennett's screen acting that he was recently engaged again by the American Company to appear in a series of Mutual pictures, and the first two—"The Sable Blessing" and "His Brother's Keeper"—have already been finished.

SARGENT HAS DIRECTED MANY BIG FEATURES

George L. Sargent is the man who is credited with a large part of the direction of the serial "The Secret of the Submarine." When Richard Bennett came to the American, Mr. Sargent relinquished the directorship of the serial to produce features starring the famous stage favorite. He is one of the few successful photoplay directors who never was a professional actor. An education at Princeton was earned by exercising his talent for managing theatricals. Later this ability secured his engagement as stage manager of the Charles B. Dillingham houses and then five years with the Cohan and Harris people as manager.

Mr. Sargent's picture experience includes Universal and Eclair, and more recently he put on the biggest part of "The Fall of a Nation." It was by reason of his success with this feature that he was engaged by the American to direct the "Submarine" serial.

KIRKWOOD DIRECTOR OF MARY MILES MINTER

James Kirkwood, a master of picture production, was recently engaged by the American to direct Mary Miles Minter and his first picture, "Dulcie's Adventure," shows that the Kirkwood-Minter combination is unexcelled.

Mr. Kirkwood's broad experience in

RICHARD BENNETT

Mr. Bennett's work in these features is the quiet, subtle, humorously dramatic sort so rare and so much sought after by picture producers, and he is sure to be as popular in these productions as he was in "Damaged Goods."

GEORGE SARGENT
Director

JAMES KIRKWOOD
Director of Mary Miles Minter

SECRET OF THE SUBMARINE COMPANY
Left to right, standing—Harry Edmondson, George Clancy, Thos. Middleton (Cameraman), Hugh Bennett, Clarence Burton, Thos. Chatterton, Frank Thorne (Assistant Director). Sitting—Wm. Tedmarsh, Juanita Hansen, George Sargent (Director), Hilda Hollis

the world of moving pictures includes the production of some of the most notable features in the history of the photoplay.

Mary Miles Minter, "Littlest" Big Star

Dainty Little Miss of 14 Enjoys Greater Popularity Than Any Other Girl of Her Age in the World

The littlest big star among the constellation at the American Studios is dainty Mary Miles Minter who with her sunny disposition, cherubic countenance and roguish smile has won greater popularity than any other girl of her age in the world. Though it has been only fourteen short years since Old Doc Stork made a flying trip down into Louisiana and left a little lacy bundle there, she has already made a warm spot for herself in the heart of nearly every person in the civilized world.

As soon as she was able to toddle

MARY MILES MINTER
snapped by the studio photographer in pergola of the Green Room

she won more praise from the metropolitan critics than did William and Dustin Farnum. Then her remarkable beauty, perfect profile and marvelous histrionic ability brought irresistible offers from the moving picture field, and she scored

Hello, everybody! Mary Miles Minter, the "littlest" big star of the American Studio, who gladdens hearts of millions

industry in America. He began directing seven years ago, after a long and successful career on the speaking stage, his entrance into the picture field being due to D. W. Griffith and Harry Solter, when they were working at the old Biograph studios in New York. Kirkwood's fame as a director grew as the industry grew, and when the Famous Players company was organized he was among the first men engaged. Here he directed Mary Pickford and played important roles in a number of his productions, including "The Eagle's Mate," "Behind the Scenes," "The Dawn of a Tomorrow" and "Rags."

When Mary Miles Minter was engaged by the American it was decided that the best director in the country was just good enough for the charming little star, and negotiations with Mr. Kirkwood resulted in his signing a long-term contract with the American.

little Goldie Mary adopted the profession of her ancestors, playing a baby part in "Shore Acres." Next came the inevitable "Little Eva," bosom friend of old Uncle Tom, a part that won the full recognition of her wonderful talents. After several seasons of valuable experience with touring stock companies, in which she memorized more than a score of plays, she made her Metropolitan debut with Eleanor Robson in "Salomy Jane," which played a full season in New York. Later she played with Dustin Farnum in "Cameo Kirby," with Charlotte Walker in "The Warrens of Virginia," playing a part which also gave early training to Mary Pickford, and with Mrs. Fiske and other famous legitimate stars.

Her greatest stage success was attained three years ago in "The Littlest Rebel," in which she played the title role, and

immediate success and popularity in the shadowland drama.

Dainty Mary recently joined the American forces, feeling that that organization offered the widest scope for the expression of her art, and has already been featured in two pictures to be released soon — "Youth's Endearing Charm" and "Dulcie's Adventure". Although still a child in years, but with a personality that charms and an ability that wins, she is sure to increase her host of friends and attain the very pinnacle of success.

Willis and Inglis

Starting With One Small Office Firm Grows by Leaps and Bounds

The firm of Willis and Inglis, composed of Richard Willis and Gus Inglis is unique in several ways.

Starting with one small office some eighteen months back, they now occupy five offices in the Wright and Callender Building in Los Angeles and two in Hollywood. They were the first to do "personal publicity" for the photoplayers in the west and later were the first to open a branch for the engagement of professional people. A branch to handle the photoplay rights to noted books and plays followed.

Kolb and Dill, Famous Comedy Team

Laugh Provokers at Work on Scenes of Rip-Roaring Pictures at American's Santa Barbara Studio

Kolb & Dill at the Flying A, in their "Oxmobile" racer

Many big deals have been made in their offices and more than one concern has been financed through their efforts; and it is their boast that every one of them is in a flourishing condition today.

Their last effort in this direction is an Electrical Equipment Corporation, the first of its kind devoted to the Motion Picture industry.

The firm is unique, too, in that the partners have both been active participators in the pictures and also have been actors. They understand the requirements of the studios and of the managements as well as the artists. They manage a number of the recognized stars.

Both gentlemen attribute their success to solid hard work as well as to their general knowledge of all branches of the industry.

The firm of Willis and Inglis is affiliated with Arthur S. Kane of 220 West 42nd Street, New York, and the connection has proven of inestimable value to all parties interested.

RAE BERGER, DIRECTOR, HAS HAD VARIED CAREER

Rae Berger, who is directing the famous comedians, Kolb and Dill, has been a preacher, soldier, photographer, actor and stage manager. Prior to directing Kolb and Dill he put on the great Audrey Munson feature "Purity," which is now having its premier performances in New York, Chicago and other principal cities.

Left to right—Max Dill, of Kolb & Dill; Rae Berger (Director), and William Kolb, chatting in front of the fountain after a strenuous day in the studios.

As a journeyman photographer in his younger days Mr. Berger paid his way through college. He was ordained a minister and left the pulpit to serve in the Spanish war with the Second Ohio infantry. When the war ended he went on the stage, appearing in drama, farce and musical comedy. He has been an American-ite for about two years, and his optimism and general affability have made him one of the best liked people on the American's big lot.

The American Company will shortly release a series of pictures featuring W. Clarence Kolb and Max Dill, the famous vaudeville team of German comedians. The productions are now in the making at the American studios and the first, entitled "A Million for Mary," will make its appearance late in August.

For the last twenty years America has been amused by the inimitable mannerisms and original stunts of the tall lean fellow and the little fat chap. Their stage career began when a Cleveland burlesque manager offered a salary of sixty dollars a week to the cleverest team of German comedians in the city.

Kolb and Dill, boyhood chums, got together and decided to take a shot at the offer, though neither of them had ever attempted German dialect or designed a costume. Their ingenuity and their natural ability won the competition for them, and then and there they decided to stick to the stage.

After several successful seasons Kolb and Dill appeared on Broadway in the musical comedy success, "Fiddle Dee Dee," which played throughout the principal eastern cities for several years, finally coming to California in 1904, where they were received with such enthusiasm that the Pacific Coast claimed them for its own, always speaking of them as "Kolb and Dill of San Francisco."

Among the comedies in which the famous comedians starred in the past few years are "Hoity Toity," "Hurly Burly," "I. O. U.," "Pousse Cafe," "The Beauty Shop," and their greatest success, "Peck of Pickles," which is now being prepared for screen production by the American Company.

DON'T ARGUE! There's none that equals

Malthoid Roofing

It covers the American Film Co., Inc., Studios; BECAUSE— it is the best on earth and we stand back of it.

Santa Barbara Roofing Company
1206 State Street, Santa Barbara, California
Home Phone 602   FRANK D. ADAMS, Manager

Acts and Directs

William Russell One of Busiest Men on American Lot.

One of the busiest men on the big American lot is William Russell, usually known as "Big Bill," who directs his own company as well as playing leading parts, which are usually strenuous roles. After

WILLIAM RUSSELL,
directs own company

his day at the studio is done, he puts in most of his evenings at rebuilding his plays, for he has a wide experience in life and has always made his productions stand out above the creation of the author. He is gifted with the knowledge of human emotions and understands how to express them.

Six feet is considered an exceptional height for a man, but Russell tops the mark by two inches. His muscles are "hard as nails" and he tips the Fairbanks at over two hundred pounds. His splendid physique stands him in good stead in the vigorous characters he portrays and he has built up a wide following chiefly through his manly personality.

Big Bill came to the American studios from the Famous Players where he had divided honors with famous stage stars in a number of features. His first appearance in American pictures was made in "The Diamond from the Sky" and his characterization of the heavy lead in this serial distinguished him as one of the foremost screen actors. At the conclusion of the serial he was starred in his own features with the co-direction of Jack Prescott, an arrangement which is still in force. Russell is an all round athlete and has won laurels as an amateur boxer. His daily exercise, taken early in the morning while the average man still sleeps, consists of bag-punching, horseback riding and swimming.

From the moment Big Bill makes his appearance on the screen the spectator knows that here is a man able to perform a man's work entirely upon his own resources.

CHARLOTTE BURTON IS BEST DRESSED ACTRESS

Charlotte Burton, who plays leads in the William Russell productions, came to the American in 1912 after years of stage

CHARLOTTE BURTON

experience in stock and road companies. She was first seen in a large number of Western pictures, but when those of the East and society began to be put on she was chosen to do "societies" only.

It being a natural accomplishment with Miss Burton to "dress" her parts well, she has persevered in this art until the honor of being one of the very best dressed personages of the screen is rightfully hers. In a leading role in the serial, "The Diamond from the Sky," her excellent work and her interesting clothes win much favorable comment.

HELENE ROSSON COMES TO FRONT WITH RAPIDITY

Helene Rosson of the American company is developing with almost startling rapidity. In a wonderfully short space of time she has become well known to the fans and her popularity is steadily rising. Although she is only seventeen and has not been in the profession for very long, she has talents far above the ordinary and is working hard to achieve the success which is bound to come her way. Her first engagement was with the Eastern Vitagraph two and a half years ago under the direction of Ralph Ince.

A little later Miss Rosson came to the Pacific Coast with the Universal, playing important parts from the outset. Then she came to the American and has been playing important leads ever since. She is very ambitious and never fully satisfied with what she does, which is a sure sign that she is going to do better things.

HELENE ROSSON
enjoying a leisure moment while waiting for the big set

---

829 STATE STREET   **Telephone 347**

Trenwith's

Dry Goods, Suits and Millinery

SANTA BARBARA, CAL.

FRANK BORZAGE WINS HIGH PLACE AS DIRECTOR

Although one of the youngest directors in the motion picture field, Frank Borzage has already won a high place for himself in the rapidly-growing industry. He is a keen student of character and his

FRANK BORZAGE—ANNA LITTLE
Comparing mash notes

productions show unusually artistic finish and individuality.

Recently he has been playing leads with Anna Little in Western features, the first of which is "Land O' Lizards" which will soon be seen in Mutual theaters.

Borzage started his stage work ten years ago, spending six of those years on the speaking stage in stock work and on the road. Then he joined the Universal company and had his first picture experience. Later he went over to the New York Motion Picture Company and stayed two and a half years, when he joined the American at Santa Barbara. While with the Ince forces he played the leads in "The Wrath of the Gods," and "The Cup of Life" and had a character lead in "The Typhoon."

His late successes in the American-Mustang pictures include "The Courtin' of Calliope Clew," "Nell Dale's Men Folks," and "Matchin' Jim."

Although only twenty-four years old, the future looks brights for the assured success of the liking and likable Frank Borzage.

ANNA LITTLE TYPICAL GIRL OF GOLDEN WEST

Whether she is working in front of the camera, armed with a six-shooter, or in the garden of her home, armed with a pair of rose shears, Anna Little is the typical outdoor girl of the golden West. She was born right here in California, at Sisson, twenty-two years ago, and most of her life has been spent in the Sunshine State. She is an excellent vocalist, hav-

ANNA LITTLE AND ANGEL,
her favorite mustang

ing played several seasons with a comic opera company.

Miss Little's picture experience began with Broncho Billy Anderson at the Essanay, then went to Inceville where she played Western leads for more than a year. A year at Universal proved that her talents were not limited to Western roles and she appeared in a leading part in "Damon and Pythias." She also played a principal role in "The Black Box" serial while at Universal City. A year ago she came to the American and has lately been playing Western leads with Frank Borzage.

The Quality Store

E. F. ROGERS & SON

Furniture, Rugs, Carpets and Draperies

Both Phones 390   928 State
SANTA BARBARA, CAL.

Consult Us
Everything in the Electric Line
FANS, FIXTURES, MOTORS, APPLIANCES, WIRING, ETC.
First installation of wiring at American Film Company Studio installed by us

The Nielson-Smith Electric Co.
ELECTRICAL CONTRACTORS
13-15 West Ortega St.
Either Phone 588   Santa Barbara

Men's Clothiers and Haberdashers

LADIES' SPORT ATTIRE

Left to right—Harry Keenan, Leona Hutton, John Prescott, Charlotte Burton, S. S. Hutchinson and Wm. Russell, talking over a new production with Mr. Hutchinson, the president of the company.

DOWLAN, RECENT ARRIVAL, NOTED FOR ARTISTIC WORK

One of the most recent additions to the directing force of the American studios is William C. Dowlan, whose ability in the way of artistic production is an established one.

WILLIAM C. DOWLAN

For four and a half years previous to his affiliation with the American, Mr. Dowlan had been a director for the Universal, his long engagement with one firm being a record one in an industry as changeable as that of the motion picture. He had left the Belasco theater in Los Angeles at a time when he was the most popular leading man of that city and his connection with the Universal followed. The subjects produced under his direction have become noted for the accuracy of detail and the true-to-life portrayals.

American Scenario Staff

Originators of Ideas at Flying A Graduates of Newspaper Game

Back of the splendid pictures of the American is a battery of scenario writers, the equal of which would be hard to find. Recognizing the superior opportunity newspaper men have to acquaint themselves with all conditions of life and plan and write stories that "get over" the Flying A executives have wisely chosen for their plot department men trained to the work of the big dailies. This is one of the principal reasons why the American's film dramas have punch and finish.

After several months as head of the scenario department George Wight has resumed full charge of the American publicity department. Before coming to the Pacific Coast Mr. Wight was identified with the newspapers of New York and Chicago, and late with the San Francisco Examiner.

He is a man of keen perception, knows news when he sees it, and further knows how to handle and get it "across."

Harold W. Hoadley, one of Mr. Wight's assistants, began his career as a newspaper man, giving this work up to become assistant manager of the old Imp studio. When that concern was absorbed by the Universal he went with it to manage the circulation of the Universal Weekly. Later he joined the scenario department, afterwards going to the Vitagraph as a comedy writer.

At the head of the American scenario staff is Clifford Howard, who has been promoted to that position after a year of splendid work with the Flying A. He is the author of a number of books and scientific works—among which are "April," in which Helen Rosson scored such a success, and also "Purity," in which Audrey Munson was featured, besides several other note-worthy pieces.

Earl Coolidge was identified with several newspapers in the capacity of city editor before taking up scenario work. He joined the western Kalem Company as editor in 1910 and later was employed by the Keystone Film Company as its first scenario editor. He left the Keystone to go to the St. Louis motion picture company as editor and publicity man and joined the American a year ago. His record credits him with over 300 photoplays.

C. B. (Pop) Hoadley, father of Harold W., began literary work as a newspaper man at the age of 18, leaving it to take up magazine work. He has had ten years' experience as scenario writer and has written close to 500 produced scripts.

John Wall supervises the titles and prepares the property inserts required in the filming of stories. He is a newspaper man of long experience and has been connected with the publicity end of two expositions.

Anthony W. Coldewey gave up newspaper work to become a scenario writer. He came to the American in February of this year. His current releases are "The Power of Mind," "Enchantment," "The Vanity of Man" and "The Lawmakers," under production, featuring Richard Bennett.

Arthur Henry Gooden was a successful writer of short stories before becoming a scenario author. He has written some splendid stories for the films since joining the American.

Al Santell has a wide reputation as a writer of comedies. His principal work is the framing of plots and writing of stories for the famous Kolb and Dill team.

Left to right—Director Ed. Sloman, Richard Willis of Willis & Inglis, and Harry Von Meter, caught unawares on the studio grounds by the camera man.

Sterling Drug Co.
S. C. PINKHAM
Everything for the Make Up
San Marcus Bldg. Opp. New Postoffice
SANTA BARBARA, CAL.

TOM CHATTERTON ASPIRED TO STAGE AS YOUNGSTER

Tom Chatterton, more often called "Lieutenant Hope" since he played the debonair naval officer in "The Secret of the Submarine" serial, had a leaning to-

THOS. W. CHATTERTON

ward things theatrical when he was a youngster, and when his father refused to let him go to the stage he brought the stage to himself, rigging up a playhouse in his father's barn and playing star parts in plays of his own authorship to an audience of neighboring kids. This was as far as his ambition progressed until his college days, when he organized a college dramatic company.

Then followed several seasons of stock company work, and he was also leading man for three years on the road with "The Man of the Hour." He later headed his own company over the Orpheum circuit.

He broke into pictures in 1913 with the New York Motion Picture Company, and after acting in several features he was given the direction of his own company, also appearing in the leads. In 1915 he came to the American as director and leading man of one of the Mustang companies, later being selected to play the leading role in the "Submarine" serial.

While in high school and college he was prominent in athletics and is still an enthusiastic amateur sportsman.

RELIABLE INFORMATION ON
Santa Barbara Real Estate

Insurance in All Lines

Harvey T. Nielson
4-5 Howard Canfield Bldg.
SANTA BARBARA, CAL.

SLOMAN DIRECTOR OF COXEN AND GREENWOOD

Edward Sloman, who is at present directing pictures featuring Edward Coxen and Winnifred Greenwood, came to the American from Lubin's studio a few months ago. Although he is devoting his talent solely to directing now, he has had considerable experience as a screen actor, having played leading parts in a number of features, including Universal's twelve-reel serial "Under the Crescent."

Born in England and inheriting stage ability from his mother, who was a noted actress and a cousin to David Belasco, Mr. Sloman played child parts in London and the Provinces and came to America at an early age. Here he appeared in a number of notable stage plays, forsaking the "legitimate" for the screen three years ago.

WINNIFRED GREENWOOD WIDELY FEATURED STAR

Winnifred Greenwood has been a well known screen personage for as many as five years. A successful stage career

WINIFRED GREENWOOD

gave her a distinctive introduction into the picture world, and hers was one of the first big names to be exploited by the Selig company. She played leads with this concern for more than two years and came to the American three years ago, where she since has been featured in a variety of its releases.

COXEN HEADS COMPANY UNDER SLOMAN'S DIRECTION

Edward Coxen recently won the distinction of being elected to head a feature company of the American under Edward Sloman's direction. For the last year or more he has been co-starring with Winnifred Greenwood in American dramas, for a time in one and two-reel pictures. More recently he has appeared with Miss Greenwood in three-reelers, and his new promotion to leading roles in a feature company is in recognition of his greater powers of dramatic interpretation.

EDWARD COXEN

GEO. FIELD

JACK PRESCOTT SPENT TEN YEARS ON BROADWAY

Jack Prescott, co-director with William Russell in the latter's feature productions, came into the world of films two years ago, breaking off a record of more than ten years spent in the successful production of Broadway hits. Before his picture career began he had been stage manager of the Madison Square and the Belasco theaters in New York, and also of a number of the Henry B. Harris successes. Not long ago a vaudeville tour with Theodore Roberts brought him to Los Angeles. Here he dabbled in the movies, on the principle of "trying anything once," but his first venture did not make a hit with him and he went back to the stage for a short time.

The American company tempted Prescott into the game again and he played

FRANKLIN RITCHIE GOES FROM SCHOOL TO STAGE

a heavy lead in "The Diamond from the Sky." When the serial was finished, the William Russell feature company was organized and Mr. Prescott was selected to share the responsibility of directing these features with "Big Bill."

Franklin Ritchie, leading man at the American studios, was born in Ritchie, Pa. (Yes, the town was named after him.) Immediately following his school days he took up the theatrical profession and for a number of years was on the legitimate stage, playing under the managements of Frohman and Belasco. He

FRANKLIN RITCHIE

starred in "The Clansman," originating the male lead and playing it for four years. His motion picture experience began in 1913 when he became affiliated with the Biograph producing staff, later appearing in a number of Klaw & Erlanger-Biograph features.

Less than a year ago Ritchie came to the American studio and has since starred in a number of big productions. He has won many friends among screen fans and has been commended by the critics and reviewers for his handling of difficult roles in screen dramas.

EUGENIE FORDE
leading character woman with American Film Co.

ALAN FORREST
playing leads with American

EDWARD LANGLEY BORN TO PROFESSION

Edward Langley, the art director and technical chief of the American studios, seemingly was born to his profession. He is an artist, designer, decorator and an expert photographer. Some famous artists of other days are included in his ancestry. He is a versatile man, equally at home superintending the technical equipment of all the great sets that are put up on the American's stages, painting masterpieces to adorn famous drawing rooms or artist's studios, or acting as an architect in any capacity.

Mr. Langley is a hunter of wild game, an expert angler, knows the mountains like a ranger and is an enthusiastic motorist. He is chief of a large staff of assistant technical men and his handsomely appointed office, standing detached from the other buildings on the studio grounds, is unique because of its furnishings, designed by himself, and because of the trophies of woods and stream which decorate its walls.

Fred S. Tucker

Interior Decorator

919 State Street

SANTA BARBARA, CAL.

LOUIS MIRATTI   E. H. LOMAS

Santa Barbara Drug Co.

MIRATTI & LOMAS, Props.

Both Phones 71

609 State Street
SANTA BARBARA, CAL.

"WE ALWAYS MAKE GOOD"

Santa Barbara Lumber Company

Building Material of All Kinds

BOTH PHONES 19   SANTA BARBARA, CAL.   H. W. GORDON, Manager

A GALAXY OF AMERICAN FILM STARS

GEORGE PERIOLAT

MAY CLOY

WM. TEDMARSH

"Come in, the water's fine!" Rhea Mitchell, leading woman with Richard Bennett, enjoying a dip

WM. STOWELL

RICHARD BENNETT
with two of his children feeding pet deer of American Studio

Split Reels
By Dick Willis

ANNA LITTLE, AMERICAN

"Miss Little?"
"No, I'm always with her."
"Favorite occupations?"

"Mustang brand—ing."
"American?"
"Surely, a Native Daughter."
"Manage to have a good time?"
"I Miss Little."

MARY PICKFORD, FAMOUS PLAYERS

"If you had your choice of an auto, what would you pick?"
"Pick? Ford."
"Are you happier now than you were?"
"Much Moore."
"What would you do if you met Owen all over again?"

"Mary."
"Do you think you and Owen are pretty good?"
"Well, we are both Famous Players."

GRACE CUNARD, UNIVERSAL

"When were you born?"
"In the year of Grace—no matter."
"You were born in Paris—how did you come over?"
"Cunard line."
"How are you feeling?"
"Like a square Peg in a round Ring."
"What form of photoplay do you prefer?"
"To be continued in our next."

APPENDIX B

FILMOGRAPHY

APPENDIX B

FILMOGRAPHY

American Film Manufacturing Company
1910-1921

Films are arranged chronologically according to release date. Split reels are indicated by the notation, (with). Subsidiary production companies credited with American-produced films are indicated in parentheses after the release date. All films are one reel unless listed otherwise. Films marked with an asterisk (*) are re-releases.

Film Title	Release Date
	1910
Romantic Redskins	November 14
Lure of the City, The	November 17
Starlight's Devotion	November 21
Nothing But Money (with)	
Big Joke, A	November 24
Regeneration	November 28
Touching Affair, A	December 1
Vera, the Gypsy Girl	December 5
Two Lucky Jims	December 8
Rummage Sale, The	December 12
Binding Shot, The	December 15
Her Fatal Mistake	December 19
Troublesome Parcel, A (with)	
Her Husband's Deception	December 22
Girlies	December 26
Squaw and the Man, The	December 29
	1911
Mrs. Gaylife's Visitors	January 2
Tenderfoot's Round Up, The	January 5
Arizona Romance, An	January 9
Lucy's Lover (with)	
Borrowed Flat, The	January 12

1911 (Cont'd.)

Dental Disaster, A (with)	
Bartered Bridegrooms, The	January 16
Bonanza King, The	January 19
When a Man's Single	January 23
Bertie's Bandit	January 26
Genius, The	January 30
Mission in the Desert, The	February 2
Pittsburg Millionaire, A	February 6
Too Much Aunt (with)	
On the Installment Plan	February 9
Quiet Evening at Home, A	February 13
In the Land of Cactus	February 16
College Spendthrift, The	February 20
Strategy	February 23
Silence System, The (with)	
Sheriff's Sweetheart, The	February 27
College Chums	March 2
Memories (with)	
Hypnotizing a Hypnotist	March 6
Rich and the Poor, The	March 9
Penalty, The	March 13
Do you Know This Woman? (with)	
Job and the Girl, The	March 16
Field of Honor, The	March 20
Harem Skirt, The	March 23
Talisman, The	March 27
Two Girls (with)	
Osteopathy	March 30
Oh! You Suffragette (with)	
Cure for Laziness, A	April 3
Reddy's Redemption	April 6
Cupid's Pocketbook	April 10
Jimmy Minds the Baby (with)	
Bungelow Craze, The	April 13
Two Plucky Girls	April 17
One Month to Live	April 20
Bud Nevins -- Bad Man	April 24
Boss of Lucky Ranch, The	April 27
California Love Story, A (with)	
United States Cavalary Drill	May 1
Crazy Gulch (with)	
Hobo's Round Up	May 4
Opium Smuggler, The	May 8
Sheriff's Captive, The	May 11
Ranchman's Vengeance, The	May 15
Cowboy's Sacrifice, A	May 18

1911 (Cont'd.)

Brandishing a Bad Man (with) Western Dreamer, A	May 22
Daughter of Liberty, A (with) Trouper's Heart, A	May 25
Rattlesnakes and Gunpowder (with) Ranch Tenor, The	May 29
Sheepman's Daughter, The	June 1
Sage Brush Phrenologist, The (with) Elopements on Double L Ranch, The	June 5
$5000 Reward -- Dead or Alive	June 8
Witch of the Range, The	June 12
Cowboy's Ruse, The (with) Law and Order on Bar L Ranch	June 15
Yiddisher Cowboy, The (with) Broncho Buster's Bride, The	June 19
Hermit's Gold, The	June 22
Actress and the Cowboys, The (with) Sky Pilot's Intemperance, The	June 26
Western Waif, A	June 29
Call of the Open Range, The	July 3
School Ma'am of Snake, The (with) Ranch Chicken, The	July 6
Cupid in Chaps	July 10
Outlaw's Trail, The	July 13
Ranchman's Nerve, The	July 17
When East Comes West	July 20
Cowboy's Deliverance, The	July 24
Cattle Thief's Branch, The	July 27
Parting Trails, The	July 31
Cattle Rustler's End, The	August 3
Cattle, Gold, and Oil	August 7
Ranch Girl's Rustler, The	August 10
Poisoned Flume, The	August 14
Brand of Fear, The	August 17
Blotted Brand, The	August 21
Auntie and the Cowboys, The (with) Anne Harris in Chicago Swimming Marathon	August 24
Western Doctor's Peril, The	August 28
Smuggler and the Girl, The	August 31
Cowboy and the Artist, The	September 4
Three Million Dollars	September 7
Stage Robbers of San Juan, The	September 11
Mother of the Ranch, The	September 14
Gunman, The	September 18
Claim Jumpers, The	September 21
Circular Fence, The	September 25

1911 (Cont'd.)

Rustler Sheriff, The	September 28
Love of the West, The	October 2
Miner's Wife, The	October 5
Land Thieves, The	October 9
Cowboy and the Outlaw, The	October 12
Three Daughters of the West, The (with)	
Caves of La Jolla, The	October 16
Lonely Range, The	October 19
Horse Thief's Bigamy, The	October 23
Trail of the Eucalyptus, The	October 26
Stronger Man, The	October 30
Water War, The	November 2
Three Shell Game, The	November 6
Mexican, The	November 9
Eastern Cowboy, The	November 13
Way of the West, The	November 16
Test, The	November 20
Master of the Vineyard, The	November 23
Sloppy Bill of the Rollicking R	November 27
Sheriff's Sisters, The	November 30
Angel of Paradise Ranch, The	December 4
Smoke of the Forty-Five, The	December 7
Man Hunt, The	December 11
Santa Catalina, Magic Isle of the Pacific	December 14
Last Notch, The	December 18
Gold Lust, The	December 21
Duel of Candles, The	December 25
Bonita of El Cajon	December 28

1912

Midwinter Trip to Los Angeles, A	January 1
Broncho Busting for Flying "A" Pictures (with)	
Misadventures of a Claim Agent, The	January 4
Winning of La Mesa, The	January 8
Locket, The	January 11
Relentless Outlaw, The	January 15
Justice of the Sage	January 18
Objections Overruled	January 22
Mormon, The	January 25
Love and Lemons	January 29

1912 (Cont'd.)

Best Policy, The	February 1
Real Estate Fraud, The	February 5
Grubstake Mortgage, The	February 8
Where Broadway Meets the Mountains	February 12
Innocent Grafter, An	February 15
Society and Chaps	February 19
Leap Year Cowboy, The (or) February 29th	February 22
Land Baron of San Tee, The	February 26
Assisted Elopment, An	February 29
From the Four Hundred to the Herd	March 4
Broken Ties, The	March 7
After School	March 11
Bad Investment, A	March 14
Full Value, The	March 18
Tramp's Gratitude, The	March 21
Fidelity	March 25
Winter Sports and Pastimes of Coronado Beach (or) Coronado's New Year's Day	March 28
Maid and the Man, The	April 1
Agitator, The (or) Cowboy Socialist, The	April 4
Ranchmen's Marathon, The (with) Checkmate	April 8
Coward, The	April 11
Distant Relative, The	April 15
Range Detective, The	April 18
Driftwood, The	April 22
Eastern Girl, The (or) Her Mountain Home	April 25
Pensioners, The	April 29
End of the Feud, The	May 2
Her Wedding Dress	May 6
Mystical Maid of Hamasha Pass, The	May 9
Other Wise Man, The	May 13
Haters, The	May 16
Thread of Life, The	May 20
Wandering Gypsy, The	May 23
Reward of Valor, The	May 27
Brand, The	May 30
Green-Eyed Monster, The	June 3
Cupid Through Padlocks	June 6
For the Good of Her Men	June 10
Simple Love, The	June 13
Weaker Brother, The (with) Fifty-Mile Auto Contest, A	June 17

1912 (Cont'd.)

Wordless Message, The	June 20
Evil Inheritance, The	June 24
Marauders, The	June 27
Girl Back Home, The	July 1
Hour of Terror, An	July 3
Under False Pretenses	July 4
Where There's a Heart	July 8
Fall of Black Hawk, The (2 reels)	July 10
Vanishing Race, The	July 11
Fatal Mirror, The (with)	
Point Loma, Old Town	July 15
In the Nick of Time	July 17
Telltale Shells, The	July 18
Indian Jealousy (with)	
San Diego	July 22
How He Made Good	July 24
Canyon Dweller, The	July 25
It Pays to Wait	July 29
Fight At the Mill (with)	
Giants of Steel	July 31
Life For a Kiss, A	August 1
Meddlers, The	August 5
Saved By an Auto	August 7
Girl and the Gun, The	August 8
Battleground, The (2 reels)	August 12
Badman and the Ranger, The	August 14
Outlaw Colony, The	August 15
Land of Death, The	August 19
Wooing of Wathena, The	August 21
Bandit of Point Loma, The	August 22
Jealous Rage, The	August 26
Lonesome Trail Pioneers, The	August 28
Will of James Waldron, The	August 29
Greaser and the Weakling, The	September 2
Marked Gun, The	September 4
Stranger At Coyote, The	September 5
Dawn of Passion, The	September 9
Geronimo's Last Raid (2 reels)	September 11
Vengeance That Failed, The	September 12
Fear, The	September 16
Wun Lung's Strategy	September 18
Foreclosure, The	September 19
White Treachery	September 23
Bad Pete's Gratitude	September 25
Their Hero Son	September 26
Calamity Anne's Ward	September 30

1912 (Cont'd.)

Renegade, The	October 2
Father's Favorite (or)	
Favored Son, The	October 3
Jack of Diamonds (Queen of Hearts)	October 7
Sister's Devotion, A	October 9
Lost Watch, The (or)	
Reformation of Sierra Smith, The	October 10
Promise, The	October 14
Border Detective, The	October 16
New Cowpuncher, The	October 17
Best Man Wins, The	October 21
Way of the Transgressor, The	October 23
Wooers of Mountain Kate, The	October 24
One, Two, Three	October 28
Chiquita, The Dancer	October 30
Wanderer, The	October 31
Maiden and Men	November 4
God's Unfortunate	November 7
Starbucks, The (2 reels)	November 9
Man's Calling	November 11
Intrusion at Lompoc, The	November 14
Jim Bentley's Adventure	November 16
Thief's Wife, The	November 18
Would-Be Heir, The	November 21
Idyl of Hawaii, The	November 23
Jack's Word	November 25
Her Own Country	November 28
Hidden Treasure, The (or)	
The Philanderings of Puddenfoot Pete (with)	
On Board the "S.S. Dubuque," Naval Training Ship	November 30
Pals	December 2
Animal Within, The	December 5
Bludsoe's Dilemma	December 7
Law of God, The	December 9
Nell of the Pampas	December 12
Heart of a Soldier, The	December 14
Daughters of Senor Lopez, The	December 16
Power of Love, The	December 19
Saving the Innocents (with)	
Mrs. Brown's Baby	December 21
Recognition, The	December 23
Blackened Hills	December 26
Girl of the Manor, The	December 28
Loneliness of Neglect	December 30

1913

Love and the Law	January 2
Fraud That Failed, The	January 4
Another Man's Wife	January 6
Trail of Cards, The	January 9
Calamity Anne's Inheritance	January 11
Their Masterpiece	January 13
Awakening, The	January 16
His Old-Fashioned Mother (with) English Walnut Industry, The	January 18
Where Destiny Guides	January 20
Silver-Plated Gun, The	January 23
Rose of Old Mexico, A	January 25
Latent Spark, The	January 27
Building the Great Los Angeles Aquaduct	January 30
Women Left Alone	February 1
Andrew Jackson (2 reels)	February 3
His Sacrifice	February 6
Calamity Anne's Vanity	February 8
Fugitive, The	February 10
Pecos Pete in Search of a Wife	February 13
Romance, The	February 15
Finer Things, The	February 17
Cowboy Heir, The	February 20
Love is Blind	February 22
Famous Illinois Canyons and Starved Rock (with) Father's Finish, A	February 27
When the Light Fades	February 24
High and Low	March 1
Greater Love, The	March 3
Jocular Winds, The	March 6
Transgression of Manuel, The	March 8
Calamity Anne, Detective	March 10
Brother Love	March 13
Orphan's Mine, The	March 15
When a Woman Won't	March 17
Lesson, The	March 20
Eastern Flower, An	March 22
Cupid Never Ages	March 24
Lonesome Joe	March 27
Calamity Anne's Beauty	March 29
Renegade's Heart, The	March 31
Matches	April 3
Mute Witness, The	April 5
Cupid Throws A Brick	April 7

1913 (Cont'd.)

Homestead Race, The	April 10
Woman's Honor	April 12
Suspended Sentence	April 14
In Another's Nest	April 17
Ways of Fate, The	April 19
Boobs and Bricks	April 21
When Jim Returned	April 24
Calamity Anne's Trust	April 26
Oil on Troubled Waters (2 reels)	April 28
Tattooed Arm, The	May 1
Road to Ruin, The	May 3
Brothers, The	May 5
Human Kindness	May 8
Youth and Jealousy	May 10
Angel of the Canyons	May 12
Kiss, The	May 15
Great Harmony, The	May 17
Her Innocent Marriage	May 19
Calamity Anne Parcel Post	May 22
Modern Snare, A	May 24
Ashes of Three, The	May 26
On the Border	May 29
Her Big Story	May 31
When Luck Changes	June 2
Wishing Seat, The	June 5
Via Cabaret	June 7
California Poultry	June 9
Hearts and Horses	June 12
Reward of Courage, The	June 14
Soul of A Thief, The (2 reels)	June 16
Unwritten Law of the West, The	June 19
Marine Law, The	June 21
Husband's Mistake, A	June 23
Calamity Anne Takes a Trip	June 26
Dead Man's Shoes	June 28
Quicksand (2 reels)	June 30
Pride of Lonesome, The	July 3
Tale of Death Valley, A	July 5
San Francisco, The Dauntless City	July 7
Foreign Spy, The	July 10
Song of the Soup, The (with)	
Garden City in California, A	July 12
Truth in the Wilderness (2 reels)	July 14
To Err is Human	July 17
At the Half-Breed's Mercy	July 19
Jealousy's Trail	July 21

1913 (Cont'd.)

Tom Blake's Redemption (or) Redemption	July 24
She Will Never Know	July 26
Scapegoat, The (2 reels)	July 38
Mission Bells	July 31
Single-Handed Jim	August 2
When Chemistry Counted	August 4
Golden Gate Park and Environs	August 7
His Sister Lucia	August 9
Adventures of Jacques, The (2 reels)	August 11
Mystery of Tusa, The	August 14
Even Exchange, An	August 16
Tide in the Affairs of Men, A	August 18
Golden Heart, The	August 21
Flesh of His Flesh	August 23
For the Flag	August 25
From the Portals of Despair	August 28
Jack Meets His Waterloo	August 30
Where There's Life	September 1
Poisoned Chop, The	September 4
Mysterious Eyes, The	September 6
For the Crown	September 8
Through the Neighbor's Window	September 11
Red Sweeney's Defeat	September 13
Calamity Anne, Herione	September 15
Fall Into Luck, A	September 18
Travelers of the Road, The (with) Jim Takes a Chance	September 20
Ghost of the Hacienda, The	September 22
Mrs. Carter's Campaign	September 25
Master of Himself	September 27
Flirt and the Bandit, The	September 29
Badge of Honor, The	October 2
Crooks and Credulous	October 4
Pitfall of the Installment Plan, A (2 reels)	October 6
Taming a Cowboy	October 9
Calamity Anne's Sacrifice	October 11
Making Pig Iron (with) Courage of Sorts	October 13
End of Black Bart, The (or) The Duel in the Mountains	October 16
Making of a Woman, The	October 18
Hidden Treasure Ranch	October 20
Step Brothers, The	October 23
In the Mountains of Virginia	October 25
In the Days of Trajan (2 reels)	October 27
In Three Hours	October 30

1913 (Cont'd.)

Follies of a Day and Night (or) The Mishaps of E. Z. Smithers	November 1
Girl and the Greaser, The	November 3
What Her Dairy Told	November 6
Haunted House, The	November 8
Martha's Decision	November 10
Assisted Proposal, An (or) The Difficulties of a Bashful Cowboy	November 13
Drummer's Honeymoon, The	November 15
Trail of the Lost Chord, The (2 reels)	November 17
Tale of the Ticker, The (with) Modern Stool Plant, A	November 20
Calamity Anne's Dream	November 22
Occult, The	November 24
Spartan Girl of the West, A	November 27
At Midnight	November 29
American Born (2 reels)	December 1
Divorce Scandal, A	December 6
Trapped in a Forest Fire	December 8
His First Cake	December 11
Armed Intervention	December 13
Where the Road Forks (2 reels)	December 15
Personal Magnetism	December 18
Fate's Round-Up	December 20
Shriner's Daughter, The (2 reels)	December 22
Rose of San Juan, The	December 27
In the Firelight (2 reels)	December 29

1914

Miser's Policy, The	January 3	
Power of Light, The (2 reels)	January 5	
Son of Thomas Gray, The	January 10	
Destinies Fulfilled (3 reels)	January 12	
Withering Roses	January 14	(Beauty)
Unto the Weak	January 17	
Return of Helen Redmond, The (2 reels)	January 19	
Fooling Uncle	January 21	(Beauty)
At the Potter's Wheel	January 24	
Blowout at Santa Banana, A (2 reels)	January 26	
Bess, the Outcast	January 28	(Beauty)
Calamity Anne in Society	January 31	

1914 (Cont'd.)

Hermit, The (2 reels)	February 2	
Sally's Elopement	February 4	(Beauty)
True Western Hearts	February 7	
Lost Treasure, The (3 reels)	February 9	
Wife, The	February 11	(Beauty)
Money Lender, The	February 14	
Cricket On the Hearth (2 reels)	February 16	
Sacrifice, The	February 18	(Beauty)
"Pote Lariat" of the Flying A, The	February 21	
Dream Child, The (2 reels)	February 23	
Professor's Awakening, The	February 25	(Beauty)
Carbon Copy, The	February 28	
Crucible, The	March 2	
Italian Love	March 4	(Beauty)
Pursuer Pursued, The	March 5	
Child of the Desert, A	March 7	
Call of the Traumerei (3 reels)	March 9	
Closed at Ten	March 11	(Beauty)
Story of Little Italy	March 14	
Modern Free-Lance, A (2 reels)	March 16	
Girl Who Dared, The	March 17	(Beauty)
Coming of the Padres, The	March 18	
Turning Point, The (2 reels)	March 23	
Peacock Feather Fan, The	March 24	(Beauty)
Decree of Justice, A	March 25	
Town of Nazareth, The (2 reels)	March 30	
Sweet Land of Liberty	March 31	(Beauty)
Certainty of Man, The	April 1	
Like Father, Like Son (2 reels)	April 6	
Retribution	April 7	(Beauty)
Happy Coercion, A	April 8	
Second Clue, The	April 10	
Last Supper, The (2 reels)	April 13	
Mlle. La Mode	April 14	(Beauty)
Independence of Susan, The	April 15	
Widow's Investment, The (2 reels)	April 20	
Man Who Came Back, The	April 21	(Beauty)
David Gray's Estate	April 22	
Her Fighting Chance (2 reels)	April 27	
Flurry in Hats, A	April 28	(Beauty)
Smouldering Spark, The	April 29	
In the Moonlight (2 reels)	May 4	
Eugenics Versus Love	May 5	(Beauty)
Story of the Olive, The	May 6	
Calamity Anne's Love Affair	May 8	
Soul Astray, A	May 11	
Her Heritage	May 12	(Beauty)

1914 (Cont'd.)

Navy Aviator, The	May 13	
In the Footprints of Mozart (2 reels)	May 18	
Courting of Prudence, The	May 19	(Beauty)
Beyond the City	May 20	
Lost Sermon, The (2 reels)	May 25	
Jane, the Justice	May 26	(Beauty)
Sheltering an Ingrate	May 27	
Metamorphosis (2 reels)	June 1	
Drifting Hearts	June 2	(Beauty)
Prince of Bohemia, A	June 3	
Oath of Pierre, The (2 reels)	June 8	
Nancy's Husband	June 9	(Beauty)
Sparrow of the Circus	June 10	
Unmasking, The	June 12	
Jim (2 reels)	June 15	
Dream Ship, The	June 16	(Beauty)
Painted Lady's Child, The (2 reels)	June 22	
Tale of a Tailor, The	June 23	(Beauty)
Blue Knot, King of Polo	June 24	
Little House in the Valley, The (2 reels)	June 29	
Via the Fire Escape	June 30	(Beauty)
Nature's Touch	July 1	
Mein Lieber Katrina Catches the Convict	July 3	
Cameo of the Yellowstone (2 reels)	July 6	
Other Train, The	July 7	(Beauty)
Feast and Famine	July 8	
Lure of the Sawdust, The (2 reels)	July 13	
Joke on Jane, A	July 14	(Beauty)
Youth and Art	July 15	
Man's Way, A (2 reels)	July 20	
Her "Really" Mother	July 21	(Beauty)
Business Versus Love	July 22	
Broken Barrier, The (2 reels)	July 27	
Midsummer Love's Triangle, A	July 28	(Beauty)
Does It End Right?	July 29	
All on Account of a Jug	July 31	
At the End of a Perfect Day (2 reels)	August 3	
Suspended Ceremony, A	August 4	(Beauty)
Widow, The	August 5	
Trap, The (2 reels)	August 10	
Butterfly, The	August 12	
Susanna's New Suit	August 14	(Beauty)
False Gods (2 reels)	August 17	
Silence of John Gordon, The	August 18	(Beauty)
Their Worldly Goods	August 19	

1914 (Cont'd.)

Susie's New Shoes	August 25	(Beauty)
Lodging for the Night	August 26	
This Is th' Life (or) Converting Dad	August 28	
Song of the Seashell, The (or) The Shepherd's Dream	August 28	
Aftermath (2 reels)	August 31	
Modern Othello, A	September 1	(Beauty)
Wrong Birds, The	September 2	
Lola (2 reels)	September 7	
Motherless Kids, The	September 8	
Break! Break! Break!	September 9	
Cocoon and the Butterfly (2 reels)	September 14	
Only Way, The	September 15	(Beauty)
Mirror, The	September 16	
Redemption of a Pal, The (2 reels)	September 21	
Caught in a Tight Pinch	September 22	(Beauty)
His Faith in Humanity	September 23	
Taming of Sunnybrook Nell, The	September 25	
Modern Rip Van Winkle, A (2 reels)	September 28	
Legend of Black Rock, The	September 29	(Beauty)
Ingrate, The (2 reels)	September 30	
Daphnia	October 5	
Nieda	October 6	(Beauty)
Billy's Rival	October 7	
Jailbirds (2 reels)	October 12	
Winsome Winnie	October 13	(Beauty)
Down By the Sea	October 14	
Daylight	October 19	
Dad and the Girls	October 20	(Beauty)
In the Open	October 21	
Final Impulse, The	October 23	
Sir Galahad of Twilight (2 reels)	October 26	
Rude Awakening, A	October 27	(Beauty)
Sweet and Low	October 28	
Redskin's Reckoning, A	October 31	
Ruin of Manley, The (2 reels)	November 2	
Tightwad, The	November 3	(Beauty)
When the Road Parts	November 4	
Slice of Life, A (2 reels)	November 9	
Motherhood	November 10	(Beauty)
Stolen Masterpeice, The	November 11	
Redbird Wins (2 reels)	November 16	
When Queenie Came Back	November 17	(Beauty)
Beppo	November 18	
Old Enough to be Her Grandpa	November 20	
In the Candlelight (2 reels)	November 23	

1914 (Cont'd.)

As a Man Thinketh (So He Is)	November 24	(Beauty)
Archaeologist, The	November 25	
Beggar Child, The (2 reels)	November 30	
Cupid and a Dress Coat	December 1	(Beauty)
Strength o' Ten, The	December 2	
Out of the Darkness (2 reels)	December 7	
Limping Into Happiness	December 8	(Beauty)
Girl in Question, The	December 9	
In Tune (2 reels)	December 14	
Her Younger Sister	December 15	(Beauty)
Silent Way, The	December 16	
Trapped By Heliograph	December 18	
Sower Reaps, The (2 reels)	December 21	
Brass Buttons	December 22	(Beauty)
Tin Can Shack	December 23	
When a Woman Waits (2 reels)	December 28	
Love Knows No Law	December 29	(Beauty)
Unseen Vengeance, The	December 30	

1915

Legend Beautiful, The (2 reels)	January 4	
In the Vale of Sorrow	January 5	(Beauty)
Alarm of Angelone, The	January 6	
Restitution (2 reels)	January 11	
Spirit of Giving, The	January 12	(Beauty)
Black Ghost Bandit, The	January 13	
Clubman's Wager, The (with)		
Producing a Nation's Pride	January 15	
Refining Fires (2 reels)	January 18	
Girl and Two Boys, A	January 19	(Beauty)
Crucifixion of Al Brady, The	January 20	
Silence (2 reels)	January 25	
Evan's Lucky Day	January 26	(Beauty)
Coals of Fire	January 27	
Law of the Wilds, The (2 reels)	February 1	
Which Would You Rather Be?	February 2	(Beauty)
Imitations	February 3	
Justified (2 reels)	February 8	
Mrs. Cook's Cooking	February 9	(Beauty)
Heart of Gold, A	February 10	
Wily Chaperone, The	February 12	
In the Twilight (2 reels)	February 15	
Happier Man, The	February 16	(Beauty)
Saints and Sinners	February 17	
Decision, The (2 reels)	February 22	
Constable's Daughter, The	February 23	(Beauty)

1915 (Cont'd.)

She Never Knew	February 24	
Heart of Flame (2 reels)	March 1	
Haunting Memory, The	March 2	(Beauty)
Derelict, The	March 3	
Truth of Fiction, The (2 reels)	March 8	
Doctor's Strategy	March 9	(Beauty)
Echo, The	March 10	
His Mysterious Neighbor	March 12	
Two Sentences, The (2 reels)	March 15	
In the Mansion of Loneliness	March 16	
Competition	March 17	
First Stone, The	March 20	(Beauty)
Ancestry (2 reels)	March 22	
When the Fire Bell Rang	March 23	(Beauty)
In the Heart of the Woods	March 24	
In the Sunlight (2 reels)	March 29	
Reformation	March 31	
Quest, The (5 reels)	March	(Mutual Masterpiece)
His Brother's Debt (2 reels)	April 5	
Once Over	April 6	(Beauty)
Touch of Love, The	April 7	
Problem, The	April 9	
Poet of the Peaks, The	April 12	
Persistence Wins	April 13	(Beauty)
Wishing Stone, The	April 14	
Castle Ranch (2 reels)	April 19	
Oh, Daddy	April 20	(Beauty)
She Walketh Alone	April 21	
Day of Reckoning, The	April 26	
No Quarter	April 27	(Beauty)
Wanted--A Wife	April 28	
Heritage of Hate, The (2 reels)		
<u>Episode One</u>		
The Diamond from the Sky	May 3	(North American)
One Summer's Sequel (2 reels)	May 3	
Face Most Fair, The	May 4	(Beauty)
When Empty Hearts Are Filled	May 5	
Dreams Realized	May 7	(Beauty)
Eye for an Eye, An (2 reels)		
<u>Episode Two</u>		
The Diamond from the Sky	May 10	(North American)
Altar of Ambition, The (2 reels)	May 10	(American Mutual)
Life's Staircase	May 11	(Beauty)
Broken Window, The	May 12	
Silent Witness, The (2 reels)		
<u>Episode Three</u>		
The Diamond from the Sky	May 17	(North American)

1915 (Cont'd.)

Greater Strength, The (2 reels)	May 17	
Lure of the Mask, The (4 reels)	May 17	(Mutual Masterpictures)
Naughty Henrietta	May 18	(Beauty)
At the Edge of Things	May 19	
Prodigal's Progress, The (2 reels)		
Episode Four		
The Diamond from the Sky	May 24	(North American)
In the Purple Hills (2 reels)	May 24	
Stay-At-Homes, The	May 25	(Beauty)
Reprisal, The	May 26	
Resolve, The (2 reels)	May 31	
For the Sake of a False Friend (2 reels)		
Episode Five		
The Diamond from the Sky	May 31	(North American)
Little Chrysanthemum	June 1	(Beauty)
Golden Rainbow, A	June 2	
Lonesome Heart, The (4 reels)	June 3	(Mutual Masterpictures)
Guiding Light, The	June 4	
Shadows at Sunrise (2 reels)		
Episode Six		
The Diamond from the Sky	June 7	(North American)
Right to Happiness, The (2 reels)	June 7	(Flying A)
Redemption of the Jasons, The	June 8	(Beauty)
Soul of the Vase, The	June 9	(Flying A)
Fox and the Pig, The (2 reels)		
Episode Seven		
The Diamond from the Sky	June 14	(North American)
His Obligation (2 reels)	June 14	(Flying A)
Mollycoddle, The	June 15	(Beauty)
Her Musical Cook	June 16	(Flying A)
Mind in the Past, A (2 reels)		
Episode Eight		
The Diamond from the Sky	June 21	(North American)
Peggy Lynn, Burglar	June 21	(Flying A)
Deal in Diamonds, A	June 22	(Beauty)
One Woman's Way	June 23	(Flying A)
Runaway Match, A (2 reels)		
Episode Nine		
The Diamond from the Sky	June 28	(North American)
By Whose Hand? (2 reels)	June 28	(Flying A)
Madonna, The	June 29	(Beauty)
Good Business Deal, A	June 30	(Flying A)
Woman Scorned, A	July 2	(Flying A)

1915 (Cont'd.)

Old Foes with New Faces (2 reels)		
Episode Ten		
The Diamond from the Sky	July 5	(North American)
Mountain Mary (2 reels)	July 5	(Flying A)
Guy Upstairs, The	July 6	(Beauty)
High Cost of Flirting, The	July 7	(Flying A)
Secretary of Frivolous Affairs (4 reels)	July 8	(Mutual Masterpictures)
Zaca Lake Mystery (2 reels)	July 12	(Flying A)
Web of Destiny, The (or) The Plaything of the Papoose		
Episode Eleven		
The Diamond from the Sky	July 12	(North American)
Applied Romance	July 13	(Beauty)
To Melody a Soul Responds	July 14	(Flying A)
Honor of the District Attorney, The (2 reels)	July 19	(North American)
To the Highest Bidder (2 reels)		
Episode Twelve		
The Diamond from the Sky	July 19	(North American)
His College Wife	July 20	(Beauty)
Wait and See	July 21	(Flying A)
Man in the Mask, The (2 reels)		
Episode Thirteen		
The Diamond from the Sky	July 26	(North American)
Newer Way, The (2 reels)	July 26	
Betty's First Sponge Cake	July 27	(Beauty)
Deception, The	July 28	(Flying A)
After the Storm	July 30	
Detective Blinn (2 reels)	August 2	
For Love and Money (2 reels)		
Episode Fourteen		
The Diamond from the Sky	August 2	(North American)
Cupid Takes a Taxi	August 3	(Beauty)
Mighty Hold, The	August 4	
Girl from His Town, The (4 reels)	August 5	(Mutual Masterpictures)
Desperate Chances (2 reels)		
Episode Fifteen		
The Diamond from the Sky	August 9	(North American)
Exile of Bar K Ranch (2 reels)	August 9	
Jimmie on the Job	August 10	(Beauty)
Comrades Three	August 11	
Jilt, The (2 reels)	August 16	
Path of Peril, The (2 reels)		
Episode Sixteen		
The Diamond from the Sky	August 16	(North American)

1915 (Cont'd.)

Honeymooners, The	August 17	(Beauty)
Assayer of Lone Gap, The	August 18	
What's In a Name?	August 21	(Beauty)
Drawing the Line (2 reels)	August 23	
King of Diamonds, The (2 reels)		
Episode Seventeen		
The Diamond from the Sky	August 23	(North American)
His Mysterious Profession	August 24	(Beauty)
Mixed Wires	August 27	
Uncle Heck, By Heck!	August 28	(Beauty)
Charm Against Harm (2 reels)		
Episode Eighteen		
The Diamond from the Sky	August 30	(North American)
Divine Decree, A (2 reels)	August 30	
Green Apples	August 31	(Beauty)
Infatuation (4 reels)	September 2	(Mutual Masterpictures)
Spirit of Adventure, The	September 3	
Bully Affair, A	September 4	(Beauty)
Question of Honor, A	September 4	
Fire, Fury and Confusion (2 reels)		
Episode Nineteen		
The Diamond from the Sky	September 6	(North American)
In Trust (2 reels)	September 6	
Forecast, The	September 8	
When His Dough Was Cake	September 11	(Beauty)
Soul Stranglers, The (2 reels)		
Episode Twenty		
The Diamond from the Sky	September 13	(North American)
Señor's Silver Buckle, The (2 reels)	September 13	
Incognito	September 14	(Beauty)
Man from Oregon, The (5 reels)	Septmeber 16	(Mutual Masterpictures)
Little Lady Next Door, The	September 17	
Great Question, The (3 reels)	September 18	(American Star Feature)
Friend In Need, A	September 18	(Beauty)
Lion's Bride, The (2 reels)		
Episode Twenty-One		
The Diamond from the Sky	September 20	(North American)
Barren Gain, The (2 reels)	September 20	
Everyheart	September 21	(Beauty)
House of a Thousand Scandals, The (4 reels)	September 23	(Mutual Masterpictures)
It Was Like This	September 24	

1915 (Cont'd.)

Cats, Cash and A Cook Book	September 25	(Beauty)
Rose in the Dust, The (2 reels)		
Episode Twenty-Two		
The Diamond from the Sky	September 27	(North American)
Terror of Twin Mountains, The	September 27	
Love and Labor	September 28	(Beauty)
Hearts in Shadow	October 1	
Mixed Males	October 2	(Beauty)
Man-Afraid-Of-His-Wardrobe (3 reels)	October 2	(Mustang)
Damaged Goods (7 reels)	October 4	(Mutual Special Feature)
Double Cross, The (2 reels)		
Episode Twenty-Three		
The Diamond from the Sky	October 4	(North American)
Mother's Busy Day	October 5	(Beauty)
Breezy Bill--Outcast	October 8	(Mustang)
Sting of It, The	October 8	
Pardoned (3 reels)	October 9	(Clipper)
Curing Father	October 9	(Beauty)
Mad Millionaire, The (2 reels)		
Episode Twenty-Four		
The Diamond from the Sky	October 11	(North American)
Let There Be Light (2 reels)	October 11	
Billie--The Hill Billie	October 12	(Beauty)
Profit from Loss	October 15	
"Two Spot" Joe (2 reels)	October 15	(Mustang)
Aided by the Movies	October 16	(Beauty)
House of Cards, A (2 reels)		
Episode Twenty-Five		
The Diamond from the Sky	October 18	(North American)
Bolt on the Shield, The (2 reels)	October 18	
Alias James--Chauffeur	October 19	(Beauty)
Miracle of Life, The (4 reels)	October 21	(Mutual Masterpictures)
Sheriff of Willow Creek, The (2 reels)	October 22	(Mustang)
Visitors and Visitees	October 22	
Buck's Lady Friend (3 reels)	October 23	(Mustang)
Deserted At the Auto	October 23	(Beauty)
Garden of the Gods, The (2 reels)		
Episode Twenty-Six		
The Diamond from the Sky	October 25	(North American)
Out of the Ashes (2 reels)	October 25	
Touring With Tillie	October 26	(Beauty)
Playing for High Stakes (2 reels)	October 29	(Mustang)

1915 (Cont'd.)

Smuggler's Cave, The	October 29	
Idol, The (2 reels)	October 30	(Clipper)
Auto-Bungalow Fracas, An	October 30	(Beauty)
Mine Own People (2 reels)		
Episode Twenty-Seven		
The Diamond from the Sky	November 1	(North American)
Wasp, The (2 reels)	November 1	
One to the Minute	November 2	(Beauty)
On Secret Service	November 5	
Trail of the Serpent, The (2 reels)	November 5	(Mustang)
Billy Van Deusen's Campaign	November 6	(Beauty)
Midnight Intruder, A (or)		
The Falling Aeroplane (2 reels)		
Episode Twenty-Eight		
The Diamond from the Sky	November 8	(North American)
Alice of Hudson Bay (2 reels)	November 8	
Her Adopted Father	November 9	(Beauty)
End of the Road, The (5 reels)	November 11	(Mutual Masterpictures)
Man to Man (2 reels)	November 12	(Mustang)
To Rent, Furnished	November 12	
Almost a Widow	November 13	(Beauty)
This Is the Life (3 reels)	November 13	(Mustang)
Deal With Destiny, A (2 reels)		
Episode Twenty-Nine		
The Diamond from the Sky	November 15	(North American)
Substituted Minister, The (2 reels)	November 15	
Johnny the Barber	November 16	(Beauty)
Drifting	November 19	
Warning, The (2 reels)	November 19	(Mustang)
Anita's Butterfly	November 20	(Beauty)
Alternative, The (3 reels)	November 20	(Clipper Star Features)
American Earl, An (2 reels)		
Episode Thirty		
The Diamond from the Sky	November 22	(North American)
Key to the Past, The (2 reels)	November 22	
Drummer's Trunk, The	November 23	(Beauty)
Valley Feud, The (2 reels)	November 26	(Mustang)
Bluffers, The	November 26	
Cupid Beats Father	November 27	(Beauty)
Silver Lining, The (2 reels)	November 29	
Billy Van Deusen and the Merry Widow	November 30	(Beauty)
Broadcloth and Buckskin (2 reels)	December 3	(Mustang)
Spider Barlow Cuts In	December 3	
Making Over Father	December 4	(Beauty)
Film Tempo (3 reels)	December 4	(Mustang)

1915 (Cont'd.)

Title	Date	Brand
Author! Author!	December 5	(Mustang)
Water Carrier of San Juan, The (2 reels)	December 6	
Pretenses	December 7	(Beauty)
Buzzard's Shadow, The (5 reels)	Decmeber 9	(Mutual Masterpictures)
Broken Cloud, A	December 10	
There's Good In the Worst of Us (2 reels)	December 10	(Mustang)
Curly (3 reels)	December 11	(Clipper)
Nobody's Home	December 11	(Beauty)
Solution of the Mystery, The (2 reels)	December 13	
Girl, A Guard and A Garret, A	December 14	(Beauty)
In the Sunset Country (2 reels)	December 17	(Mustang)
Spider Farlow's Soft Spot	December 17	
Two Hearts and a Thief	December 18	(Beauty)
Clean-Up, The (2 reels)	December 20	
Making a Man of Johnny	December 21	(Beauty)
Pitch of Chance, The (2 reels)	December 24	(Mustang)
That Country Gal	December 25	(Beauty)
Tragic Circle, The (2 reels)	December 27	
Kiddus, Kidds and Kiddo	December 28	(Beauty)
Cactus Blossom, The (2 reels)	December 31	(Mustang)
Mender, The	December 31	

1916

Title	Date	Brand
Settled Out of Court	January 1	(Beauty)
Wraith of Hadden Towers, The	January 1	(Clipper)
Matching Dreams (2 reels)	January 3	
Billy Van Deusen's Shadow	January 4	(Beauty)
Other Side of the Door, The (5 reels)	January 6	(Mutual Masterpictures)
Time and Tide	January 7	
Hills of Glory, The (2 reels)	January 7	(Mustang)
To Be or Not To Be	January 8	(Beauty)
Gamble, The (2 reels)	January 10	
Viviana (2 reels)	January 10	
First Quarrel, The	January 11	(Beauty)
Secret Wife, The (2 reels)	January 14	
Spider Barlow Meets Competition	January 14	
Getting In Wrong	January 15	(Beauty)
Water Stuff (3 reels)	January 15	(Mustang)
Thoroughbred, The (5 reels)	January 17	(Mutual Masterpictures de Luxe)

1916 (Cont'd.)

Silent Trail, The (2 reels)	January 18	
Johnny's Birthday	January 19	(Beauty)
Wild Jim Reformer (2 reels)	January 21	(Mustang)
Thunderbolt, The	January 21	
Mischief and a Mirror	January 23	(Beauty)
Man in the Sombrero, The (2 reels)	January 25	
Some Night	January 26	(Beauty)
Lord Loveland Discovers America (5 reels)	January 27	(Mutual Master-pictures de Luxe)
Sanitarium Scramble, A	January 28	
Smugglers of Santa Cruz, The (3 reels)	January 28	(Clipper)
Walk This Way	January 30	(Beauty)
Broken Cross, The (2 reels)	February 1	
Billy Van Deusen's Wedding Eve	February 2	(Beauty)
Extra Man and the Milk-Fed Lion, The (3 reels)	February 4	(Mustang)
Mammy's Rose	February 4	
White Rosette, The (5 reels)	February 5	(Mutual Master-pictures de Luxe)
Laird O'Knees, The	February 6	(Beauty)
Lille of the Sulu Sea (3 reels)	February 8	
Won By One	February 9	(Beauty)
Powder (5 reels)	February 10	(Mutual Master-pictures de Luxe)
According to St. John (3 reels)	February 11	(Mustang)
Billy Van Deusen and the Vampire	February 13	(Beauty)
Modern Sphinx, A (3 reels)	February 15	
Ella Wanted to Elope	February 16	(Beauty)
Life's Blind Alley (5 reels)	February 17	(Mutual Master-pictures de Luxe)
When the Light Came (3 reels)	February 18	(Mustang)
Battle of Cupidovich, The	February 20	(Beauty)
Life's Harmony (3 reels)	February 22	
Too Much Married	February 23	(Beauty)
Double Crossed (3 reels)	February 25	(Mustang)
Craving, The (5 reels)	February 26	(Mutual Master-pictures de Luxe)
Cooking His Goose	February 27	(Beauty)
Happy Masquerader, The (3 reels)	February 29	
Johnny's Jumble	March 1	(Beauty)
Embers (5 reels)	March 2	(Mutual Master-pictures de Luxe)
Margy of the Foothills (3 reels)	March 3	(Mustang)
Dad's College Widow	March 5	(Beauty)

1916 (Cont'd.)

Silken Spider, The (3 reels)	March 7	
Gay Blade's Last Scrape, A	March 8	(Beauty)
True Nobility (5 reels)	March 9	(Mutual Master-pictures de Luxe)
Quagmire, The (3 reels)	March 10	(Mustang)
Persistent Percival	March 12	(Beauty)
Suppressed Order, The (3 reels)	March 14	
Curfew Corliss (3 reels)	March 17	(Mustang)
Overalls (5 reels)	March 18	(Mutual Master-pictures de Luxe)
Tips	March 19	(Beauty)
Code of Honor, The (3 reels)	March 21	
Cupid at Cohen's	March 23	(Beauty)
Bruiser, The (5 reels)	March 23	(Mutual Master-pictures de Luxe)
Snow Stuff (3 reels)	March 24	(Mustang)
Bubbles and the Barber	March 25	(Beauty)
In the Shuffle (3 reels)	March 28	
Trunk an' Trouble, A	March 29	(Beauty)
Revelations (5 reels)	March 30	(Mutual Master-pictures de Luxe)
Ranger of Lonesome Gulch (3 reels)	March 31	(Mustang)
Bumble's Job	April 2	(Beauty)
Ways of the World, The (2 reels)	April 3	
Billy Van Deusen's Muddle	April 5	(Beauty)
Bonds of Deception (3 reels)	April 6	
Two Bits (2 reels)	April 7	(Mustang)
Under Azure Skies (3 reels)	April 8	(Mustang)
Art and Arthur	April 9	(Beauty)
April (5 reels)	April 10	(Mutual Master-pictures de Luxe)
Peanuts and Powder	April 12	(Beauty)
Pendulum of Chance (2 reels)	April 13	
Silent Selby (3 reels)	April 13	(Mustang)
Flickering Light, A (2 reels)	April 14	(Mustang)
Improbable Yarn of McQuirk, The	April 16	(Beauty)
Wayfarers, The (3 reels)	April 16	
His Masterpiece (2 reels)	April 17	
Return, The (2 reels)	April 21	(Mustang)
Realization (3 reels)	April 22	
Bookworm's Blessed Blunders, The	April 23	(Beauty)
Counterfeit Earl, The (2 reels)	April 24	
Bugs and Bugles	April 26	(Beauty)
Broken Genius, A (3 reels)	April 27	
Unlucky Luke (2 reels)	April 28	(Mustang)
Two Beds and No Sleep	April 30	(Beauty)

1916 (Cont'd.)

Pierre de Brissac, The Brazen (2 reels)	May 1	
Billy Van Deusen's Ancestry	May 3	(Beauty)
Lying Lips (5 reels)	May 4	(Mutual Master-pictures de Luxe)
All for Nuttin'	May 7	(Beauty)
Overcoat, The (5 reels)	May 8	(Mutual Master-pictures de Luxe)
Touch On the Key, The (2 reels)	May 8	
Skelly's Skeleton	May 10	(Beauty)
Profligate, The (3 reels)	May 11	
Gulf Between, The (2 reels)	May 12	(Mustang)
Deacon's Card, The	May 14	(Beauty)
Pretender, The (2 reels)	May 15	
Billy Van Deusen's Fiancée	May 17	
Courtesan, The (5 reels)	May 18	(Mutual Master-pictures de Luxe)
Four Months	May 18	
Blindness, The (2 reels)	May 19	(Mustang)
Twenty Minutes Magic	May 21	(Beauty)
Repaid (2 reels)	May 22	
Secret of the Submarine, The (2 reels)		
Episode One	May 22	
Adjusting His Claim	May 24	(Beauty)
Reclamation, The (5 reels)	May 25	(Mutual Master-pictures de Luxe)
Jack (2 reels)	May 26	(Mustang)
Pork Plotters, The	May 28	(Beauty)
Man from Manhattan, The (5 reels)	May 29	(Mutual Master-pictures de Luxe)
Release of Dan Forbes, The (2 reels)	May 29	
Secret of the Submarine, The (2 reels)		
Episode Two	May 29	
Comet's Come-Back, The	May 31	(Beauty)
Trail of the Thief, The (3 reels)	June 1	
Ima Knutt Gets a Bite	June 4	(Beauty)
Secret of the Submarine, The (2 reels)		
Episode Three	June 5	
Billy Van Deusen's Operation	June 7	(Beauty)
Soulmates (5 reels)	June 8	(Mutual Master-picutres de Luxe)
Pilgrim, The (2 reels)	June 9	(Mustang)
Thinim Shout!	June 11	(Beauty)
Inner Struggle, The (5 reels)	June 12	(Mutual Master-pictures de Luxe)
Convicted for Murder (2 reels)	June 12	

1916 (Cont'd.)

Secret of the Submarine, The (2 reels)		
Episode Four	June 12	
Billy Van Deusen's Egg-Spensive Adventure	June 14	(Beauty)
Abandonment, The (5 reels)	June 15	(Mutual Master-pictures de Luxe)
Sheriff of Plumas (2 reels)	June 16	(Mustang)
Pedigrees, Pups and Pussies	June 18	(Beauty)
Gentle Conspiracy, The (2 reels)	June 19	(Mutual-American)
Secret of the Submarine, The (2 reels)		
Episode Five	June 19	
House on Hokum Hill	June 21	(Beauty)
Modern Knight, A (2 reels)	June 23	(Mustang)
Jealousy's First Wife (2 reels)	June 25	
Day's Work, The	June 25	(Mutual-Beauty)
Fate of the Dolphin, The (2 reels)	June 26	
Secret of the Submarine, The (2 reels)		
Episode Six	June 26	
Sign of the Spade, The (5 reels)	June 26	(Mutual Master-pictures de Luxe)
When Adam Had 'Em	June 28	(Beauty)
Tangled Skins (3 reels)	June 29	
Demon of Fear (2 reels)	June 30	(Mustang)
Gink from Kankikee, The	July 2	(Mutual-Beauty)
Killed By Whom? (2 reels)	July 3	(Mutual-American)
Secret of the Submarine, The (2 reels)		
Episode Seven	July 3	
Billy Van Deusen, Masquerader	July 5	(Mutual-Beauty)
Highest Bid, The (5 reels)	July 6	(Mutual Star Productions)
Gink Lands Again, The	July 9	(Mutual-Beauty)
Dust (5 reels)	July 10	(Mutual Master-pictures de Luxe)
Love's Bitter Strength (2 reels)	July 10	(Mutual-American)
Secret of the Submarine, The (2 reels)		
Episode Eight	July 10	
Two Slips and a Miss	July 12	(Mutual-Beauty)
Quicksands of Deceit (3 reels)	July 13	(Mutual-American)
Purity (7 reels)	July 13	(Mutual Master-pictures de Luxe)
Nugget Jim's Partner (3 reels)	July 14	(Mutual-Mustang)
Secret of the Submarine, The (2 reels)		
Episode Nine	July 17	
Dancer, The (2 reels)	July 17	(Mutual-American)
Dyspeptic, The (2 reels)	July 21	(Mutual-Mustang)
Studio Satire, A	July 23	(Mutual-Beauty)

1916 (Cont'd.)

Secret of the Submarine, The (2 reels) Episode Ten	July 24	
Pastures Green	July 24	(Mutual-American)
Out of the Rainbow (3 reels)	July 27	(Mutual-American)
That Gal of Burke's (2 reels)	July 28	(Mutual-Mustang)
Gamblers in Greenbacks	July 29	(Mutual-Beauty)
Germ Gem	July 30	(Mutual-Beauty)
Secret of the Submarine, The (2 reels) Episode Eleven	July 31	
Dreamer, The (2 reels)	July 31	(Mutual-American)
Daredevils and Danger	August 2	(Mutual-Beauty)
Madonna of the Night, The (3 reels)	August 3	(Mutual-American)
Strength of Donald McKenzie, The (5 reels)	August 3	(Mutual Star Productions)
Sandy Reformer (2 reels)	August 4	(Mutual-Mustang)
Just As He Thought	August 6	(Mutual-Beauty)
Secret of the Submarine, The (2 reels) Episode Twelve	August 7	
Little Troubadour, The (2 reels)	August 7	(Mutual-American)
Billy Van Deusen, The Caveman	August 9	(Mutual-Beauty)
Power of the Mind, The (3 reels)	August 10	(Mutual-American)
Courtin' of Calliope Clew, The (2 reels)	August 11	(Mutual-Mustang)
Too Bad Eddie	August 13	(Mutual-Beauty)
Secret of the Submarine, The (2 reels) Episode Thirteen	August 14	
Ruth Ridley's Return (2 reels)	August 14	(Mutual-American)
Perkin's Mystic Manor	August 16	(Mutual-Beauty)
Holly House, The (3 reels)	August 17	(Mutual-American)
El Diablo (2 reels)	August 18	(Mutual-Mustang)
Secret of the Submarine, The (2 reels) Episode Fourteen	August 21	
Enchantment (2 reels)	August 21	(Mutual-American)
Million for Mary, A (5 reels)	August 21	(Mutual Star Productions)
In a Prohibition Town	August 23	(Mutual-Beauty)
Nell Dale's Men Folks (2 reels)	August 25	(Mutual-Mustang)
Secret of the Submarine, The (2 reels) Episode Fifteen	August 28	
Two of a Kind	August 30	(Mutual-Beauty)
Man Who Would Not Die, The (5 reels)	August 31	(Mutual Star Productions)
Forgotten Prayer, The (3 reels)	August 31	(Mutual-Mustang)
Gambler's Lost Love, The (2 reels)	September 1	(Mutual-Mustang)
Atonement (2 reels)	September 4	(Mutual-American)
Youth's Endearing Charm (5 reels)	September 4	(Mutual Star Productions)

1916 (Cont'd.)

Boomerang Gold Brick, A	September 6	(Mutual-Beauty)
Light, The (5 reels)	September 7	(Mutual Masterpictures de Luxe)
Matchin' Jim (2 reels)	September 8	(Mutual-Mustang)
Sable, Blessing, The (5 reels)	September 11	(Mutual Star Productions)
Three Pals, The (5 reels)	September 18	(Mutual Star Productions)
Stinger Stung, The	September 18	(Mutual-Beauty)
Land o' Lizards, The (5 reels)	September 21	(Mutual Masterpictures de Luxe)
Torch Bearer, The (5 reels)	September 25	(Mutual Star Productions)
Slicking the Slickers	October 3	(Mutual-Beauty)
Shadow, The (5 reels)	October 5	(Mutual Masterpictures de Luxe)
Woman's Daring, A (5 reels)	October 5	(Mutual Masterpictures de Luxe)
Phillip Holden--Waster (5 reels)	October 9	(Mutual Star Features)
Citizens All (2 reels)	October 9	(Mutual-American)
That Sharp Note (2 reels)	October 10	(Mutual-Beauty)
Dulcey's Adventure (5 reels)	October 12	(Mutual Star Productions)
Bluff (5 reels)	October 16	(Mutual Star Productions)
Franchise, The (2 reels)	October 16	(Mutual-American)
Voice of Love, The (5 reels)	October 19	(Mutual Masterpictures de Luxe)
Undertow, The (5 reels)	October 23	(Mutual Masterpictures de Luxe)
Love Hermit, The (5 reels)	October 26	(Mutual Star Productions)
Faith (5 reels)	October 30	(Mutual Star Productions)
Spartan Spleen	October 31	(Mutual-Beauty)
Last Thrust, The	October 31	(Mutual-Beauty)
Pearl of Paradise, The (5 reels)	November 2	(Mutual Star Productions)
And the Law Says (5 reels)	November 6	(Mutual Masterpictures de Luxe)
*Fight on the Dam, The	November 9	(Mutual-American)
Peck o' Pickles (5 reels)	November 13	(Mutual Star Productions)
*Calamity Anne, Guardian	November 23	(Mutual-American)
Lone Star (5 reels)	November 23	(Mutual-American)
*Starbucks, The (2 reels)	November 23	(Mutual-American)

1916 (Cont'd.)

Sequel to the Diamond from the Sky (2 reels)		
<u>Episode One</u>: Fate and Death	November 25	
Dream or Two Ago, A (5 reels)	November 27	(Mutual Star Productions)
*Calamity Anne, Vanity	November 30	(Mutual-American)
*Capture of Rattesnake Ike, The	December 2	(Mutual-American)
Sequel to the Diamond from the Sky		
<u>Episode Two</u>: Under Oath	December 2	
Valley of Decision, The (5 reels)	December 4	(Mutual)
Sequel to the Diamond from the Sky		
<u>Episode Three</u>: Sealed Lips	December 9	
Miss Jackie of the Army (6 reels)	December 11	(Mutual Star Productions-Pollard)
Lonesome Town (5 reels)	December 11	(Mutual-American)
Twinkler, The (5 reels)	December 18	(Mutual Star Production)
Sequel to the Diamond from the Sky (2 reels)		
<u>Episode Four</u>: The Climax	December 18	
Innocence of Lizette, The (5 reels)	December 25	(Mutual Star Productions)

1917

Gilded Youth, A (5 reels)	January 1	(Mutual Star Productions)
Butterfly Girl, The (5 reels)	January 8	(Mutual Star Productions)
*Honeymooners, The	January 13	(Mutual-American)
Beloved Rogues (5 reels)	January 15	(Mutual Star Productions)
Gentle Intruder, The (5 reels)	January 19	(Mutual Star Productions)
*Almost a Friar	January 20	(Mutual-American)
*Double Revenge	Janaury 27	(Mutual-American)
Pardners (5 reels)	January 29	(Mutual Star Productions)
*Nature's Calling	February 3	(Mutual-American)
Where Love Is (5 reels)	February 5	(Mutual Star Productions)
*Old Sheriff, The	February 10	(Mutual-American)
*Damaged Goods ("New Edition") (7 reels)	February 12	(Mutual-American)

1917 (Cont'd.)

*Calamity Anne's Legacy	February 16	(Mutual-American)
*Hermits Hoard, The	February 17	(Mutual-American)
*Calamity Anne's New Job	February 23	(Mutual-American)
*Mouth Organ Jack (2 reels)	February 24	(Mutual-American)
My Fighting Gentlemen (5 reels)	March 1	(Mutual Star Productions)
*Calamity Anne's Protege	March 2	(Mutual-American)
Girl from Rectors, The (5 reels)	March 5	(Mutual Star Productions)
*Tell-Tale Arm, The	March 9	(Mutual-American)
*Homicide's Weapon, The	March 10	(Mutual-American)
*Lonesome Mariner, The	March 16	(Mutual-American)
*Cupid and a Button	March 21	(Mutual-American)
Motherhood (5 reels)	March 26	(Mutual Star Productions)
*Bearded Fisherman, The	March 28	(Mutual-American)
Devil's Assistant, The (5 reels)	April 2	(Mutual Star Productions)
*Artist's Intrigue, An	April 4	(Mutual-American)
High Play (5 reels)	April 9	(Mutual Star Productions)
Environment (5 reels)	April 16	(Mutual Star Productions)
Whose Wife? (5 reels)	April 30	(Mutual Star Productions)
Frame-Up, The (5 reels)	May 7	(Mutual Star Productions)
Annie for Spite (5 reels)	May 14	(Mutual Star Productions)
Serpent's Tooth, The (5 reels)	May 28	(Mutual Star Productions)
Shackles of Truth (5 reels)	June 4	(Mutual Star Productions)
Periwinkle (5 reels)	June 11	(Mutual Star Productions)
Melissa of the Hills (5 reels)	July 26	(Mutual-American)
Charity Castle (5 reels)	September 13	(Mutual-American)
Sands of Sacrifice (5 reels)	September 24	(Mutual Star Productions)
Rainbow, Girl, The (5 reels)	September 27	(Mutual Star Productions)
Her Country's Call (5 reels)	October 1	(Mutual Star Productions)
Southern Pride (5 reels)	October 8	(Mutual Star Productions)
Calendar Girl, The (5 reels)	October 15	(Mutual Star Productions)

1917 (Cont'd.)

Sea Monster, The (5 reels)	October 22	(Mutual Star Productions)
Peggy Leads the Way (5 reels)	October 29	(Mutual Star Productions)
Game of Wits, A (5 reels)	November 5	(Mutual Star Productions)
Please Help Emily (5 reels)	November 7	(Mutual Star Productions)
Betty and the Buccaneers (5 reels)	November 12	(Mutual Star Productions)
Snap Judgment (5 reels)	November 19	(Mutual Star Productions)
Mate of Sally Ann, The (5 reels)	November 26	(Mutual Star Productions)
Miss Jackie of the Army (5 reels)	December 10	(Mutual Star Productions)
New York Luck (5 reels)	December 17	(Mutual Star Productions)
Her Sister (5 reels)	December 31	(Mutual Star Productions)

1918

Molly Go Get 'Em (5 reels)	January 7	(Mutual Star Productions)
Imposter, The (5 reels)	January 14	(Mutual Star Productions)
In Bad (5 reels)	January 21	(Mutual Star Productions)
Beauty and the Rogue, The (5 reels)	January 28	(Mutual Star Productions)
Jilted Janet (5 reels)	February 11	(Mutual Star Productions)
Midnight Trail, The (5 reels)	February 25	(Mutual Star Productions)
Powers That Pray (5 reels)	March 4	(Mutual Star Productions)
Ann's Finish (5 reels)	March 11	(Mutual Star Productions)
Bit of Jade, A (5 reels)	April 1	(Mutual Star Productions)
Primitive Woman, The (5 reels)	April 15	(Mutual Star Productions)
Hearts of Diamonds (5 reels)	April 29	(Mutual Star Productions)
Mum's the Word (5 reels)	May 3	(Mutual Star Productions)

1918 (Cont'd.)

Social Briars (5 reels)	May 27	(Mutual Star Productions)
Square Deal, A (5 reels)	June 10	(Mutual Star Productions)
Up Romance Road (5 reels)	June 24	(Mutual Star Productions)
Ghost of Rosy Taylor, The (5 reels)	July 8	(Mutual Star Productions)
Eyes of Julia Deep, The (5 reels)	September	(Pathe-American)
Money Isn't Everything (5 reels)	September	(Pathe-American)
Hobbs in a Hurry (6 reels)	October	(Pathe-American)
Rosemary Climbs the Heights (5 reels)	October	(Pathe-American)
Mantle of Charity, The (5 reels)	November	(Pathe-American)
All the World to Nothing (6 reels)	November	(Pathe-American)
Wives and Other Wives (5 reels)	December	(Pathe-American)
Fair Enough (5 reels)	December	(Pathe-American)
When a Man Rides Alone (5 reels)	December	(Pathe-American)
Girl o' Dreams, The (5 reels)	December	(Pathe-American)

1919

Amazing Imposter, The (5 reels)	January	(Pathe-American)
Molly of the Follies (5 reels)	January	(Pathe-American)
Where the West Begins (5 reels)	February	(Pathe-American)
Put Up Your Hands (5 reels)	March	(Pathe-American)
Intrusion of Isabel, The (5 reels)	March	(Pathe-American)
Brass Buttons (5 reels)	March	(Pathe-American)
Charge It to Me (5 reels)	April	(Pathe-American)
Some Liar (5 reels)	April	(Pathe-American)
Bachelor's Wife, A (5 reels)	May	(Pathe-American)
Trixie From Broadway (5 reels)	June	(Pathe-American)
Sporting Chance, A (5 reels)	June	(Pathe-American)
Yvonne From Paris (5 reels)	July	(Pathe-American)
Tiger-Lily, The (5 reels)	July	(Pathe-American)
This Hero Stuff (5 reels)	July	(Pathe-American)
Six Feet Four (6 reels)	September	(Pathe-American)
Hellion, The (5 reels)	September	(Pathe-American)
Eve in Exile (5 reels)	November	(Pathe-American)

1920

Valley of Tomorrow, The (5 reels)	January	(Pathe-American)
Dangerous Talent, The (6 reels)	March	(Pathe-American)
Honey Bee, The (6 reels)	April	(Pathe-American)

1920 (Cont'd.)

*Slam Bang Jim (5 reels)	April	(Pathe-American)
Thirtieth Piece of Silver, The (6 reels)	May	(Pathe-American)
House of Toys, The (6 reels)	June	(Pathe-American)
*Peggy Rebels (5 reels)	June	(Pathe-American)
*Live Wire Hick, A (5 reels)	July	(Pathe-American)
Weekend, The (6 reels)	August	(Pathe-American)
Light Woman, A (6 reels)	October	(Pathe-American)
Gamesters, The (6 reels)	September	(Pathe-American)
Blue Moon, The (6 reels)	October	(Pathe-American)
Their Mutual Child (6 reels)	December	(Pathe-American)
*Virtuous Outcast, The (5 reels)	December	(State Rights Productions)
*From the West (5 reels)	Decmeber	(State Rights Productions)

1921

*Crook's Romance, A (5 reels)	January	(State Rights Productions)
*Loggers of Hell-Roarin' Mountain (5 reels)	January	(State Rights Productions)
*Man From Medicine Hat, The (5 reels)	January	(State Rights Productions)
*Marriage Bargain, The (5 reels)	January	(State Rights Productions)
*Moonshine Menace, The (5 reels)	Janaury	(State Rights Productions)
*Quick Action (5 reels)	January	(State Rights Productions)
*Rough-Shod Fighter, A (5 reels)	January	(State Rights Productions)
*Sally With a Past (or) Sally Shows the Way (5 reels)	January	(State Rights Productions)
Sunset Jones (5 reels)	March	(Pathe-American)
Payment Guaranteed (5 reels)	March	(Pathe-American)
Silent Shelby (5 reels)	March	(State Rights Productions)
*High Gear Jeffrey (5 reels)	June	(State Rights Productions)
*Youth's Melting Pot (5 reels)	June	(State Rights Productions)

APPENDIX C

PERSONNEL

APPENDIX C

PERSONNEL

The following list includes members of American's personnel for whom information could be found. The list does not include the hundreds of temporary employees hired by American for such positions as carpenters and painters. Personnel are listed by production responsibilities; the year or years in parentheses indicate the dates during which they were in American's employ.

The Executive Branch

Atkinson, Eddie	Personnel Manager (1917-18)
Camp, Claude	Purchasing Agent (1913-18)
Crone, J. R.	Studio Manager (1916-21)
Doud, Omer F.	Publicity Director (1910-14)
Freuler, John R.	Secretary/Treasurer (1910-21)
Hamilton, Gilbert P.	Superintendent (1910-11)
Hutchinson, M. D.	Vice-President (1916-21)
Hutchinson, J. Hobart	Advertising Manager (1918-21)
Hutchinson, Samuel S.	President (1910-21)
Hutchinson, Winston S.	Sales and Distribution (1918-21)
Kennedy, Aubrey M.	General Manager (1910-12)
Kerrigan, Wallace W.	Business Manager (1910-13)
Lynch, P. G.	Studio Manager (1913-18)
McKnight, Robert B.	Publicity (1918)
Morrison, C. P.	Superintendent (1910-16)
Nehls, Richard R.	General Manager (1910-21)
Stebbins, R. E.	Assistant Studio Manager (1916-19)
White, C. D.	Purchasing Agent (1914-1920)
Ziebarth, Charles A.	Laboratory Superintendent (1910-21)

Directors

Ayres, Sidney (1913-14)	Borzage, Frank (1915-16)
Bartlett, Charles E. (1916?)	Bowman, William. J. (1911-14)
Beal, Frank (1910-11)	Clements, Hal (1914?)
Berger, C. Rea (1915-16)	Cooley, Frank (1915-18)
Bertram, William (1914-15)	Cox, George L. (1919-21)

Directors (Cont'd.)

Dillon, Jack (1914)
Dowlan, William (1916)
Dwan, Allan (1910-13)
Douglas, James S. (1914-18)
Eason, B. Reeves (1913-15)
Ellsworth, Warren (1916)
Flynn, Emmett J. (1919)
Forbes, Harris L. (1916?)
George, Burton (1919)
Halloway, John (1917?)
Heffron, T. N. (1916-17)
Hillyer, Lambert (1914?)
Humphrey, Oral (1915-16)
Ingraham, Lloyd (1917-19)
Jaccard, Jacques (1915)
Johnston, Lorimer (1913-14)
Julian, Rupert (1920)
King, Henry (1917-19)
Kirkwood, James (1916-17)

MacQuarrie, Murdock (1916)
Maude, Arthur (1916?)
McDonald, Donald (1916?)
McMakin, Archer (1915-16)
Neill, Roy William (1919)
Otto, Henry (1914-15)
Pollard, Harry (1914-16)
Prescott, John (1916)
Ricketts, Thomas (1910-11, 1913-16)
Santell, Al (1915-16)
Sargent, George (1916)
Sloman, Edward (1917-19)
Steppling, John (1915)
Sturgeon, Rollin S. (1917)
Taylor, William D. (1915)
Thorne, Frank A. (1918)
Watt, Nate C. (1915-16)
Withey, Chester (1913-16)

Scenarists

All of the following have been credited with authorship of American films. Some, however, were free-lance writers and never actually on American's staff.

Algier, Sidney (1920)
Attwool, Hima (1913)
Baker, Hettie Gray (1914)
Ballard, E. S. (1915)
Banks, Perry (1914)
Banks, Mrs. Perry (1914)
Barry, Richard (1916)
Black, Ruth (1914)
Boyers, Bertie B. (1914-15)
Bridson, T. H. (1913)
Brooks, Virginia (1915)
Brown, C. M. (1915)
Brush, Charlotte M. (1913)
Calif, Jessie F. (1914)
Campbell, A. Bruce (1913)
Campbell, Clyde C. (1915)
Campbell, Webster W. (1914-15)
Cantwell, George G. (1913)
Carpenter, Elizabeth R. (1915)

Caskins, Elizabeth (1914)
Carr, Catherine (1915)
Child, Richard Washburn (1913)
Cittel, Harry E. (1914)
Clapp, Chester Blinn (1920)
Clark, Frank Howard (1915, 1919)
Clark, Olga P. (1912, 1915)
Coldwey, Anthony Weller (1916-17)
Cooke, Caroline (1914)
Cooley, Mrs. Frank (1914)
Coolidge, Karl (1916-18)
Cooper, Frank C. (1914)
Cooper, Verdinal (1915)
Cox, Effie L. (1914)
Coxetal, William R. (1914)
Curwood, James Oliver (1919)
Dazey, Charles Turner (1917-18)
Duff, Nellie Brown (1914)
Eckels, C. Eddy (1917)

Scenarists (Cont'd.)

Evans, Guy T. (1914)
Everson, Grace (1915)
Felkner, Marjorie (1914)
Feltus, P. L. (1914)
Field, George (1914)
Fitzroy, Louis (1914)
Frambers, Clarence A. (1918)
Furthman, Jules (1917-19)
Futrelle, May (1915)
Gaddis, Pearl (1913)
Gibson, Tom (1915)
Giebler, A. H. (1913)
Glenz, Mrs. George (1915)
Glick, Carl C. (1914)
Goldberg, Max (1913, 1915)
Gordon, Edward (1913)
Gormley, Helen V. (1914)
Gooden, Arthur Henry (1916-20)
Graham, Carl (1915)
Hamilton, Cosmo (1919)
Harris, Adele (1914)
Harris, Clarence J. (1913-15)
Harris, Theodosia (1913-15)
Harvey, M. B. (1913)
Hawes, L. B. (1915)
Jeck, Robert (1914)
Heffernam, Marion (1915)
Heiskell, F. A. (1913)
Himes, A. B. (1914)
Hoadley, Charles Byron (1916-18)
Hoadley, Harold William (1916-18)
Hoffman, Aaron (1916?)
Hogan, R. (1914)
Hopkins, Milton S. (1915)
Horton, Kate L. (1915)
Howard, Clifford (1915-18)
Hungerford, J. Edward (1913-18)
Isaacson, Florence (1914)
Jefferson, L. V. (1919)
Johnston, Agnes C. (1915, 1919)
Johnstone, Calder (1915?)
Jones, F. A. (1914)
Jones, Marc E. (1914-15)
Justice, Maibelle (1916-17)
Kamm, S. J. (1914)
Kaufman, Edward A. (1915-16)
Kennedy, Margaret (1913)
King, W. M., Jr. (1914)
Kinkead, Eleanor (1914)
Kirtley, Virginia (1915?)
Lamothe, Julian Louis (1916-17)
Lavergne, Anna (1914)
Lavin, Louis M. (1914)
Layet, Marie (1914-15)
Lenoir, Phil A. (1915)
Levin, Louis N. (1913)
Lloyd, John (1914)
Lockwood, Anna I. (1913)
Lonsdale, Mary F. (1913)
Looney, Jere F. (1917)
Loos, Anita (1914)
MacGrath, Harold (1915)
Mahoney, Elizabeth (1918-19)
Mallock, Douglas (1914)
Manley, D. L. (1914)
Martyn, Wyndham (1918)
Matkin, Mary (1914)
May, Gordon V. (1913)
McAuliffe, T. E. (1913)
McCandless, George Lee (1918)
McCardell, Roy L. (1915)
McConville, Bernard (1918)
McDonald, Wallace (1915)
McFarland, Peter C. (1919)
McKinstry, M. R. (1914-15)
Methley, Alice A. (1913)
Montague, F. J. (1914)
Myers, Charles D. (1913)
Nelson, Abraham (1915)
Nelson, O. A. (1913, 1914)
Newsum, Sallie P. (1914)
O'Connor, Mary H. (1915-17)
O'Leary, J. R. (1914)
Osborne, William Hamilton
    (1913, 1915)
Parker, William (1915)
Peck, Charles Mortimer (1917?)
Phillips, Henry Albert (1916-17)
Phillips, Nell V. (1915)
Pigott, William (1913-18)
Poland, Joseph Franklin (1914-15)
Posner, George A. (1914)

Scenarist (Cont'd)

Printzlau, Olga (1915?)
Reyonolds, Isobel M. (1914)
Rich, Vivian (1914)
Riesener, George M. (1913)
Roach, J. Anthony (1918)
Roberts, Ethel (1914)
Robertson, Frances M. (1915)
Rockfort, Dorothy (1915)
Sanborn, Robert A. (1914)
Sayre, J. Willis (1913-14)
Schroeder, Doris (1917)
Schrumon, R. S. (1913)
Shafer, Mollie (1915)
Shipley, Mrs. E. N. (1915)
Slocum, Daisy Mayer (1915)
Smith, Frank E. (1913)
Smith, Russell E. (1916)
Snyder, Flora B. (1913, 1915)
Stearns, Myron Morris (1918)
Stillman, Al (1915)

Stone, Alan E. (1915)
Sutton, H. M. (1913)
Terrell, S. J. (1915)
Van Vorst, Marie (1915)
Wall, F. G. (1914)
Wallace, Grant (1914)
Webb, W. J. (1915)
West, Billie (1913)
Whitcomb, Daniel F. (1918-21)
Whitcomb, Eva R. (1914-15)
Whitcomb, O. F. (1914)
White, S. S. (1914)
Whitmore, Mrs. E. V. (1914)
Whitmore, Virginia (1914-15)
Wilcox, Winifred (1914)
Willis, F. McGrew (1915)
Wright, Frances M. (1913)
Wulze, Harry (1914)
Zellner, Lois (1920, 1921)
Zellner, Arthur (1920)

Actors and Actresses

Abbott, Marguerita (1917?)
Abraham, Jake (1917?)
Acord, Art (1915-16)
Aitken, Spottiswoode (1915)
Allison, May (1915)
Arbuckle, Andrew (1917)
Ashton, Sylvia (1917?)
Banks, Perry (1916-19)
Barrows, Henry A. (1917)
Beal, Scott (1910-13)
Bennett, Hugh (1916)
Bennett, Richard (1915, 1916-17)
Billington, Francelia (1917)
Bronti, Mrs. Adelaide (1915?)
Burton, Charlotte (1911-16)
Burton, Clarence F. (1916-17)
Bush, Pauline (1910-13)
Butterworth, Ernest (1913)
Butterworth, Ernest, Jr. (1913)
Carroll, William A. (1916-19)
Chatterton, Thomas (1915-16)
Christy, Lillian (1912-16)
Clancy, George (1916)

Clark, Harvey (1916-20)
Clark, J. King (1916)
Cloy, May (1916-17)
Cody, Lewis J. (1917)
Conklin, William (1917)
Cooley, Hal (1916)
Coxen, Edward (1912-16)
Crawley, Constance (1916?)
Cummings, Irving (1915)
Day, Juliette (1917)
DeBrullier, Nigel (1915)
DeCamp, Frank (1917?)
Dearholt, Ashton (1915-17)
Devere, Harry T. (1913)
Ditt, Josephine (1910-11, 1915-16)
Edmondson, Al (1917)
Edmundson, Harry (1916)
Eidson, O. C. (1918?)
Farley, Dot (1910-11)
Farley, James Lee (1917?)
Farrington, Adele (1917)
Field, George (1915)
Finley, Mrs. Peggy (1916?)

Actors and Actresses (Cont'd.)

Fischer, David G. (1910-11)
Fischer, Margarita (1914-20)
Fisher, George (1917)
Ford, Fred (1916?)
Forde, Eugenie (1912-17)
Forrest, Alan (1916-18)
Frazen, Nell (1912?)
Gamble, Fred A. (1912-13)
Gebhardt, Geroge M. (1917)
Gerber, Neva (1913-15)
Gleason, Adda (1917)
Greenwood, Winnifred (1912-16)
Grey, R. Henry (1910)
Halloway, Carol (1916?)
Hansen, Juanita (1916)
Harding, Guy (1917?)
Harris, Sidney A. (1916?)
Hayward, Lillian (1917)
Hayes, Tommy (1915-16)
Hollingsworth, Alfred (1915-17)
Hollis, Hylda (1916-19)
Johnstone, Lamar (1916)
Kane, Gail (1917)
Kerrigan, J. Warren (1910-13)
Kingsbury, Gladys (1914-15)
Kirkham, Kathleen (1917)
Klein, Robert (1915-17)
Kolb, C. W., and Dill, Max (1916)
Kromarm, Ann (1916?)
La Reno, Dick (1917?)
Lester, Louise (1910-17)
Lewis, Ida (1913?)
Little, Anna (1915-16)
Lloyd, Billy (1917)
Lockwood, Harold (1915-16)
Lorraine, Leota (1916)
MacDonald, Wallace (1916)
MacLean, Douglas (1916)
Maye, Jimsy (1916)
McCabe, Harry (1916)
Minter, Mary Miles (1916-18)
Mitchell, Rhea (1916-17)
Morrison, Pete (1910-16)
Mower, Jack (1916)
Munson, Audrey (1916, 1918)
Neilan, Marshall (1911-12)
Newton, Charles L. (1916-17)
Nichols, Marguerite (1916)

Pallette, Eugene (1912-14)
Payton, Gloria (1911?)
Peil, Edward (1916?)
Periolat, George (1910-18)
Peyton, Larry (1915?)
Pickford, Lottie (1915)
Rich, Vivian (1916)
Richardson, Jack (1910-17)
Ridgeway, Fritzie. (1917)
Reid, Wallace (1912-13)
Ritchie, Franklin (1915-18)
Rosson, Dick (1913)
Rosson, Helene (1916)
Russell, J. Gordon (1916-17)
Russell, William (1915-19)
Schaeffer, Anne (1917)
Sheehan, John (1916)
Shumway, Leonard C. (1918?)
Sills, Milton (1920)
Singleton, Joseph E. (1913?)
Spencer, Walter (1915)
Steppling, John (1916-17)
Stewart, Roy (1915-16)
Stockdale, Carl (1917-18)
Stowell, William H. (1916-18)
Stuart, Dixie (1915)
Sulky, Leo (1911?)
Taylor, E. Forrest (1916)
Tedmarsh, William J. (1916)
Templeton, Olive (1915)
Thorne, Lizette (1916)
Trunnelle, Mabel (1917)
Ullman, Ethel (1916)
Van, Beatrice (1915-16)
Van Tassell, Marie (1916)
Van Trump, Jessalyn (1911-12)
Vinton, Horace (1914?)
Von Meter, Harry (1914-17)
Vosburgh, Jack (1917)
Ward, Lucille (1917)
Webb, George (1916)
Weigel, Paul (1917)
Wells, Estelle (1911?)
Whitman, Alfred (1914?)
Whitman, Jack (1917)
Wicki, Norbert (1913?)
Younge, Lucille (1917)

Production Personnel

Abel, David	Cameraman (1916)
Alder, William F.	Cameraman (1912-13)
Alley, Alfred Wright	Art Director (1918)
Armstrong, Roger Dale	Cameraman (1910-15)
Baldrige, Sidney Allen	Technical Director (1910-21)
Benoit, George	Cameraman (1915?)
Brown, John W.	Cameraman (1915)
Carpenter, Gerald	Still Photographer (1912-21)
Coffee, Robert	Property Head (1910-12?)
David, Charles N.	Cameraman (1910-11?)
Dean, Faxon M.	Cameraman (1915-16)
Fowler, H. M.	Cameraman (1916?)
Heimerl, A. J.	Manager, Photographic Department and Laboratory (1910, 1913-19)
Howland, Louis A.	Assistant Director (1914?)
Kennedy, Peter Benjamin	Costumer (1917?)
Klaffki, Roy	Cameraman (1916)
Lampe, Ralph Clarence	Architectural Director (1918)
Langley, Edward M.	Art Director (1916)
Lundin, Walter	Laboratory (1910-12)
Marshall, Geroge	Cameraman (1915)
Middleton, Thomas B.	Cameraman (1912-16)
Morgan, Harry Dukes	Assistant Director (1914)
Morgan, Joe	Cameraman (1915)
Orenbach, Michael	Technical Director (1917)
Ormston, Frank	Art Director (1915?)
Overbaugh, Roy F.	Cameraman (1910-13, 1914-21)
Phelan, Robert V.	Cameraman (1916)
Randall, Charles Lewis	Photographer (1918)
Reeves, Arthur E.	Cameraman (1916?)
Richardson, Frank A.	Assistant Director (1915)
Rizard, George	Cameraman (1916-17?)
Roberts, George L.	Artist (1918)
Rogers, Charles E.	Assistant Director (1917)
Rothwell, Ben H.	Assistant Director (1916?)
Rubenstein, Irving B.	Cameraman (1915?)
Schoedsack, G. F.	Cameraman (1914?)
Seitz, John F.	Cameraman (1912-16)
Smith, Harry Jay	Assistant Directory (1916)
Thompson, Robert P.	Assistant Director (1912?)
VanDerVeer, Willard	Cameraman (1918)
Vaughan, William H.	Assistant Director (1915-18)
Ward, Chance E.	Assistant Director (1916)
Weight, F. Harmon	Assistant Director (1916-19)
Widen, Carl	Cameraman (1916)

The Arno Press Cinema Program

THE LITERATURE OF CINEMA
Series I & II

Agate, James. **Around Cinemas.** 1946.

Agate, James. **Around Cinemas.** (Second Series). 1948.

American Academy of Political and Social Science. **The Motion Picture in Its Economic and Social Aspects,** edited by Clyde L. King. **The Motion Picture Industry,** edited by Gordon S. Watkins. *The Annals,* November, 1926/1927.

L'Art Cinematographique, Nos. 1-8. 1926-1931.

Balcon, Michael, Ernest Lindgren, Forsyth Hardy and Roger Manvell. **Twenty Years of British Film, 1925-1945.** 1947.

Bardèche, Maurice and Robert Brasillach. **The History of Motion Pictures,** edited by Iris Barry. 1938.

Benoit-Levy, Jean. **The Art of the Motion Picture.** 1946.

Blumer, Herbert. **Movies and Conduct.** 1933.

Blumer, Herbert and Philip M. Hauser. **Movies, Delinquency, and Crime.** 1933.

Buckle, Gerard Fort. **The Mind and the Film.** 1926.

Carter, Huntly. **The New Spirit in the Cinema.** 1930.

Carter, Huntly. **The New Spirit in the Russian Theatre, 1917-1928.** 1929.

Carter, Huntly. **The New Theatre and Cinema of Soviet Russia.** 1924.

Charters, W. W. **Motion Pictures and Youth.** 1933.

Cinema Commission of Inquiry. **The Cinema: Its Present Position and Future Possibilities.** 1917.

Dale, Edgar. **Children's Attendance at Motion Pictures.** Dysinger, Wendell S. and Christian A. Ruckmick. **The Emotional Responses of Children to the Motion Picture Situation.** 1935.

Dale, Edgar. **The Content of Motion Pictures.** 1935.

Dale, Edgar. **How to Appreciate Motion Pictures.** 1937.

Dale, Edgar, Fannie W. Dunn, Charles F. Hoban, Jr., and Etta Schneider. **Motion Pictures in Education: A Summary of the Literature.** 1938.

Davy, Charles. **Footnotes to the Film.** 1938.

Dickinson, Thorold and Catherine De la Roche. **Soviet Cinema.** 1948.

Dickson, W. K. L., and Antonia Dickson. **History of the Kinetograph, Kinetoscope and Kinetophonograph.** 1895.

Forman, Henry James. **Our Movie Made Children.** 1935.

Freeburg, Victor Oscar. **The Art of Photoplay Making.** 1918.

Freeburg, Victor Oscar. **Pictorial Beauty on the Screen.** 1923.

Hall, Hal, editor. **Cinematographic Annual, 2 vols.** 1930/1931.

Hampton, Benjamin B. **A History of the Movies.** 1931.

Hardy, Forsyth. **Scandinavian Film.** 1952.

Hepworth, Cecil M. **Animated Photography: The A B C of the Cinematograph.** 1900.

Hoban, Charles F., Jr., and Edward B. Van Ormer. **Instructional Film Research 1918-1950.** 1950.

Holaday, Perry W. and George D. Stoddard. **Getting Ideas from the Movies.** 1933.

Hopwood, Henry V. **Living Pictures.** 1899.

Hulfish, David S. **Motion-Picture Work.** 1915.

Hunter, William. **Scrutiny of Cinema.** 1932.

Huntley, John. **British Film Music.** 1948.

Irwin, Will. **The House That Shadows Built.** 1928.

Jarratt, Vernon. **The Italian Cinema.** 1951.

Jenkins, C. Francis. **Animated Pictures.** 1898.

Lang, Edith and George West. **Musical Accompaniment of Moving Pictures.** 1920.

London, Kurt. **Film Music.** 1936.

Lutz, E[dwin] G[eorge]. **The Motion-Picture Cameraman.** 1927.

Manvell, Roger. **Experiment in the Film.** 1949.

Marey, Etienne Jules. **Movement.** 1895.

Martin, Olga J. **Hollywood's Movie Commandments.** 1937.

Mayer, J. P. **Sociology of Film: Studies and Documents.** 1946. New Introduction by J. P. Mayer.

Münsterberg, Hugo. **The Photoplay: A Psychological Study.** 1916.

Nicoll, Allardyce. **Film and Theatre.** 1936.

Noble, Peter. **The Negro in Films.** 1949.

Peters, Charles C. **Motion Pictures and Standards of Morality.** 1933.

Peterson, Ruth C. and L. L. Thurstone. **Motion Pictures and the Social Attitudes of Children.** Shuttleworth, Frank K. and Mark A. May. **The Social Conduct and Attitudes of Movie Fans.** 1933.

Phillips, Henry Albert. **The Photodrama.** 1914.

Photoplay Research Society. **Opportunities in the Motion Picture Industry.** 1922.

Rapée, Erno. **Encyclopaedia of Music for Pictures.** 1925.

Rapée, Erno. **Motion Picture Moods for Pianists and Organists.** 1924.

Renshaw, Samuel, Vernon L. Miller and Dorothy P. Marquis. **Children's Sleep.** 1933.

Rosten, Leo C. **Hollywood: The Movie Colony, The Movie Makers.** 1941.

Sadoul, Georges. **French Film.** 1953.

Screen Monographs I, 1923-1937. 1970.

Screen Monographs II, 1915-1930. 1970.

Sinclair, Upton. **Upton Sinclair Presents William Fox.** 1933.

Talbot, Frederick A. **Moving Pictures.** 1912.

Thorp, Margaret Farrand. **America at the Movies.** 1939.

Wollenberg, H. H. **Fifty Years of German Film.** 1948.

RELATED BOOKS AND PERIODICALS

Allister, Ray. **Friese-Greene: Close-Up of an Inventor.** 1948.

Art in Cinema: A Symposium of the Avant-Garde Film, edited by Frank Stauffacher. 1947.

The Art of Cinema: Selected Essays. New Foreword by George Amberg. 1971.

Balázs, Béla. **Theory of the Film.** 1952.

Barry, Iris. **Let's Go to the Movies.** 1926.

de Beauvoir, Simone. **Brigitte Bardot and the Lolita Syndrome.** 1960.

Carrick, Edward. **Art and Design in the British Film.** 1948.

Close Up. Vols. 1-10, 1927-1933 (all published).

Cogley, John. **Report on Blacklisting. Part I: The Movies.** 1956.

Eisenstein, S. M. **Que Viva Mexico!** 1951.

Experimental Cinema. 1930-1934 (all published).

Feldman, Joseph and Harry. **Dynamics of the Film.** 1952.

Film Daily Yearbook of Motion Pictures. Microfilm, 18 reels, 35 mm. 1918-1969.

Film Daily Yearbook of Motion Pictures. 1970.

Film Daily Yearbook of Motion Pictures. (Wid's Year Book). 3 vols., 1918-1922.

The Film Index: A Bibliography. Vol. I: The Film as Art. 1941.

Film Society Programmes. 1925-1939 (all published).

Films: A Quarterly of Discussion and Analysis. Nos. 1-4, 1939-1940 (all published).

Flaherty, Frances Hubbard. **The Odyssey of a Film-Maker: Robert Flaherty's Story.** 1960.

General Bibliography of Motion Pictures, edited by Carl Vincent, Riccardo Redi, and Franco Venturini. 1953.

Hendricks, Gordon. **Origins of the American Film.** 1961-1966. New Introduction by Gordon Hendricks.

Hound and Horn: Essays on Cinema, 1928-1934. 1971.

Huff, Theodore. **Charlie Chaplin.** 1951.

Kahn, Gordon. **Hollywood on Trial.** 1948.

New York Times Film Reviews, 1913-1968. 1970.

Noble, Peter. **Hollywood Scapegoat: The Biography of Erich von Stroheim.** 1950.

Robson, E. W. and M. M. **The Film Answers Back.** 1939.

Seldes, Gilbert. **An Hour with the Movies and the Talkies.** 1929.

Weinberg, Herman G., editor. **Greed.** 1971.

Wollenberg, H. H. **Anatomy of the Film.** 1947.

Wright, Basil. **The Use of the Film.** 1948.

DISSERTATIONS ON FILM

Beaver, Frank Eugene. **Bosley Crowther: Social Critic of the Film, 1940-1967.** First publication, 1974.

Benderson, Albert Edward. **Critical Approaches to Federico Fellini's "8½".** First publication, 1974.

Cohen, Louis Harris. **The Cultural-Political Traditions and Developments of the Soviet Cinema: 1917-1972.** First publication, 1974.

Dart, Peter. **Pudovkin's Films and Film Theory.** First publication, 1974.

Facey, Paul W. **The Legion of Decency: A Sociological Analysis of the Emergence and Development of a Social Pressure Group.** First publication, 1974.

Karpf, Stephen L. **The Gangster Film: Emergence, Variation and Decay of a Genre, 1930-1940.** First publication, 1973.

Lounsbury, Myron O. **The Origins of American Film Criticism, 1909-1939.** First publication, 1973.

Lyons, Timothy James. **The Silent Partner: The History of the American Film Manufacturing Company, 1910-1921.** First publication, 1974.

McLaughlin, Robert. **Broadway and Hollywood: A History of Economic Interaction.** First publication, 1974.

North, Joseph H. **The Early Development of the Motion Picture, 1887-1909.** First publication, 1973.

Rimberg, John. **The Motion Picture in the Soviet Union, 1918-1952.** First publication, 1973.

Sands, Pierre N. **A Historical Study of the Academy of the Motion Picture Arts and Sciences (1927-1947).** First publication, 1973

Wolfe, Glenn J. **Vachel Lindsay: The Poet as Film Theorist.** First publication, 1973.